THE HISTORY OF THAT RAMBLING great collection of eastern tales that we call The Arabian Nights is, as it should be, mysterious. We learn of a 9th century fragment, of a lost book of Persian stories ("called by the people A Thousand Nights") mentioned in a work dated 947, and of manuscript sightings through later centuries, with additions all the time. The first published volume anywhere, though, was in French (1704 to 1717), a ten-volume translation by Antoine Galland. Ever since then, translation to and fro has been brisk. Certainly, the selected versions available, with their special gifts of eastern fantasy – magic carpet, flying horse, caves of untold treasure, a lamp which summons a private genie slave, a ride on a bird whose wingspan blots out the sun itself – brought joy to countless bygone young, Byron and the Brontë children among them. Oddly, these tales are not typical.

For outside Sindbad, Aladdin and the rest, a handful only of stories, how much of the whole assembling do we know? Very little in fact. There could be a reason. The characteristic Arabian tales that occupy the opening books of the full-sized version are often so tedious and so gross (a peculiarly disagreeable compound) that early selectors may well have come to a halt. They should have persevered, for after a while other voices take over; the tales become wittier, the dialogue more entertaining, (see 'The Generous Sheikh, The Prince and the Tortoise'); we begin to remember the people, not merely the magic toys.

Folk and fairy tale motifs roam the world, but the tales reflect the region where they are told. The myths of a land of eunuchs, slaves, multiple wives, where kings and princes pass their days in slaughtering deer and gazelle are not deficient in action or scenery, but in human drama, yes. Yet even a land as vast as Arabia has its borders. If the magic rug can fly over the Moslem frontiers, other themes can equally stray within. How else can we explain the curiously Celtic note in that splendid story 'Friend So-and-So'? 'The Anklet' is of course Cinderella – or rather, the German Ashputtel, and a somewhat pleasanter version, you could say. Only one detail is specifically eastern; since segregation prevails, the women have their party in the harem while the men have their feast in the main palace. So the prince never sees the girl, only her ankle ring. In 'The Two Lives of Sultan Mahmud', one of the very few "moral" tales, a bored young king is startlingly visited by a mage or seer, an emissary of "the saints of the distant west". 'Sea Rose' has an endearing giant with a passion for home-made cake; he might have stepped out of Joseph Jacobs. The Princess Farizad succeeds in climbing the terrible mountain where her brothers, now black stones, have failed. We find mermen in 'Land Abdallah', no soulless beings, either, but "sons of Adam", on the same terms with Allah as the humans: an advance, I'd say, on the Andersen/Matthew Arnold view.

Yet, whatever their origins, they are now part of the curious enchantment that still invests the tales. This is caught, I think, most gracefully in the close of the charming tale that brings the book to an end: "Hand in hand, lighter than birds, they vanished into the friendly dark, fragrant with flowers, lit with guiding stars. Nothing more was ever heard of them in the palace. But fortunate is the dreamer who meets in dreams such happiness as theirs."

Naomi Lewis

STORIES FROM THE ARABIAN NIGHTS

Retold by NAOMI LEWIS
Illustrated by ANTON PIECK

METHUEN

First published in Great Britain 1987
by Methuen Children's Books Ltd
11 New Fetter Lane, London EC4P 4EE
in collaboration with B. V. Uitgeversmaatschappij Elsevier
Text copyright © 1987 Naomi Lewis
Illustrations by Anton Pieck copyright © 1984
B. V. Elseviers Uitgeversmaatschappij, Amsterdam
Design by Sue Ryall
Researched by Yvonne Hooker

Printed in Holland

British Library Cataloguing in Publication Data

Lewis, Naomi
  Stories from the Arabian nights.
  1. Tales – Arabia
  I. Title   II. Pieck, Anton
  398.2'1'0953   PZ8.1

  ISBN 0–416–49870–1

Contents

ᕼOW SHAHRAZAD CAME TO TELL HER TALES TO THE GREAT KING SHAHRYAR

LEGENDS TELL OF A CERTAIN pair of brothers, each a king; the older was called Shahryar, the younger Shahzaman. For a space of twenty years they had ruled their lands in power and splendour, but in that time neither had seen the other. Now King Shahryar was seized by a violent longing to meet his brother again, so he ordered his wazir to journey out to Samarkand al-Ajam, his brother's kingdom, and bring him back.

"I hear and obey," said the wazir.

King Shahzaman of Samarkand received the message and thereupon prepared for his departure. When all equipment was ready – tents, camels, mules, slaves, armed fighting men and gifts of treasure – and the wazir had been appointed to govern in his absence, the king set out. But shortly after, he remembered leaving something of importance to him at the palace, and he returned. Entering quietly (for now it was nightfall, and most were sleeping) he opened the door of his room and saw – ah, fearful sight! – his wife in the arms of a slave; they were embracing, and more. His heart turned to ice, his brain to fire; the world grew dark within him; with a single blow of his sword he smote off the heads of the pair. Then he went back to the caravan, and the journey was resumed.

As the procession approached the city, King Shahryar joyfully came forth to meet his brother; the streets were decorated; music played; crowds were waiting in welcome. But nothing could cheer Shahzaman, who advanced with hollow cheeks and heavy step. At first King Shahryar thought that the wan looks of his brother came from the weariness of travel. But after some days he began to suspect a hidden care or grief. He asked his brother to join him in a day of hunting, to refresh his mind and body, but Shahzaman had no taste for it, and refused, so the king went alone.

Now, left to himself, Shahzaman wandered through the palace to pass the time. Pausing at a window that looked on to the royal garden, he perceived the wife of his brother stepping forth, accompanied by forty slaves, twenty men and twenty girls. When they reached a pool which flowed from a sparkling fountain, they all undressed and splashed about in the waters.

Then the king's wife called out: "Masud! Masud!" At once a huge slave ran up to her, and they embraced, and more. And all the men slaves did the same with the women slaves.

The king's brother watched, amazed. At last he said to himself, "By Allah, this is even more terrible than that which happened to me." And with this thought the burden left his spirit; he felt able to eat and drink and was himself again. Presently the king returned from hunting and wondered much to find his brother restored and vigorous, with good appetite.

"Brother," he said, "is there some reason for this change?"

"I will tell you," answered Shahzaman. And he described the frightful happening in his palace, which had made him believe that none had been afflicted with such treachery as himself. This, he said, was the cause of the sickness. But (he added) while the king was out hunting he had witnessed an even worse betrayal, and that had restored his strength. For he knew now that he was not the only sufferer, nor the worst.

"What thing did you perceive?" asked Shahryar. At first the brother was loth to tell him, but at last he did so.

Shahryar was astounded. "I must see this for myself if I am to believe it," he declared.

So, on the following day, he announced that he was again going hunting, and went forth, but while his followers thought that he was sleeping in his tent, he secretly disguised himself and returned. And all that his brother had seen in the garden he also saw.

Now Shahryar felt as if reason were hurrying out of his mind. He said to his brother, "Let us go forth wherever Allah wills until we have found one with a fate even worse than ours; otherwise, death is all we can wish for." So they went out by a secret door, wandering night and day until they came to a tree in a lonely plain that bordered on the sea, and there they sat down to rest. Suddenly the waves began to swirl and boil; a black column of smoke rose from the waters, towering towards the heavens; this moved towards them, and became an enormous Jinnee, carrying a box on his head. Seating himself on the ground he opened the lid and lifted out a beautiful young girl, bright as the sun, fair as the moon. He stroked the hair of his lovely captive, gazed at her with devouring eyes, then fell asleep. The girl had noticed the brothers and at once beckoned them to her, inviting each to a close embrace.

"If you do not," she added, "I shall wake the Jinnee, and that will be your end." Then she showed them a necklace made of seal rings. "Do you know

7

what these are?" she said. "I will tell you. They are the seal rings of passers like yourself, five hundred and seventy of them, princes, merchants, beggars even, for it is my chief and only abiding pleasure to deceive the Jinnee who stole me away on my wedding night. Now I would have your seal rings also." And they complied, and did as she wished, and gave the rings to her.

Then one brother said to the other, "If such things can happen to a Jinnee, with all his power, then we should be consoled." And each returned to his own home, after fitting ceremony. As for King Shahryar, he ordered his wife to be beheaded, and the forty slaves also. Then he commanded his wazir to bring him every night a virgin girl; every morning he had the girl put to death; thus he would have no betrayal.

For three years this continued, until the whole city was deep in grief for their slain daughters, and those who still had girl children fled the land. So a day came when the wazir could not find a single maiden for the king's pleasure. He returned to his home in fear.

Now the wazir himself had two daughters, Shahrazad and Dunyazad, lovely, witty, charming, each a jewel of damsels. Shahrazad was especially gifted. She had read much, knew unnumbered legends, and possessed a thousand books telling of kings and princes and people of bygone ages, also of the poets and their songs throughout past centuries. To listen to her was music.

When she saw her father so bowed down with care, she said: "Father, nothing lasts for ever, neither joy nor grief. Tell me now of your trouble." Then the wazir told the tale of the king and his commands.

Shahrazad listened, then she said, "Father, you must arrange for me to marry this king, for – if Allah wills – I shall by certain means be the preserver of all other maidens in our land." The wazir had no wish to lose his daughter and tried to dissuade her, but to no avail. So the usual preparations were made.

King Shahryar was filled with pleasure at the news of this fresh and lovely virgin. But before the evening came, Shahrazad gave certain instructions to her younger sister, little Dunyazad.

"When I am with the king," she said, "I will ask him to send for you. And when the time comes, you must say to me, 'Sister, the night before us is long. Tell us some of your tales of marvels, that the hours may be delightful.' Then I shall do what I shall do. Have no fear!"

At nightfall, the wazir took Shahrazad to the king. But first the young girl begged for a favour.

"O noble and virtuous king," she said, "I have a little sister, and I have not said my last farewell to her." So the king sent for the sister, and after the two girls had embraced and spoken together, little Dunyazad sat quietly by the bed.

And when the time came, she said, as she had been told, "Dear sister Shahrazad, tell us one of your tales of marvels, so that the rest of the night may pass delightfully." Shahrazad then began to relate a story, and the king listened enraptured. But when dawn approached she left the tale at a point, so that the king longed for the second night, in order to hear what next befell. And in this way she survived the first night, and the next, and the next again, as you shall now discover.

THE TALE OF THE ONE-EYED BEGGAR

LISTEN, O KING, SAID SHAHRAZAD, to a tale strange beyond imagining, told to me by a one-eyed beggar. These are the words he spoke.

I was a king, and son of a king. When my father died, I came to the throne and my reign was thought wise, just and generous. But I loved sea-voyaging; and since my kingdom was bordered by the sea, and many fortified islands were under my protection, I decided to visit these islands. And so I set out with ten ships, each provisioned for a month. After twenty days, a strong wind rose up against us, blowing us out of course all through the night. At dawn the false wind dropped and we set sail again, thinking that we were on course; but after a further twenty days we found ourselves lost in strange waters, unknown even to the captain.

A look-out was sent to the mast-head to search for signs of land. He came down, saying: "Master, on my right hand I saw fish floating on the water, but further ahead, in the distance, I perceived a looming shape, now black, now white."

Hearing this, the captain uttered a loud cry, threw his turban on the deck and tore at his beard, saying: "These things mean death for us all. Not one of us will escape." Everyone joined in weeping and wailing; but I begged the man to tell me more.

"My lord," said the captain, "we are being powerfully drawn towards a mountain of black stone, rising out of the sea: the Magnetic Mountain, it is called, and no wind can help us avoid our fate. For every nail and every piece of iron in our vessel will burst and fly towards that terrible mound and cleave to its sides: such is its mysterious power. Who knows but Allah how many ships it has destroyed through the ages! I must tell you that on the summit is a dome of brass resting on ten columns; on the top of this is a horseman made out of brass on a brazen horse, with a brass spear in his hand. Hung against his breast is a leaden tablet engraved with secret runes and signs, unknown to living man. It is said that so long as the rider stays on the horse, every ship which comes too near is doomed." The captain then again wept bitterly and all on board lamented too, and exchanged farewells.

The next day had scarcely dawned when we were violently drawn towards the magnetic rock: all metal in our ship flew towards its sides with a great clanging and clattering, and the vessel fell to pieces. Most on board were drowned. Some floated for a while, but what became of them I do not know, because the waves swirled them away. But it was Allah's will to preserve me for further affliction. A plank came to my hand; I clung to it and was cast on to a hard surface – the base of the Magnetic Mountain itself. There I found that a path of steps, cut into the stone, led upwards. With toil and fear, clinging to metal parts from murdered ships, I reached the summit. The brass dome lay before me, just as I had been told. I gave thanks to Allah, and, overcome with exhaustion, fell asleep.

In my sleep I heard a voice saying, "O son of Kasib, when you wake, dig beneath your feet and you will find a bow of brass and three arrows of lead, engraved with runes and signs. Take the bow and arrows and shoot at the rider on the dome, and you will free the world from a great evil. The horseman will fall into the sea and the bow will drop at your feet. Where it lies you must bury it. As soon as this is done the sea will boil and rise until it reaches the mountain top where you are standing. Then a boat will appear with a man within, carrying oars. He will look exactly like the rider; but do not fear; he is not that one but another. You must enter the boat, and in ten days you will reach safe and friendly waters; then one will appear to take you to your own country. But there is one condition – that you do not utter the sacred name of Allah: no, not once. Remember."

Then I awoke, and did as I had been told in the dream. With a leaden arrow I shot the horseman, who fell into the sea. I buried the bow where it had dropped from my hand and saw the waters boil and rise to the mountain top. Then the boat appeared, rowed by a man of brass. I embarked, saying not a word, and after ten days we reached a safe and friendly sea, with land in sight.

In my joy I cried out: "There is no God but God! Praise be to Allah!"

At once the man hurled me into the sea and vanished. I swam for many hours until night, when I could do no more. I thought my end had come, but then a great wave, huge as a castle, rose up and tossed me on to land. When morning came I found myself on a small island, green with trees, but remote and uninhabited, with wide seas all around. What could I do? Despair began to fill my heart, when I suddenly saw a ship approaching fast, with a number of men on board, all looking towards the island.

Fearing danger, I quickly climbed a tree and watched unseen as ten black slaves stepped ashore carrying spades. They made for the centre, dug in the earth and uncovered a trap-door; then they returned to bring back from the vessel supplies of rich foods and exquisite and costly clothes. Finally, a most ancient man left the ship, one so eaten up by time that he scarcely seemed human. He led by the hand a boy of perfect beauty, slender and graceful as a sapling tree: a sight to melt the heart. Then all of them, old man, boy and slaves, went through the trap-door. Presently they returned – all but the boy. The slaves replaced the earth, then with the old man, left the shore. I watched the ship sail away.

When they were well out of sight I climbed down the tree, removed the earth, lifted the heavy trap-door and peered within. A long flight of steps led down: I descended and came at last to a great room, richly carpeted and hung about with silks and lustrous cloths. And there, on a low couch, fanning himself, with delicate fruits and sweetmeats and sweetly-scented flowers all about him, was the boy. Seeing me, he turned pale with terror.

I greeted him in the name of peace, saying, "You have nothing to fear. I am no evil spirit but a man, a king and son of a king; fate has brought me to this strange place to lighten your solitude and to save you from this prison." At my words he seemed to lose his dread; then, sweetly smiling, he asked me to sit beside him on his couch while he told his story.

"I must tell you," he said, "that I am in this sunless cell not to die but to escape the doom of death. Shortly after my birth, my elderly father was given this warning by soothsayers: 'The boy will live for fifteen years, but he will then be killed by a king, son of a king, and this will come to pass forty days after this same man has caused the brass rider on the Magnetic Mountain to fall into the sea.' When my father learnt that the rider had indeed been shot by a leaden arrow and was now deep in the ocean, he was overcome with dread. He brought me at once to this secret subterranean hiding place. At the end of the fortieth day he will return and fetch me home, since the danger will be over."

When the boy had spoken, I thought to myself, "What liars are those who claim to read the stars, for I would rather kill myself than do this young boy harm."

Then I said aloud, "My child, Allah has sent me here to guard you from all dangers. And when the forty days are over I shall ask your father to let you come to my kingdom to be my companion and heir."

The boy thanked me in his gentle way and great affection grew daily between us. We passed the hours from dawn until dusk in laughter, singing, feasting, talk and play.

At last came the fortieth day, when the father was to return. At dawn the boy woke and wished to eat. I brought him a water melon, and, to carve it open, climbed upon the bed to bring down a sharp knife which hung on the wall above. But I slipped, and the knife pierced the boy's heart. He died at once. So, destiny defeated our hopes and plans.

An hour later the old man and his slaves arrived; I was hiding once more in the tree. Their grief on finding the boy dead echoed my own. Lamenting and wailing, they set sail again and once more I was alone on the island.

After a few days I noticed a strange happening: the waters were retreating daily on the western edge of the island, and quite soon a stretch of sand lay between my seeming prison and the nearest coast. So I stepped along the ribbed and marshy causeway, until I reached firm land. A fiery glow lit the distance, no doubt from a great fire. But as I drew nearer I saw that the flame-coloured light was none other than the setting sun reflected from a palace whose walls were of shining copper. As I stood marvelling at the sight, the gates opened and a venerable sheikh, followed by ten young men, came towards me. These young men were all of exceptional beauty, except for one defect; in each, one eye was blind. They greeted me courteously and asked to hear my story; as I told it they listened with wonder. Then they invited me into the palace, where we passed through many spacious halls adorned with beautiful hangings, of exquisite design. At last we came to the great hall in the centre, where the young men invited me to sit. The greybeard served us with food and wine.

Then they said to me, "Young man, watch if you will, but ask no question about anything you see." The old man brought each one a tray covered over with a silken cloth, also a candle. I gazed with increasing wonder, for the trays held ashes, charcoal, lampblack and soot; and the young men began to sprinkle their heads with the ashes and rub the black on their faces and round their remaining eye, all the while crying out: "We were happy and fortunate but we could not be content. Our punishment is just!" They continued in this fashion until daybreak; then the sheikh brought them warm water and they washed away the dirt and changed their clothes.

I was tormented by curiosity, but dared not speak, for I had been warned to ask no questions. The next night and the next they went through the same performance. At last I could no longer keep silent and I cried out: "I will die if I am not told why you have each lost an eye; and why you behave in this strange fashion night after night."

They replied, "We advised you only for your own good. For if you persist in desiring to know what you should not, you will suffer the same fate as

ourselves. And you will not be able to join us either, for our permitted number is ten and our company is complete."

"Nevertheless," I said, "whatever the cost, I must know and I will."

At this they argued no more, but saying, "What will be will be," they ordered the old man to fetch a live sheep, kill it and take off the skin.

Then I was told, "We will sew you into this sheepskin and place you on the green slope outside the palace walls. A giant bird called the rukh will swoop down and carry you through the clouds to its home in the mountain peaks. But you must slit the skin with a sharp knife; then, seeing a human, the bird will fly away. Now you must walk to the east for half a day and you will see before you a towering palace with walls of gold, encrusted with emeralds, rubies, sapphires, amethysts and other radiant stones. Our palace would seem a hovel beside it. It is easy enough to enter for the gates stand open – but if you ever do so, beware! For our fate will be yours."

Then they took me into the grounds, gave me a knife, sewed me in the sheepskin and left me there alone. Suddenly I heard a thunderous whirr of wings and felt sharp talons seizing the fleecy hide. Away we flew, at what dizzying heights I dared not guess. At last I was set down. At once I ripped the hide and leapt out, uttering weird noises to alarm the bird, and it heavily rose and flew away. It was indeed a huge creature, white in colour, taller than twenty camels, with wings that spread out over many leagues. I had no wish to linger in that fearsome place, so set out along a winding path which led to an immense and dazzling building, the golden palace, undoubtedly, of which I had been warned. Indeed its beauties and splendours, within and without, were more than words could conjure, more than dreams.

When I entered I found in the first hall a throng of the fairest damsels, forty in number, each one a moon of loveliness; their beauty made me faint. One brought water and washed my feet; another my hands; a third offered me a refreshing drink, perfumed with flowers; this one danced, that one sang, others brought wine and fruits, all gathered about me, calling me sweet and teasing names. Then, as the day drew to a close one would offer me her company for the night. And so passed a twelvemonth of sweet joys.

But on the year's last day the damsels came to me weeping and letting loose their hair. I asked the cause of their grief.

"Lord of our hearts," they said, "others have come and gone, but none has pleased us so much as you. And we fear that you will go the way of all the rest – by disobeying one request."

"That is not possible," I said. "But what is the request?"

"You must know," they answered, "that we are all daughters of a king by different mothers. This palace has been granted to us as our home, to live as we will. But every year we must visit our parents for forty days and forty nights, and we leave this day. However, you will remain here while we are gone. Here are a hundred keys, to the hundred doors of the palace. Only one must not be tried – the key to the red-gold door that faces the garden. But beware! If you disobey, you are lost. You will never see us again, or know this place, or taste again the joys that we have shared."

And so, with many a kiss and tear and tender look, they departed. Now I was for the first time alone, and began a tour of the palace. I turned the key of the first door – and found myself in a garden where all the fruits of the world hung from trees, intoxicating the senses, a perfection of joy to eat. The second door led to a paradise of flowers, of ravishing perfume, an enchantment to eye and heart. The third opened on to a jewelled hall filled with cages of singing birds whose songs thrilled every organ in my being. The fourth held precious stones that dazzled the sight and mind; the fifth – but how can I convey the wonders that lay behind the doors?

By the fortieth day, when the damsels would return, I had opened all but the red-gold door in the garden. A violent temptation came over me. I placed the key in the lock. I paused. I turned the key and I found myself in a spacious hall, strewn with saffron and lit with golden lamps and candles, which gave out a mingled odour of musk and ambergris, or incense of a kind unknown to me. And then I perceived a great black horse that gleamed like a sky of stars; he seemed a prince of horses, a miracle to see. His manger was of white crystal filled with well-cleaned sesame seeds; his drinking vessel held perfumed rosewater. His saddle, bridle and trappings were of wrought gold. I had pride in my horsemanship and leapt on to his back, but he did not move. This angered me and I struck him with his own gold bridle chain. At this he uttered a terrible cry, spread out two vast black wings and rose up into the air, reaching a sickening height. Half-dead with fear I clung to his mane and sides, but at last he descended. The place was familiar – it was the green terraced slope outside the palace of the ten young men. There, he threw me off his back, and with a blow from his wing tip thrust out my left eye.

As I stood there, weeping and lamenting, the young men all came forth.

"You would not heed our advice," they said, "and there is no place for you here. But take the road beyond and make for the city of Baghdad, where a beggar may find alms."

And that is how I, a king and the son of a king, came to be a one-eyed beggar, wandering the streets of Baghdad. What lies in the future, only Allah can tell.

THE TALE OF THE GENEROUS SHEIKH

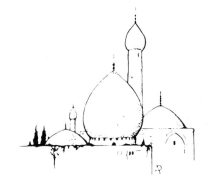

THIS CURIOUS TALE WAS TOLD to the great Khalifah Harun al-Rashid, whose pleasure it was to wander through the city and learn of the lives of his people. It happened on one of these occasions that he saw a venerable man giving bountifully to a beggar under a bridge. He asked the worthy sheikh to come to his palace.

"You appear to be a man of substance, who yet has known toil," said the Khalifah. "I greatly wish to know the path by which Allah has brought you to this fortunate state."

And this is the sheikh's strange story.

"O Prince of the Faithful, I was born to the trade of rope-making, specializing in hemp, as were my father and my grandfather before me. My takings were meagre at the best of times, and scarcely fed my wife and children; but since I knew no other skill I was content enough. If I were poor, it was the will of Allah, who had not given me wit or knowledge enough to rise any further in the world. So I spent the years.

Late one day, as I sat making a hemp rope, which was fastened about my heel, two wealthy friends, Saad and Saadi, came to sit before my shop and chat, as they often did in the cool of the evening. They would talk of all things in heaven and earth, neither interrupting the other, and in so clear and measured a fashion that even I could follow the argument. On this particular day the conversation was on the matter of poverty, destiny, and the will of man. The one named Saad was putting forth the view that a man cannot be happy unless he has wealth enough to be free and independent of servitude.

"The poor," he was saying, "are poor through the mischance of birth and other forms of ill-luck. They remain so because they never have a sufficient sum to lift them out of their sorry state. I hold that, given a little capital, any man, however poor, could become quite wealthy if he gave his mind to it."

"My friend," said Saadi, "it grieves me that I cannot share your opinion. Wealth itself may be a burden, whereas a man like our companion here, Hasan

the ropemaker, seems content without possessions. If a poor man is meant by Destiny to become a wealthy one, he will become so without all this calculation. No, he who trusts in Allah should take no thought for the morrow, but each day give his surplus to relieve the needy. Such is my philosophy."

"I perceive," the other said, "that neither of us will win the argument by talk alone. So let us try a test. We will find a poor but honest man and give him a little capital. In a few months' time we shall see if he has started on the ladder to wealth, or whether Destiny has other plans."

"As you will," said Saadi, "but why should we look any further than our ropemaker here?"

"You are right," said Saad. Then he turned to me, saying, "O Hasan, you have many small children to feed, and the price of hemp alone takes almost all your profits. If I give you two hundred golden dinars, could you use them in a manner to lift yourself out of poverty?"

I replied at once, "Noble master, even with a lesser sum I could transform myself into the richest ropemaker in my guild."

He smiled and handed me a purse, saying, "I have confidence in you, Hasan. We both hope that you will gain from this start and find pleasure in your prosperity." Then he waved away my grateful thanks, and the two friends went off, talking on other matters.

When they had gone, I began to wonder where I could hide the money. My house had only one small room, and not a shelf, not a cupboard in that. At last I decided to place it in my turban, which I did, after taking out ten dinars for immediate use. Then I went to the market, bought some hemp, and also, as a luxury, a leg of lamb from the butcher. Alas! as I walked back, dreaming of the feast we would enjoy, a hawk dropped out of the clouds, seized the lamb in its beak and my turban in its claws, and sailed back into the sky. Sadly, I purchased another turban and made my way home. When the few dinars were spent we returned to our usual poverty. Foolishly, I told all to my wife, and she never ceased to lament the loss and reproach me for my carelessness. So passed ten months. Then, one day, the two friends Saad and Saadi stopped before my shop and asked for news.

"I am hoping," said Saad, "that our friend is living in some prosperity. We shall find a change, I am sure."

"As for that," said Saadi, "I see little difference here. Hasan is still making rope with the hemp attached to his heel. His turban is slightly less filthy and disgusting than it was ten months ago, but otherwise things appear very much the same."

from The Generous Sheikh

"Well, Hasan," said Saad, "I have to say that your face lacks joy. Business worries, perhaps? The cares of wealth?"

"O master," I replied, "I am in worse trouble than before. Destiny is my foe." And I told the tale of the hawk.

Both were silent for a moment, then Saad observed, "Well, the experiment has not gone as well as I had hoped. Did I not know that truth is truth, I would say that the matter of the hawk has a fine ring of invention about it. For all this, I am prepared to make a second attempt; I have no wish for my friend Saadi to think that he has proved his point by a single trial." Then he counted out another two hundred dinars, saying, "I trust that you will not hide them in your turban." He waved off my thanks and the two departed, talking in their usual fashion.

This time, after careful thought, I decided on a new hiding place. First setting aside ten dinars, I knotted the rest in a cloth and put it in the bottom of a large jar filled with bran. Then I replaced the jar in its corner and went out to buy a supply of hemp. While I was at the market a pedlar passed along the street with a supply of a certain kind of earth which is used by women for washing their hair. My wife had not washed her hair for a considerable time and since she had no money for the purchase she exchanged our jar of bran for a quantity of this earth.

I did not learn this until I came back with the hemp. At once I looked towards the corner to see that my treasure was safe – but it was not there!

When I discovered the terrible truth I fell to the ground, crying, "O wife! You have bartered my destiny and your own destiny and our children's destinies for a handful of earth with which to wash your hair! We are lost indeed – lost beyond recall." And I revealed to her what she had done. She screamed and raved, reviling me for not having shared the secret.

At last I said, "Enough, enough. We are poor, it is true, but the rich are only mortal like ourselves. They breathe the same air; they die when Allah appoints; do we do otherwise?" And so we returned to our accustomed poverty, with no more than the usual complaints.

Only one thing troubled me: what was I to say to my benefactor? The dreaded moment came at last, when I saw the pair coming towards my shop, one with a hopeful look, one with a knowing smile. I pretended not to see them, and busily plied my work. But they called to me with greetings, and I was obliged to answer. Quickly I told the sad tale and with lowered eyes continued twisting the rope. But Saad was not angry.

"Well, Hasan," he said mildly, "your story could be true – though it is a curious chance that the hawk and hawker were so promptly at hand at these moments. If I did not know your honesty I would credit you with quite a gift of invention. Still, I do not think that I will make any more experiments for the time being. Nevertheless –" and here he turned to Saadi – "I still hold that a poor man must have a little capital if he is to change his state at all."

"My generous friend," said Saadi, "you are quite wrong, and you have thrown away four hundred dinars, half to a hawk, half to a hawker, to prove it. Well, I am prepared to risk a trifle to prove that a poor man is the toy of Destiny, and that nothing can alter that." He picked up a small lump of lead from the dust and gave it to me, saying, "I am not as rich as my companion here, but something is better than nothing, and, if Destiny wills, this may turn out to be of more use than a bran jar full of gold dinars." Gravely I accepted the gift, thanking both men for their kindnesses, and they left in the usual manner.

That night, an hour or so after midnight, I was awakened by a knocking at the door.

"Who is there?" I asked.

"I am the wife of your neighbour, the fisherman," was the answer. "I am black with shame to disturb you, but my husband rose to go to his work and found a leaden weight missing from his nets. Without it, the net is useless. Moreover, if he does not get to the waterside well before sunrise he will not make his expenses for the day. So he begged me to ask if by chance you had a piece of lead to lend him." At once I recalled the leaden weight I had been given a few hours earlier, and told my wife to give it to the woman. She said with delight, "In return for your goodness, my husband will make his first cast in your husband's name and will bring you any fish that he catches with that cast."

In the morning, on his way to the market, the fisherman brought the catch from his first cast, bedded in sweet herbs. It consisted of one fish only, but that one was large and fine, a prince of fishes. My wife rejoiced, but wondered how to cook it since it was too large for any of her pans.

"Cut it in pieces," said I, "and make a stew." She started to clean the fish and found in its centre an oval of smooth glass, the size of a pigeon's egg, and as clear as water. She washed it, and gave it to the children as a plaything while the fish was being prepared. But when evening came, the egg gave out a radiant glow that lit the whole room; we had no need of a lamp. Finally, well pleased with our supper and the day's events, we went to sleep.

But the next day my wife could not keep silent. By noon, the news of our find had spread through the neighbourhood. A certain butcher, grown rich from the slaughter of lambs, was known to increase his wealth by looking out for rare and curious objects on behalf of some officials at the palace.

The wife of this man came to our door saying, "As Allah lives, dear neighbour, I wish to do you a good turn. I hear that you have a glass bauble which appears to be a pair to one I already have. So to help your neediness I will give you ten gold dinars for this trifle."

But the children did not wish to part with their toy and held it behind their backs; moreover, my wife was finding it useful instead of a lamp, so she said, "I can do nothing without my husband's permission. You must ask him when he returns." The woman was not pleased.

"As one Moslem wife to another," she said, "I must tell you that I am with child, and my wishes should not be thwarted, however foolish they may seem." And she settled down to wait.

As soon as I entered the house the woman made her offer again. I said nothing, for I was thinking, and this, for a ropemaker, is not done with speed.

"Will you take twenty?" she said. "A pregnant woman's wishes must not be crossed. That is why my husband allows me gold for this purchase."

It seemed to me that, if this wealthy woman were so determined to have the toy, it might be of more worth than I knew, so I said, "I must reflect on the matter." She offered me fifty, then a hundred dinars, but when I told her that I was not yet ready to sell the thing, she gathered her veils about her and left, in a thunder of rage.

All this made me think that the glass egg might be, perhaps, some marvellous jewel of the ocean, fallen from the crown of a great sea-king. I had heard that many treasures lie deep beneath the waves, and I resolved to show the pretty thing to a jeweller, to the leading jeweller of the city, no less. Wrapping it in a cloth I made my way to his shop and asked if I might show my goods in a darkened room at the back. Though puzzled, the man agreed; but when the egg was unwrapped the place seemed lit by a multitude of torches.

The master jeweller looked at the source of the light, and then cried out, "That is one of the lost gems of Sulaiman, a jewel from his crown!" Then he took it in his hand, saying, "The price of this is hard to estimate, but I offer you a hundred thousand dinars. I hope that you will accept it, for I cannot do more."

And so, in a single day, my meagre poverty was transformed into fabulous wealth. What did I do? First, I called together all the ropemakers of Baghdad and told them of my good fortune.

"Brothers," I said, "it is my view that all of our craft should benefit. From this day I take you into my service, so that you will be sure of regular payment for your work, and never need fear for the morrow." The ropemakers thanked

from Sweet-Friend and Ali-Nur

me, and, indeed, the plan has given them easier lives and a steady profit for all. It has also given me a highly respected position in the market. I then moved my family from our hovel to a splendid mansion set within flowering gardens, groves and orchards. But all this was not known at the time to Saad and Saadi, and when they found my old shop closed and derelict, they thought that I must be dead. Great was their astonishment when they learnt that I was not only alive, in excellent health, but had become one of the richest merchants in Baghdad, that I lived in a palace circled with gardens, and that I was now known as Hasan the Magnificent.

They made their way to my new home, where slaves conducted them through bowers of orange and lemon trees, refreshed by trickling streams, to my reception hall. I would have kissed the hem of their robes, but they would have none of this, and embraced me as their brother. We moved to a small pavilion overlooking the grounds, and when they were served with fruits and sherbet, I told my story, omitting not a single detail.

"You see, O Saad," said Saadi, "Destiny, not capital, was the making of his fortune."

"Yet think again," said the other; "did he not choose to give the weight to the fisherman? Did he not show choice in refusing the offer of the lamb-slaughterer's wife? Has he not employed thought in the spending of his gains? The fault, dear Saadi, is not in our stars . . ." So they argued, in pleasant amity, and are about it still, for at my wish they have made their home with me. Which of the two has the truth of the matter I find it prudent not to say, but the thought is in my mind. I give to the poor from my plenty wherever I can, and that is how I came to be on the bridge when you, O king, were passing. Such is my story."

"O sheikh Hasan," said the Khalifah, "wonderful are the ways of Allah. Now I will provide a pendant to your delightful tale." He whispered into the ear of his treasurer, who went away, returning with a carved box in his hand. Harun al-Rashid opened it, and showed it to his guest saying, "This came into my possession on the day you parted from it."

There lay the egg of glass, the wondrous gem from the crown of Sulaiman.

THE EXTRAORDINARY TALE OF SWEET-FRIEND AND ALI-NUR

O MOST AUSPICIOUS KING, THERE was once a good and worthy Sultan of Basrah, who held his throne by favour of the mighty Khalifah Harun al-Rashid. The name of this Sultan was Mohammed, and he had two wazirs. Now the wazir al-Fadl was the most generous and virtuous of men, admired and loved by all for his knowledge and wisdom. But the wazir al-Muin was a man of evil; wherever he walked the people moved away in fear and loathing.

One day the Sultan Mohammed called to his wazir al-Fadl, saying, "I wish you to find me a female slave – but the one I have in mind must be of the rarest quality, unmatched in the world for beauty, gifts, accomplishments and pleasing ways."

The wazir al-Muin, enraged that his rival should have been chosen for this assignment, said with a sneer, "The price of such a one could hardly be less than ten thousand pieces of gold!" But this only made the Sultan more eager, and he ordered al-Fadl to begin the search at once. As for the purchase money, he commanded his treasurer to take ten thousand gold pieces to the wazir's house, to be there when he should require it.

So, day after day, al-Fadl went to the market, having arranged with the brokers that all their choicest slave girls should be brought first to him. After a month had passed he had inspected more than a thousand damsels, yet none seemed the perfect answer to the Sultan's wish.

One morning, however, a broker brought him a female slave of utmost beauty. Her eyes were the colour of midnight, seen through long curved lashes, blacker than ebony; her skin was silk, her mouth a rose, her lips sweeter than syrup; her waist was like that of a bee; her voice resembled a light west wind which had passed over a garden of flowers. She was dressed in shimmering robes made of the costliest stuffs ever woven. The wazir rejoiced in himself and asked the price of the damsel.

"The owner spoke of ten thousand pieces of gold," said the broker, "though even that he admits will not meet the cost of the sumptuous clothes she is wearing, the chicken meat and delicacies that have been her food, nor of her many teachers; for she has studied fine calligraphy, philosophy, poetry, singing, composing, and playing on beguiling instruments. She has also so pleasing a nature that she has been named Sweet-Friend."

The wazir agreed to the price and, when the money had been weighed out, the broker spoke again. "O wazir," he said, "it is my opinion that the damsel should not be taken at once to the Sultan; she has just arrived from a long journey and suffers a little from fatigue and change of climate. I suggest that you keep her for ten days or so in your palace, where she can rest and recover the full flower of her beauty."

This advice seemed good to the wazir; he had the damsel brought to his home where she was given a private apartment with every luxury that she might desire.

Now the wazir al-Fadl had a son, Ali-Nur by name, who was as beautiful as the shining moon, but a rascal for pretty women. For several days he knew nothing of the damsel in his home, then he entered his mother's apartment when that noble woman was at the bath and saw Sweet-Friend in all her beauty. Immediately he was consumed with desire and made her his own.

When the wazir heard what had happened he pulled out the hairs of his beard in his fury.

"If al-Muin hears of this, he will tell the Sultan and ruin me," he cried.

But his wife said, "Listen to me. The Sultan knows nothing of the damsel; outside our household she has not been seen. I will replace the money, for I have jewels enough to sell, and another beauteous slave girl may yet be found for the Sultan. Now cease your torment, and leave all in the hands of Allah."

At last the wazir agreed, and a year of happiness passed for the young couple, while Allah took from the Sultan's mind all thought of the perfect slave girl. But news of the affair soon reached the evil al-Muin, who was ever alert to whispers. And yet, because al-Fadl was so much esteemed by the Sultan, nothing could be done – at least for the time being. But then it chanced that the good wazir came from the bath into the cold air and thus caught a malady, which consumed him night and day until he died.

Great grief filled the city of Basrah at the news of the good man's death. Even the schoolboys wept. Ali-Nur lamented long, shutting himself from the world, until at last a friend of the old wazir came to the house to reproach him.

"A father lives again in a son," said the wise man. "It is your duty now to end your mourning and look outwards once again." And this Ali-Nur began to do, with such zest that soon he was entertaining friends and guests every day and night of the week, with feasting, singers and dancers. More than once the steward tried to warn him that his gold was dwindling fast, but he took no heed, handing out gifts to every casual caller.

One night the steward came to him with sad looks, saying: "Master, what I feared has come about. You have no gold left."

"Then," said the young man, "I will go to my friends, who have had so much from me. They will surely help me now in time of trouble."

But at each door where he knocked he was told that the master was from home, or occupied, or lying sick. Dejected, he returned home.

Then Sweet-Friend said, "Do not despair. You must sell the furniture, clothes and ornaments of this house, a few at a time."

This he did and so they were able to live. But again the money came to an end.

"Do not forget," said Sweet-Friend, "that you have another property, myself. You must go to the broker who sold me and he will inform the wealthy purchasers."

This Ali-Nur did, but news of the arrangement reached the ears of the evil al-Muin and he seized the opportunity to bring harm to the son of his old rival. He went to the Sultan and reminded him of the money he had given al-Fadl to buy the perfect slave girl. He told the Sultan that al-Fadl had bought Sweet-Friend and that Ali-Nur had kept her for himself. The Sultan was consumed with rage. He called to him, with a single sign, a group of forty guards, each armed with a naked sword.

"Go with all speed to the house of Ali-Nur," he commanded, "and raze it to the ground. Bind the youth and the girl with ropes and drag them here with their faces to the earth. Away!"

"We hear and obey," said the leader, and they were off.

But there was in the court a young chamberlain called Sanjar who had been in the service of the old wazir and had long been a friend of Ali-Nur. Swiftly he mounted his horse and raced to the young man's home.

"You must go at once," he told him. "Al-Muin has spread a net about you which will mean your death. Already forty guards are on the way. Take this gold – " he gave Ali-Nur a handful – "it is all that I have at this moment, and fly. Go now; go fast!"

Ali-Nur rushed to fetch Sweet-Friend, and Allah arranged that they passed unseen to the water's edge, where a ship was about to sail to Baghdad. The two embarked; a fair wind sped the ship, which flew through the waves like a bird with outspread wings, towards the fabled city.

Now when the ship reached port, it was the will of Destiny that Sweet-Friend and Ali-Nur did not take the usual road but one which led to a place of trees and greenery, beautifully tended. A long path caught their interest for it seemed to end at a private garden which had high walls all around. A door was in the facing wall, exquisitely carved and hung about with coloured lamps, but this door was firmly locked. The path had several benches, and they decided to rest on one of these. They washed their hands and faces in a sparkling fountain, lay down, and very soon fell asleep.

Ah, the hidden garden beyond the door was truly a marvel. It was known as the Garden of Delight and in its centre was a palace called the Palace of Wonders. All this belonged to the Khalifah Harun al-Rashid: when his heart was burdened he would come here to forget his cares. The palace had a great hall pierced with eighty windows, in each of which hung a golden lamp. When the Khalifah came these were lit – never at any other time. The guardian of the place was a good old man called Ibrahim, who kept watch to see that no thieves or trespassers entered the grounds. On this day he was making his usual inspection when he perceived two people asleep on one of the seats. He was inflamed with anger, and cut a thin branch from a tree, swishing it through the air as he prepared to give them a beating. But then he reflected that the travellers might be beggars or travellers sent by Allah. With careful fingers he lifted the cloth which covered their faces, and beheld a young man and a girl, both of extraordinary beauty. All thought of beating them vanished, and he began to stroke the feet of Ali-Nur.

The young man woke in alarm, but seeing that the kindness came from an aged man, he rose up to show respect, and carried the old man's hands to his lips and brow.

Then the sheikh Ibrahim asked him, "O my son, where are you from?"

"My lord, we are strangers," Ali-Nur replied.

"Allah has written," said the old man, "that strangers must be treated with kindness. Come, my children, and taste the delights of the garden and palace which lie beyond the door."

"Whose is this place?" asked Ali-Nur.

"It is mine," said the old man, who did not wish to disturb his guests with the truth. "It came to me as an inheritance."

So they passed through the arched door and into grounds of surpassing beauty and wonder. Rich clusters of grapes, red as rubies, black as midnight, hung from arches. The trees were heavy with fruit, beguiling all the senses, the lustrous cherry, the tender apricot, the fig, white or green, sweeter than sugar; nightingales sang in the boughs; the turtle doves cooed of their longings, melting the heart; flowers shone in the emerald grass like jewels – violet, myrtle, rose; the lemons were gold lamps against the green. Waterfalls made a silver tinkling; the light west wind fanned the air with its own music. But perceiving that the two were almost swooning with the enchantments, the sheikh Ibrahim led them into the palace, which dazzled them even more with its splendours. Then he seated them by a window and brought them food.

Ali-Nur said, "Truly, the anguish that burned in my soul has been quenched by all these marvels."

After feasting, they washed their hands and gazed out at the rising moon and the trees and flowers touched by the moon's white light. The old man became more and more enraptured by the couple's youth and beauty – so much so that he became heedless of the Khalifah's orders. When Ali-Nur asked for wine, Ibrahim opened the Khalifah's own wine store. And when Sweet-Friend asked if she might light a lamp, since night had come, he said, "Yes, yes, damsel, what you will," though this was wholly forbidden.

Now Allah decreed that the Khalifah was sitting in his main palace, gazing out at the moon on the shimmering river. But what was that fiery light, dimming the moon itself? It seemed to come from his own Palace of Wonders. He called for his wazir, Jafar al-Barmaki.

"Dog of a wazir!" he said. "Why am I not told what is happening in my own city? Baghdad might be seized by rebels and you would not know it. Look! My own Palace of Wonders is ablaze!"

The kind wazir, thinking to protect old Ibrahim, who might have committed some folly, said quickly, "O prince, I omitted to tell you that the sheikh came to me last week asking if he might perform a family religious ceremony in the palace. I advised him to make his plans and I would obtain your leave, but Allah decreed that the matter left my head."

"That was a double fault," said the Khalifah. "Not only did you fail to tell me but you gave me no chance to help the old man, who clearly needed money. However I forgive you. And now let us visit old Ibrahim. He is a good, religious man, and is now, I am sure, surrounded by holy men and the poor. Someone there may offer up a prayer for us which will do us good in the hereafter. And Ibrahim will benefit from our presence."

"But," said Jafar, somewhat troubled, "the night is late; the guests will be departing."

"Nevertheless we shall go," said the Khalifah, and they set off. When they arrived, he paused and said, "First, I wish to see, without being seen, how the holy men perform their ceremonies. They must be deep in meditation for I hear no sound of praying." A walnut tree stood by the wall and he climbed up, branch by branch, until he reached a window and peered in.

What he saw was no religious gathering, but a youth and a damsel, each a moon of beauty, seated with cups of wine, and between them drinking too, was old Ibrahim. They were singing and chanting verses, turn by turn.

"Oh if I had but a lute," declared Sweet-Friend. The old man rose and left the hall, returning with a beautiful instrument.

"This is too much," cried the Khalifah in his tree. "That is the lute of my own sweet singer, Ishak! Well, if the girl plays out of tune, I will crucify them all three, and you too, Jafar. If she sings well, I shall pardon them and merely punish you."

"In that case," said Jafar, "I hope she sings badly, for then I shall have good company."

The Khalifah laughed in cheerful humour; but the laughter turned to amazement when he heard the damsel's music. "I must enter the hall and hear that young slave again," he declared.

"But not as you are, my lord," cried Jafar. "She will be too fearful to sing, and Ibrahim will die of fright."

At that moment, the Khalifah saw a movement in the grounds near a stream which flowed from the Tigris. It was a poor fisherman trying his luck in forbidden waters; already he had made a good haul. It was an easy matter to get the man to change his filthy rags for the Khalifah's silken clothes and to buy the basket of wriggling, leaping fish. In this disguise the Khalifah was welcomed by the three revellers who were ready for further feasting; Ali-Nur bought the fish for three gold pieces.

Then the Khalifah said: "Dare I ask a favour? What I most desire in the world is to hear this damsel sing and play the lute."

"Sing for the fisherman, Sweet-Friend," said Ali-Nur, and this she did.

So moved was the Khalifah that he cried out: "Allah be praised! Allah be praised! I have not heard the like!"

"So the damsel's music pleases you," said Ali-Nur. "Then she is yours. Take her, O fisherman, as my gift."

He was making for the doorway when Sweet-Friend cried out, "Can you leave me so without even a word of farewell? If you desert me, the only lover I can desire is death!"

The Khalifah, who wondered much what lay behind the strange events of

from Ghanim, the Slave of Love

the evening, called Ali-Nur back and begged him to tell his tale. And having heard it, he asked him: "Where do you go now?"

"The world is wide," said Ali-Nur.

"Wait," said the Khalifah, "I will write you a letter to take to the Sultan of Basrah; it will serve you well. And if you wonder how a poor fisherman can be on such terms with kings, I must tell you that as a child I learnt to read and write under the same master as the Sultan Mohammed and we have remained friends. If I make a request he will grant it for friendship's sake." He called for paper and pen and ink-holder, and after the proper forms of greeting to the Sultan Mohammed, he requested him to resign the throne of Basrah and to anoint the young man Ali-Nur, son of his former wazir al-Fadl, in his place. He signed it with his name, sealed it with his seal and gave it to Ali-Nur who set out straightaway.

Then the sheikh Ibrahim spoke. "Wretched fisherman!" he said. "You are not content with a bounty of gold for your miserable fish but you are taking this girl as well. If you don't wish for trouble I advise you to share both the gold and the girl with me – and she will come with me first!"

At this the Khalifah frowned with a terrible anger, clapped his hands and made a sign to Jafar and the real fisherman who were waiting outside. The fisherman rushed in and seized the old man, while Jafar advanced with a kingly robe to replace the filthy rags.

"Do I sleep or wake?" cried Ibrahim and cast himself on the floor.

"All is forgiven," said the Khalifah. Then turning to Sweet-Friend he said: "Damsel, you will soon be reunited with the young man, for whom good fortune awaits. In the meantime, we shall go to my palace for you belong to me by right of gift."

Now what of Ali-Nur? By the grace of Allah he arrived at the Sultan's palace at Basrah and handed him the letter. Seeing the seal and handwriting, the Sultan rose to his feet, kissed the paper three times, then read the message with care.

"The will of the Prince of the Faithful is the will of Allah," he said and was about to step down from the throne when the wazir al-Muin asked to see the letter, then tore it to pieces and chewed them in his mouth.

"What have you done!" cried the Sultan.

"My lord, I have saved you from a forgery. If the announcement had been genuine the Khalifah would have sent a chamberlain or wazir with a document properly set out by the palace scribe."

As the wazir al-Muin went on, the Sultan began to believe his words. He ordered his guards to seize the young man, then to place him in chains in the deepest dungeon, where the chief dungeon master was ordered to have him tortured night and day. The dungeon master, who had loved the old wazir, closed the cell door that none might see, swept the floor, set out a prayer carpet and a bench and said: "Master, have no fear. You are the son of a noble father, and shall be treated so." But he sent to the wazir each day a full account of the imaginary tortures inflicted on the prisoner.

On the forty-first day after Ali-Nur's arrival, a magnificent present arrived from the Khalifah for the Sultan of Basrah. The Sultan Mohammed was puzzled by the extreme richness of the gift, until one of his advisers suggested that it might be for the young man now condemned as a forger. The Sultan had forgotten him! Where was he now? In dungeon vile, the wazir reminded him, adding, "Would it not be better to rid yourself of the imposter altogether?"

"By Allah, you are right," replied Mohammed. "That is always the best solution in the name of peace."

"Then I have your permission, my lord, to announce the execution through the city? It will be good for all to see your strength and wisdom."

"Do as you will," said the Sultan.

When the people heard the announcement, many wept and grieved, for Ali-Nur was a favourite. Nevertheless multitudes both young and old hastened to the palace to be sure of a good close view.

As soon as the order came to bring the young man to the place of execution, the dungeon master hastily dressed him in prisoner's rags, wished him luck, and handed him over to the wazir. Placed on a mule, the youth was paraded through the city that all might see his shame. Finally they halted at the Place of Blood, as it was known, beneath the Sultan's window.

The executioner came and said to him quietly: "I am a slave under command but if you have any wish that I can fulfil, tell it now, for your span of life lasts only until the Sultan looks out of the window overhead." Ali-Nur asked for a drink of water. But before he could take the cup, the wazir al-Muin struck it to the ground, shouting: "Why this delay, executioner?" So the man bound the eyes of the prisoner and prepared to do his task. But the people were enraged and the sound of their anger rose like the sound of a storm. And then all heads turned. For a cloud of dust, and the thundering sound of hoofs drew nearer and nearer.

And where all this time was Sweet-Friend? After one night the Khalifah had forgotten all about her and she had stayed in her apartment weeping. One day, as the Khalifah wandered through his palace, he heard her sobs and asked who she was. Sweet-Friend reminded him of his promise to reunite her with Ali-Nur and the Khalifah sent at once for Jafar.

"For thirty days," he said, "no news has come of Ali-Nur, who should be on the throne of Basrah. I swear by the tombs of my ancestors that anyone who has harmed the young man will be put to death, even if it be my dearest friend. I charge you to set out at once to Basrah and report to me what you find."

Jafar and his attendants left on their swiftest horses; and it was the dust and thunder of their arrival that held up the executioner's sword. Straightaway he entered the palace and having greeted the Sultan and wished him peace, he delivered the Khalifah's message, asking if all was well with Ali-Nur. What answer could the Sultan give? So Jafar ordered his men to arrest Mohammed and his wazir al-Muin; then he named Ali-Nur as the rightful ruler and, during the three days of celebration, he remained in the city.

On the fourth day Ali-Nur told Jafar that he had a great longing to see the Khalifah.

"Your desire is good," said Jafar. "We shall prepare to depart after morning prayers."

And so, they set off, a great company, and with them were the offenders Mohammed and the wazir al-Muin.

In swift time they reached Baghdad, and came before the Khalifah, the famed Harun al-Rashid. He listened as Jafar gave his report, then called to Ali-Nur, saying, "Take this sword and cut off the head of the wretched al-Muin, who is standing here."

But the wazir, cunning to the last, said to Ali-Nur, 'I have behaved to you according to my nature. You may now behave according to your own."

At this, Ali-Nur threw down his sword saying, "His shrewd words have disarmed me." At that the Khalifah, Prince of Peace, called on his executioner to do the deed, which he did with a single stroke. Then he asked Ali-Nur if he had any special wish; whatever he named would be granted.

"O my lord," said Ali-Nur, "I want no kingdom. All I desire is to spend the rest of my days in your service. I could wish for no greater honour or happiness."

"You have spoken well," said the prince. "And I shall add to your wish another, a promise made and kept." He sent for Sweet-Friend and restored her to Ali-Nur, and gave them a palace in Baghdad, and gold and rich possessions, and he made the young man one of his close companions. The Sultan Mohammed was restored to the throne of Basrah and advised to be more careful in choosing his wazirs. So ends the strange and wonderful tale of Sweet-Friend and Ali-Nur, but stranger still, as you will find, is the tale to come.

THE STORY OF GHANIM, THE SLAVE OF LOVE

THERE WAS ONCE, O KING, in ancient times, a merchant of Damascus called Ayyub, who had two children. The son's name was Ghanim, which means the Slave of Love; he was as beautiful as a moonlit night, and his voice was like sweet music. His sister was called Fitnah, and she was as fair as day.

When Ayyub died, he left great riches to his children, also a hundred camel-loads of silks, jewelled fabrics and vessels of pure musk pods. On the bales he had written: "These are to sell in the city of Baghdad", and now young Ghanim planned to journey there in his place. He hired a great train of camels to carry these goods, took leave of his mother and sister, and set out, with a caravan of merchants, for that city. When he reached Baghdad he settled in a beautiful house where the wealthy merchants and notable persons came to welcome him. Then the leading sheikh of the market assigned him an honoured place, and he began to sell his wares, each day making two gold pieces for the expense of one. So passed a year of good fortune.

One day, everyone in the market place went to the funeral of one of the leading merchants; Ghanim also went. But the funeral lasted long; day passed into night, and still the mourners sat around the tomb, while slaves brought them meat and pastries. Ghanim grew more and more anxious to return, for he feared that his house might be robbed in his absence. At last he requested leave of the chief mourners and started off; but darkness hid the road, and soon he was entirely lost. Searching around for a shelter until daylight he dimly saw what seemed a small burial ground surrounded by four walls, with a palm tree growing inside. He opened the door in the wall and was about to lie down when he saw a light moving towards his hiding place. Quickly he climbed to the top of the tree, where he could watch among the leaves unseen.

The light came nearer. Soon he perceived three tall black slaves, two carrying a wooden chest, the third bearing a lantern and a spade. They entered the walled enclosure, dug a deep trench in the earth, and laid the heavy box inside. Then, as if glad to be done, they hurried away.

A great desire seized Ghanim to know what the chest contained. But until the first streak of dawn he dared not move from the tree. Daylight came at last; he climbed down, dug in the soft earth with his hands until he had uncovered the chest, then looking first from right to left, he opened the lid. He uttered a cry. What was this! A human body, the body of a girl. She breathed! She was alive! But in the deepest sleep – perhaps in a trance.

This girl was of the utmost beauty and delicacy. From head to foot she was decked with gold and jewels. A king's ransom could not have paid for her adornments. Ghanim carefully lifted her from the box and laid her in the open air. The fresh breeze entered her nostrils; she sighed, she coughed, she sneezed – and out of her mouth flew a lump of benj, enough to send an elephant to sleep a full day and a night.

She opened her eyes and softly called for her maidens: "Where are you, Little Breeze? I am thirsty, give me something to drink. Where are you, Flower of the Garden, and you, my Dawn?" As no one answered she began to look about her and cried out in terror: "Woe is me! I am alone in the place of tombs! Who has taken me from the palace and cast me among the dead?"

The young man stepped forward, saying, "Queen of Beauty, I am Ghanim ibn Ayyub. You have nothing to fear. Allah has led me here, your slave, to mend your troubles and to lead you back into the way of happiness. What I have witnessed, I will tell you as soon as you wish to hear."

The girl then turned her bright eyes on Ghanim and perceived that he was real and not the creature of a dream. In a voice sweeter than clear water she replied: "O thrice welcome youth, I would indeed learn how I came to lie in this place of death." And, when Ghanim had related what he had seen, she begged him to hide her once again in the chest, then to hire a mule and so transport her secretly to his house. There she would tell him her story.

Ghanim did as she wished, helped the muleteer to carry the chest into his home, then freed the girl from her prison. Looking around, the damsel saw she was in a well-built mansion, richly carpeted, hung with silks of a thousand ravishing colours and designs, with splendid furnishings everywhere: her rescuer must surely be a great merchant. He was also handsome to look upon, and of a rare charm in his ways. Therefore she loved him.

She took the little veil from her face and said: "See, I have uncovered my face before you. But now I am very hungry; I beg you bring me something to eat."

Then Ghanim, the Slave of Love, hastened to the market and purchased a roasted lamb, baskets of almonds and fruits, jars of old wine, and flowers of many kinds. The girl thanked him with many sweet words and the two ate and drank and talked until nightfall. Then Ghanim lit the lamps and brought stringed instruments, and with songs and verse and laughter the evening slipped away. In such delights a whole month was passed. Ghanim fell deeply in love, but sorrowfully the beautiful girl told him that she could not be his.

"I am," she said, "the favourite of the Khalifah Harun al-Rashid, Prince of the Faithful. My name is Kut al-Kulub, which means the Food of Hearts. I grew up from infancy in the Khalifah's palace; such was my beauty that he was fired with love and gave me an apartment to myself, and ten delightful maidens as companions. He showered me with gold and jewels, preferring me even to his wife, Zubaidah; therefore she hated me. One day, when the Khalifah was away in battle against a rebel tribe, Zubaidah bribed a female slave to give me a sleeping draught, then to place the drug called benj in my mouth. I fell down in convulsions; I thought that I was dying. Then, as I have since learnt, the queen gave secret payments to three black slaves to carry me out at night and bury me in the tomb. You were my deliverer. Now two things trouble me. The first is, what will the Khalifah do when he returns from the wars and finds me gone. The second is, that because I am bound to him, I can never truly be yours, O Ghanim my beloved."

Now when the young man heard that Kut al-Kulub belonged to the Khalifah, he dared no longer look on her or approach her; she seemed a sacred thing. He continued to have fine food and delicacies bought for her in the market, and in the day they made verses, and sang, and wept together, but he would not come near her; so all day they sat apart.

Meanwhile, at the palace, Queen Zubaidah pondered much about the return of the Kalifah, and was much perplexed to know what to do when he asked for his loved Kut al-Kulub. At last she sent for a cunning old woman, revealed her secret, and asked for her advice.

"I could show you many ways out of your difficulty," said the old woman. "But the simplest is this. Get a carpenter to carve a wooden shape that could pass for a human corpse, and arrange a ceremonial burial. Have torches and candles lighted all about the tomb, clothe all the slaves in mourning garments, then tell the Khalifah that Kut al-Kulub is dead, and that you have given her all the rites of a worthy funeral. The Khalifah will weep bitterly. But even if he has the tomb opened you need not fear, for the wooden figure will be covered with precious stuffs and jewels. And if he desires to touch her, all who are there will tell him that it is unlawful to look on a naked woman who is dead. So he will have the tomb closed again, and believe that his favourite has gone to the peace of Allah."

Zubaidah gave the old woman a robe of honour and much gold for her advice. And when the Khalifah returned from battle it all fell out as the old woman had said. The Khalifah stayed by Kut al-Kulub's tomb for the month of mourning, then he returned to his palace and fell into a heavy slumber, watched over by two women slaves. Presently, his deep sleep faded, he began to hear their voices.

Said one: "This is a sorry business."

"What is a sorry business?" said the other.

"Only that our dear master should pass his days and nights weeping over a tomb with nothing but a wooden dummy in it."

"Where is Kut al-Kulub then?"

"I have lately heard," replied the other, "that Zubaidah had her drugged with benj and buried among the tombs. But she escaped, and has now been living for four months with a certain young merchant of Damascus, called Ghanim ibn Ayyub. Thus our master is deceived and weeps over an empty tomb."

Hearing this, the Khalifah jumped to his feet with a terrible cry, calling in his rage for his wazir, Jafar al-Barmaki.

"Take guards with you instantly," he told the wazir, "and surround the house of Ghanim ibn Ayyub; rescue from that place my favourite Kut al-Kulub, and bring the young man to me to be put to the torture."

But when Kut al-Kulub saw armed guards around the house, she quickly clothed Ghanim in rags and set on his head an earthen pot filled with scraps.

"They will simply take you for a slave," she said. "Go now. Have no fear for me. I know how to manage the Khalifah."

So Ghanim left straightaway and Allah took him unnoticed through the ranks of besiegers. And when Jafar entered the house, he found the fair Kut al-Kulub sitting alone.

"Dear mistress," said Jafar, "my orders are to seize a certain Ghanim ibn Ayyub. Can you tell me where he is?"

"Indeed I can," said the girl. "Some days ago he packed together most of his merchandise and left for his native city of Damascus, to see his mother and sister. That is all I know."

Jafar then, with every show of deference and honour, requested Kut al-Kulub to accompany him to the Khalifah. The rest of his men he left behind to sack and destroy the house, as his master had commanded. But the Khalifah's rage grew no less. Not doubting that he had been betrayed, he ordered his favourite to be imprisoned in a dark room. He turn turned his attention to Ghanim. First he sent out horsemen to seek him on the Damascus road. Then he penned a letter in his own hand, to the Sultan

Muhammed of Damascus. In this he requested the Sultan to give the young man five hundred lashes, then to send him back in chains for further punishment. The letter ended:

You will sack his house and lay it waste, so that none may know where it stood. You will strip his mother and the sister of their fine clothes, expose them for three days to the eyes of the curious, and then cast them from your city. You will execute this order with great zeal.
Peace be with you.

The Sultan was a kindhearted man, but the Khalifah's orders had to be obeyed. Against his will, he destroyed Ghanim's house and cast his mother and sister out of the city, to become wandering beggars.

But, Ghanim, too, was now a homeless wanderer. He had left Baghdad, weeping as if his heart were broken; he had walked all day without food or drink until he came to a village. There he sought the mosque and cast himself down on the mat in the courtyard, his back against the wall; and there he stayed through the night, more dead than alive. In the morning he was found by the village people; they brought him bread and honey and some rags of clothes. Too ill and despairing to move, he lay for a whole month upon the mat, feeble, pale and devoured by fleas and lice. At last the faithful of the mosque agreed to send him to the hospital at Baghdad.

A camel driver was found and told: "If you take this poor young man on your camel and leave him at the door of the Baghdad hospital, where he may be cured by medical attention, we will pay you well on your return."

"I hear and obey," said the camel driver, and Ghanim, mat and all, was lifted on to the animal's back. Just as they were setting out, they passed two poor and shabby women, none other than Ghanim's mother and sister, who were making their slow way from Damascus to Baghdad.

One said to the other: "That poor young invalid is like our Ghanim, but Ghanim could not be in so wretched a state." And so they failed to meet. But the camel driver journeyed on, and when he reached Baghdad he laid the sick man on the hospital steps, for the place was not yet open for the day. This done, he turned for home. But, presently, seeing this man like the shadow of a man, lying before the door, the people of Baghdad began to cluster round. Who was he? Guess after guess was made.

Then the leading sheikh of one of the markets said to himself: "By Allah, if I have that young man tended in my house, I may perhaps be rewarded when I come to the Garden of Delights." He ordered his slaves to carry the youth to his own home, and prepare a clean bed for him, with good mattresses and soft pillows. Then he called his wife, saying, "Allah has sent us a guest. See that he is well looked after."

"So be it," she replied, then she heated water in a great cauldron, tucked up her sleeves, and washed the young man all over. Then she dressed him in clean clothes, gave him a glass of refreshing sherbet, and sprinkled his face with rosewater. And, as Ghanim's strength began to return, so did his memory of the past and of his Kut al-Kulub, his beloved.

But where was she? As week followed week, she languished still in the same dark room, guarded by an old woman, and forgotten by all, even the Khalifah. One day, however, passing that room he heard a sad voice speaking verses, a voice that he knew well. Then he heard these words: "O Ghanim ibn Ayyub, how noble you appear compared with the one who persecutes you. You respected the woman of his house; you guarded her from shame; he brought shame and dishonour on your innocent mother and sister."

Now the Khalifah understood for the first time that he had wrongly condemned the young man. Therefore he sent for Kut al-Kulub and said to her, "My love, I heard you say that I had acted ill against one who had acted well by me, one who respected the woman of my house, while I put his mother and sister to shame. I have made a sad mistake. Ask what you will in recompense, and you shall receive it."

"Prince of Believers," replied the girl, "I would wish to be married to Ghanim ibn Ayyub, when he returns to us."

And the Khalifah, though he still felt the greatest love and desire for her, said, "He is yours, the gift of a generous giver who never takes back. Furthermore, I will raise him to honour." And he gave her permission to search for the lost young man, and a purse of a thousand gold dinars to help her on her way.

On the first day she travelled through the city, but found no clues. On the second day she visited the shops and markets, leaving with the principal sheikh of each a sum of money to give to any stranger in need. On the third day she tried the goldsmiths' and jewellers' market, again seeking the principal sheikh and giving him gold for needy wanderers. But this time the master had a tale to tell.

"I have indeed taken into my home," he said, "a strange young man, nameless and ill and poor. But I think him to be the son of noble parents, for, though he is worn to a shadow, he is beautiful to look upon, and has gracious manners. Perhaps – who knows – his sickness is caused by debt, or by some grievous love affair."

Then Kut al-Kulub's heart beat fast and she asked the sheikh if someone could be spared from work to lead her to his house. The sheikh called a young boy, and said, "Fulful, lead this lady to my house, where the stranger is lying ill." When they arrived, the sheikh's wife took her to the room of the sick man, but she could not recognise her Ghanim in the feeble ghost on the bed. However, she left much gold for his treatment and continued her search.

One day she met again the sheikh of the goldsmiths. "Mistress Kut al-Kulub," he said, "I have for your benevolence two women of high rank, a mother and daughter whom I found wandering in goatskin garments with wallets round their necks, as if they were beggars. I have brought them to you, O Queen of Goodness, knowing that you would pity and help them."

"I would like to see them," she answered. When she beheld their beauty and nobility and their rags, she wept, and they wept too.

At last the older woman said, "Generous lady, pray to Allah that we may find whom we seek, that is my son, Ghanim ibn Ayyub." At the sound of this name the girl knew that the poor wanderers were the mother and sister of her beloved. She uttered a loud cry and fell fainting to the floor.

When she came to, she turned to the sheikh and gave him a thousand dinars, saying, "Conduct these strangers to your house; tell your wife to take them to the baths and give them fair new robes. Spare no expense on their behalf."

"Honoured lady," said the sheikh, "all help to the poor and needy brings reward in the hereafter. Your will shall be done."

Next morning, when she visited the house, she beheld the mother and sister much restored to their true nobility. Then the three of them went to visit the poor invalid. As they sat and talked at his bedside, the name of Kut al-Kulub was spoken.

At once the young man opened his eyes and rose on his elbow, crying: "Kut al-Kulub! Where are you, Kut al-Kulub?" And the young woman saw that he was indeed Ghanim, and the mother and sister also perceived that their search was at an end. Great was their rejoicing and Ghanim and Kut al-Kulub wept tears of joy to be reunited at last.

The Khalifah kept his promise to Kut al-Kulub and gave Ghanim a high position in the kingdom, a royal income and a palace. Moreover, he was so enchanted by Ghanim's sister, Fitnah, that he asked for her in marriage. And his wedding took place on the same day as that of Kut al-Kulub and Ghanim, the Slave of Love.

THE PRINCE AND THE TORTOISE

A TALE IS TOLD OF a monarch, in the far-off ages of time, who had three sons: Ali, Husain and Muhammed. All were princely to look upon, valiant in war, skilled in the arts of peace; but the youngest was the most handsome, most brave and most good-hearted of the three. Their father loved them all, not favouring one more than the other, and secretly planned to leave to each an equal share of his kingdom and his wealth.

A time came when the boys were old enough for marriage, but since they had made no move to seek brides, the king called his wazir to him and asked for his advice.

The wazir, a man both wise and prudent, sat for an hour in thought, then said, "O king of the centuries, what can avail against the finger of Destiny? Therefore I suggest this plan. Bid the three princes come to the terrace of the palace, each with bow and arrows; then, blindfolded with a cloth, each in turn must shoot an arrow high into the air. The house on which it falls will surely hold a daughter or other damsel. The owner of the house will then be visited and a marriage arranged. This will indeed be the work of Destiny."

"Excellent counsel!" said the king. "All this shall be done without delay." And as soon as the boys returned from hunting, they were told to present themselves, equipped with bow and arrows, at the appointed place. First the oldest, Prince Ali, had a scarf tied over his eyes; he was turned round and round, then given the word to shoot. His arrow flew through the air and fell on the dwelling of a noble lord with a ripe young daughter. The second prince's arrow alighted on the walls of a fine mansion, the house of the king's commander-in-chief. He too had a girl who had reached the age for marriage. But the arrow of young Muhammed fell on a villa standing apart in a strange district, unknown to anyone in the palace. Messengers sent to investigate found no human inhabitant within, only a large and lonely tortoise.

Clearly chance had played a trick, and the prince was told to shoot again. For a second time he was blindfolded and turned about and about. Once more his arrow fell on the house of the lonely tortoise.

The king was enraged, and shouted to his son, "You may have one more try. Call on the name of Allah, then send forth your arrow once again." Muhammed did as he was bid – and for the third time the arrow neatly alighted on the home of the tortoise, exactly as before.

"If the hand of Destiny shows in this," murmured the king, "it must intend the boy to remain a bachelor." Aloud, he said, "My son, this tortoise is not of our race nor of our religion; indeed, I do not recall a single case of a satisfactory union of one such with our kind. Surely it is Allah's will that you withdraw yourself from any thought of marrying."

But the prince replied, "O most mighty father, I read this differently. Destiny has appointed this tortoise to be my marriage partner, and marry her I must and shall."

"Your interpretation may be right," said the king, "but in practice the notion is not only absurd – it is monstrous. How can you enter into marriage with a tortoise? I cannot understand your passion for the creature."

"Do not mistake me," said the young man. "I have no great partiality for tortoises in general; indeed, I have hitherto given them little thought. It is this particular one that I wish to marry."

Since further objection seemed useless and tiring, and since the king was fond of his son, he shrugged his shoulders, made no more protest, and gave orders for three great wedding feasts. The first two were held with widespread celebrations. But the third was a different matter; not a single guest attended, not even the other brothers and their wives, nor any court officials. Indeed, poor Prince Muhammed was mocked and scorned by all. Sneering smiles or averted faces everywhere met his gaze. And yet – though none but Allah could tell how he and the tortoise lived their lives together – the prince seemed well content with the ways of Destiny.

But the king, already weighed down by years and the burdens of state, and over-wearied by all the recent events, began to pine and dwindle; he ceased to eat; his eyesight failed; a shadow of his former self, he lay awaiting death. The three sons were much concerned; after consulting together, they went to their father's bedside, where the eldest spoke for the three.

"Dear father, we all desire to see you restored to health, and so we bring you a plan. From now on our wives will prepare whatever you eat. They will do their utmost to revive your appetite with enticing dishes, carefully cooked, and your strength, and the sight of your eyes will soon return."

The king was greatly moved. "But will not this be an unwanted toil and labour to your wives?" he asked.

At once the prince replied, "Are not our wives your slaves? Is there a better way for them to spend their time? Noble father, it has been agreed between us that, for a start, each shall prepare a dish, and you will say which you find the most tempting, most reviving, most delightful."

"All is for the best," said the father, and he lay back, weak but hopeful, to await the savoury fare.

So each wife set to work, the large and lonely tortoise no less than the other two. Smiling to herself, she sent a confidential servant to her older sister-in-law, begging her to send back any mouse and rat droppings she could spare, as these had special value as seasoning.

The wife of Ali thought to herself, "If this is so, I shall need all I have for my own use. Let her find her own." Aloud, she said, "Tell your mistress that I cannot give her what she requires as I have scarcely enough for myself."

When this answer was brought to her, the tortoise laughed and laughed, then sent to the second sister-in-law, the wife of Husain, asking if she might have all spare hen and pigeon droppings for the special dish that she was preparing.

A sour refusal came from the woman, who was thinking to herself, "There must be some rare merit in these things; I certainly will not give any of mine to that creature!"

The tortoise was so overcome with mirth when the servant brought back the message that she almost fell over; but she recovered herself and began to cook the dish that she really intended to bring to the sick monarch. At last it was done. She put it in a wicker basket, covered it with a rose-scented linen cloth, and told her servant to carry it carefully to the palace, where the offerings of the other wives were also being brought.

And now came the test. First, the dish of Prince Ali's wife was put before the king. He lifted the lid, expecting a delicious experience. But so foul an odour rose from the bowl that he fell into a swoon and had to be roused with fans and scented water. Presently he felt recovered enough to try the dish of the second daughter-in-law. He raised a spoonful to his lips – but so unpleasant and burning was the taste that he threw down the spoon, crying out to the anxious sons, "What have I done to your wives that they should wish to kill me with their messes? Away, all of you!"

The young Muhammed now stepped forward, and begged his father to try the third dish, which he was certain would make up for both the other failures. The old king angrily refused. Then the prince knelt down and swore to eat the entire dish himself if the king did not care for it.

"At least, dear father, lift the cover."

So the king signed to a slave to remove the cloth, murmuring as he did so, "May Allah protect me!" But the odour which swirled towards him was so exquisite, so enticing and so savoury that it nourished the king before he lifted a morsel to his lips. His eyes began to clear; he ate the entire vesselful without stopping, then rounded it off with an excellent sherbet drink compounded of musk and snow. Finally he gave thanks to Allah, and called his son Muhammed to him, full of praise for the cooking of his wife.

"It is not her only talent, dear father," said the prince. "She has many gifts that would give you pleasure. Meanwhile she would rejoice to have the privilege of preparing your food each day." The king agreed, and to celebrate his recovery announced a banquet, especially for his three sons and their wives.

At once the daughters-in-law began to make their plans, wishing to appear at their best before their father-in-law. The tortoise too gave careful thought to the matter. First, she sent her special servant to the older wife, asking if she would lend the great goose in her courtyard as a steed for her to ride to the palace.

The foolish woman refused, for the same jealous reasoning as before – "If she wants it, I'd do better to use it myself."

When the answer came, the tortoise laughed and laughed, then sent the servant to the other sister-in-law, asking for a loan of the he-goat in her yard, for she wished to arrive in style at the ceremony. Again the request was refused; again the tortoise was overcome with mirth. What were her own real plans? We shall know when we shall know.

And now came the hour of the feast. The old king and his queen awaited the arrival of the royal brides. Suddenly a monstrous thing seemed to be moving towards them – a huge goose was waddling along in a cloud of dust, flapping and squawking under the heavy burden of the first princess in the kingdom. Following closely was a he-goat carrying the second princess; she was desperately clutching the neck of the furious creature as it leapt and bleated under the load. Both women were covered with dust and dirt; their handsome gauzy clothes were torn to rags.

The king and queen watched aghast as the bedraggled, gibbering pair arrived, trying in vain to keep a steady seat on their frightened steeds. Words seemed to fail the monarch, but his mounting anger clearly showed in his face. At that moment messengers announced the coming of the third daughter-in-law. The king threw up his hands.

"If two humans can behave in this disgusting fashion, what can we expect from a tortoise? Strange indeed are the ways of Allah!" But, even as he spoke, a glittering palanquin was carried into the hall, borne by four handsome attendants, richly dressed. Out of it stepped an unknown princess, lovely as the moon, in robes of exquisite beauty. All were amazed as Muhammed stepped forward and greeted her as his bride.

The transformation lightened the heart of the king; he ordered all to be seated, and the banquet to begin. The first course, as always, was a great dish of rice in butter. Before anyone could start, the fair princess raised the dish and poured its contents over her hair. At once each grain became a priceless pearl, adorning the damsel's tresses and running in a bright and tinkling torrent to the floor. While the company gazed, open-mouthed at this marvel, the princess seized a large tureen full of thick green soup and poured this also over her head. The green drops became a sea of emeralds, mingling in ravishing fashion with the pearls in her hair, the overflow forming brilliant pools on the floor.

The king was quite delighted. Then the servants brought fresh supplies, and the feast was about to start. But the two other wives, gnawed with jealousy, could not bear to be outdone. The older grasped the new dish of rice, the other the tureen of soup, and they poured them over their heads. But the result for each was a horrible mess, sickening to behold. The king was altogether disgusted with the women; he banished them from the feast and from the palace, saying that he never wished to hear of them again. Their husbands led them away, and that was that. But the Prince Muhammed and his magical bride remained, for they pleased the heart of the king.

First, the monarch embraced them, saying, "From this day, my palace is your home, your home my palace." Then he wrote a will, making his youngest son the heir to his throne and kingdom.

The princess now sent her servant to fetch the large and lonely shell, and she burnt it, there and then, for she did not wish to vex her old father-in-law by appearing in it thereafter. Many were the children of Muhammed and the princess in the years to come; happy were their lives throughout. Wonderful are the ways of Allah!

from The Anklet

THE ANKLET

LEGENDS TELL THAT LONG AGO, in a certain city, there were three sisters, who lived by spinning flax. All had the same father, but the youngest was the child of a second wife. And though all three were like the moon in beauty, the youngest had the fairest face and a charm of manner that both the others lacked. What's more, she was a faster and finer spinner than either; not a single fault could be found in the thread that left her hand. As you may imagine, the sisters did not love this favoured girl, no, indeed they did not, and they suffered much from jealousy.

One day the youngest one was in the market, buying the day's supplies, when her eye was caught by a little alabaster pot, and she bought it from her spinning money. With a few flowers inside, she thought, it would give her pleasure to glance at while she worked. But her sisters looked at it scornfully.

"What extravagance!" said one.

"What a silly waste of money!" said the other. The girl felt sad, and was silent. She put a rose in the pot, set it in front of her, and went back to her spinning.

Now this was no ordinary pot; it had magic powers, as the young girl soon discovered. When she wished to eat, it brought her delicious food; when she longed for lovely clothes, it laid before her shimmering silken robes that any princess might envy. Still, she had the sense not to reveal this secret to her sisters, and she passed the days as before, saying little, spinning much, and always dressing soberly. But whenever the two went out to enjoy themselves, she shut herself in her own little room and tenderly clasped the treasure.

"Little pot, dear little pot," she would say, "I beg you to bring me – " and then she would add whatever her fancy lit on at the moment. And at once she would find before her dazzling jewels, lustrous fabrics, delicious cakes and fruits, sweets of fine-spun sugar, as ravishing to look upon as to taste. But as soon as it heard the sound of the sisters' feet, the good little pot would make all traces vanish; there was the girl, spinning away, and there before her was the pot, holding a single rose. In this way many weeks passed. When other people were present, the youngest appeared to be just a poor working girl. But when she was alone, she was a princess, lacking for nothing.

One day the king announced that he was giving a great feast, and inviting all the householders of the city. Among these were the three sisters. But the two older girls had their own views on that. They told the youngest to stay at home to mind the house; then they dressed as well as they could from a spinner's wage, and set off for the palace. As soon as they were out of sight, the young girl spoke sweetly to the pot, then asked to be given clothes so beautiful that she would outshine all at the feast.

"And I beg you too, little pot," she added, "for turquoise bracelets for my arms, sapphire and amethyst rings for my fingers, and little diamond anklets for my feet." At once these things were before her. Hastily she dressed herself and made her way to the harem part of the palace, where the women were allowed their own entertainment.

All the assembled guests, her sisters among them, marvelled at the beauty of this dazzling stranger – surely a high princess. But the girl thought it best to leave before the end; and while the women gathered to listen to an entertainment of singers, she slipped away, leaping over the sunken water trough where the royal horses came to drink, and swiftly glided home. There she was, quietly waiting in her mended clothes when the older pair returned. She did not know that in her haste she had dropped a diamond anklet in the trough.

Next morning when the palace horses were taken to drink, they backed away in terror, snorting and trembling, stamping with their hooves. The grooms looked down and saw a shining thing in the water, a ring of stars, it seemed; it was the diamond anklet.

The king's son, who had been watching the strange behaviour of his horses, looked at it curiously, then cried out, "Only the rarest of damsels could wear a thing so small, so exquisite. She is the one I shall marry, and none other!" He went to his royal father and told him of his decision.

"As you will, my son," replied the monarch. "But really, I know very little about these things. Your mother is the one to go to; she'll help you to find the girl." So the prince went to his mother and showed her the anklet.

"I am determined to marry the girl with the incredible ankle," he said, "and I put the matter in your hands, for my father says that you understand these things."

"I hear and obey," said the queen, and at once she called her women together to plan the search for the damsel. Harem after harem they visited, up and down the city, but nowhere could they find a girl whose ankle matched the jewel. One week passed, then another. They were just about to admit defeat when they came upon the modest home of the spinning sisters. The first two proffered their feet, but with no success at all. Then the youngest asked to try, and the anklet at once slipped on as if it were part of her.

"Well now, our quest is at an end, and I am glad of that," said the queen, who was quite exhausted. "She seems a charming girl as well, and the prettiest we've seen, I do believe." She embraced the happy damsel, and the wedding date was announced; there were feastings and celebrations for forty days and nights.

And where were the older sisters all this time? They too were in the palace, for the goodhearted bride had invited them to share in all the merrymaking. Happiness made her careless, though, and on the fortieth day she revealed to them the secret of the pot, which had even helped with her wedding clothes. The women whispered together, then offered to arrange her hair. They combed the long tresses, coiled them round and held them in place with seven diamond pins. But these were enchanted pins, which they had obtained from the alabaster pot; their power was to turn a human maiden into a dove. And when the last pin was inserted, no girl was there, only a white bird, which flew in fright through the window. The prince came to find his bride – but where was she? Not a trace of her could be seen.

"She told us that she was off for a stroll in the garden," said the sisters, putting on anxious looks and glancing hither and thither. Search parties were sent through the grounds, then through the city, then throughout the kingdom. The king sent ships to the farthest shores of his domain, seeking for news of his son's vanished bride. But the lost girl was not found, and the prince began to waste away; in his anguish and bitterness he refused to leave his room. So sunk in grief was he that at first he took no notice of a little dove that came to his window every morning and evening. Then he began to take comfort in the bird, and to watch for its coming. One day he put out his hand and the bird alighted on his palm. He began to stroke her softly, but his hand met several hard little objects, like the heads of pins. And pins they were. One by one he pulled them forth, and when the last was drawn, a mist obscured the dove for a moment; it seemed to vanish – and then before him was a lovely girl, his lost bride found, none other.

No more misfortunes crossed the path of the prince and the princess. They lived in happiness ever after, and their children were many and beautiful. But when the sisters saw that their plot had failed, their rage rushed into their hearts, and so they died.

THE TALE OF THE PRINCE TAJ AL-MULUK AND THE PRINCESS DUNJA

IN FAR-OFF TIMES THERE was a city called the Green City behind the mountains of Isfahin in the land of Persia. When this tale begins, it was ruled by a wise and generous king called Sulaiman Shah, and he was honoured and loved by all. He had one son, a young man of surpassing beauty, whose name was Taj al-Muluk, which means the Crown of Kings.

The young prince was brought up with every privilege and taught by the most gifted masters. But now, in his eighteenth year, he was most addicted to hunting. Wherever he went in the forests he left the creatures, from lion to gazelle, in vast dead and dying heaps. Soon he was forced to go much further afield in search of living game. He and his servants travelled four days through the desert before they found a green wood near a river; the hunt began and soon the green grass became scarlet. Tired but content with a good day's sport, the prince slept.

Awakened by the light of dawn, he saw that a large caravan with many camels and slaves was approaching. The prince sent a messenger to enquire who they were.

"We are merchants," he was told, "and we rest here on our journey because of the water and the green shade. We know too that we have nothing to fear because we are in the land of the good King Sulaiman, where all is justice and peace. Indeed, we are bringing our richest stuffs to show to his son, the Prince Taj al-Muluk."

Hearing this, the young man said, "Why should we wait! Let the merchants show us now what they are carrying. It will occupy our morning."

The newcomers at once set up a tent of crimson satin embroidered with designs of birds and flowers, and glittering with jewels; inside, they placed a silken carpet fringed with emeralds. The prince graciously seated himself upon the carpet, and looked at the merchandise as it was brought before him. Whatever took his fancy, he ordered his men to purchase and have taken to the camp.

52

This done, he was about to mount his horse to return when his eye was caught by the face of one of the merchants – a young man of great beauty, but pale and sorrowful. He felt strangely drawn to the young man and enquired his name, asking why he had not come forward with his wares.

"My lord," this young man replied, "I am called Aziz. As to my wares, I have nothing worthy of so high a prince." But this reluctance only intrigued the prince more. He made a place for the young man to sit beside him and had the goods brought in, piece by piece.

Each time, without inspecting, the prince made the sign of purchase to his attendants. The last item was a robe of sumptuous satin, woven through with gold. When this was lifted, an embroidered silken square fell to the ground. At once the young man Aziz seized the stuff and tried to hide it. But the prince put forth his hand and said, "I must see the cloth."

So Aziz opened it out, and there the prince beheld a gazelle, skilfully worked in red-gold thread; facing it was another gazelle in silver, with a red-gold collar round its neck, hung with chrysolites; in the design were other symbols, all of enchantment and desire.

"How did you come by this cloth?" asked the prince. "What is its meaning?"

Aziz replied: "It was left to me by my cousin, now with Allah, a damsel of rarest beauty, for whom I am grieving. It is the work of the Princess Dunja, whose father rules the Islands of Camphor and Crystal. With my cousin's gift to me was this message: 'Good will come to you through this princess, though not in the form of love – Allah has destined her for another – but of friendship, which will in time heal both affliction and grief.'"

When the prince heard this tale and looked at the designs he was seized by a passion of love for the Princess Dunja. Taking Aziz with him as his companion and brother he returned to his father's court, where he ordered for his friend's use a fine house and many slaves. But he himself withdrew to his own apartment, unable either to eat or drink because of his longing. King Sulaiman was greatly troubled, and scarcely less when he heard the reason.

"O my son," he said, "this princess lives in a far-off country. There are many princesses, both lovely and accomplished, among our neighbouring kingdoms."

But the prince said, "I wish only for the Princess Dunja. If I do not have her I will flee into the desert and end my life."

At this, the father said, "As you wish. I will send a deputation to the Isles of Camphor and Crystal to ask the king for his daughter's hand in marriage to my son. If he refuses, I shall send an army so great that it will cover the whole of the earth between our kingdoms." Then he called to his wazir to lead the mission, and requested Aziz, who knew the roads, to be his guide.

They journeyed many days and nights until they were in sight of the royal palace, and sent a messenger forward to announce their arrival. But when the king learned their purpose, he became silent, and sadly gazed at the floor. For he knew that his daughter, Dunja, a proud and arrogant girl, was enraged at the very thought of marriage; all suitors who came were violently rejected. At last, however, he raised his head and summoned the chief of his eunuchs.

"Go to the lady Dunja," he said. "Take her the gifts of the great King Sulaiman and tell her of his request."

All too soon the eunuch returned, breathing hard. "O king of all creatures and the centuries, and time," he said, "scarcely had I spoken when the lady was convulsed with rage; had I not fled, she would have cracked my skull with a golden stick. But she called out this message: 'If my father forces me to marry I will first kill the man, then myself.'"

The king turned to the wazir saying, "You hear what you hear. Yet my daughter's will is not mine, and this you must tell your master."

So the mission returned to the Green City and the wazir gave his report to the king. At first, King Sulaiman was enraged, and prepared to send a destroying army, but the wazir reminded him that it was not the fault of the monarch.

"The father longs for the daughter's marriage. Besides, the lady means to kill; hers was no idle threat."

But the prince would not accept refusal. "I swear by Allah," he said, "that none but the Princess Dunja shall be my wife. I shall go myself and win her in my own way, whatever the risk. I shall set out in disguise of a merchant."

"What must be must be," said the king, "but take with you our wazir and Aziz." He then ordered merchandise to be prepared to the value of a hundred thousand pieces of gold and a train of horses, camels and slaves.

When at last they reached the Isles of Camphor and Crystal, the wazir sought out the sheikh of the market place.

"I am travelling," he said, "with my two sons to give them greater knowledge of the world and some experience in the buying and selling of merchandise."

The old man's dignified aspect, his great train of attendants, and above all, the beauty of the two young men had much impressed the sheikh and he assigned them the largest and most handsome shop in the market place. News of the beautiful strangers and of their exquisite goods soon spread through the city and crowds came from dawn to dusk. This continued for many days, but

from Prince Taj al-Muluk and Princess Dunja

Taj al-Muluk began to grow restless with desire for the Princess Dunja. Once again, he could neither eat nor sleep for longing.

One day, however, an old woman followed by a pair of female slaves paused at the splendid shop. The richness of the wares and the beauty of the two young men were greater than all the rumours. The prince struck her especially.

"This is no mortal but an angel," she told herself. Then aloud she said, "Show me whatever is most beautiful in your shop, for beauty must bring beauty."

"What I have is suited only to kings and the children of kings," said the young man.

"Then I must tell you," she replied, "that I wish for some stuff to make a robe for the lady Dunja, daughter of the king."

On hearing this, the prince grew faint with joy. He brought forth from a hidden cupboard in the wall a fabric of such rare design and wondrous perfume that only a princess of legend seemed worthy to wear it. The old woman eagerly bought the stuff and hastened back to the lady Dunja.

"What a sight I have seen!" she told the damsel. "I have purchased for you a fabric of untold beauty – but the seller of this stuff is in voice and looks nothing less than an angel. He has come to this city as part of his travelling, and sells only as a pastime."

"You speak nonsense," said the damsel. But when she took the fabric in her hand, her mood changed. "Tell me again of the merchant," she said. Then, after listening, she told the old woman to return to the shop and ask if he had any request that the palace might grant, to show their approval of his exquisite goods.

The old woman hurried back to give the prince the message. Overcome with joy, he replied: "If you will do me the service of taking a letter to the lady and bringing back a reply, I shall be well rewarded." Then he called to Aziz to bring him paper and pen and ink-case, and rapidly wrote her a poem of his love and desire to meet in life one whom he had so far known only in dream. He sealed the letter and gave it to the old woman with a thousand pieces of gold as a gift.

The lady Dunja was not pleased and beat her old nurse for being the cause of this imprudence as she saw it. But the old woman, anxious not to break the correspondence, persuaded her to write a severe letter, also in verse, warning the young man that any more such propositions would bring him a terrible death. Reading the harsh letter, the young man wept.

"What is the cause of her hatred of men?" he asked.

"That I will now reveal," said the old woman. "She had a dream in which a fowler set a snare and caught a male pigeon by the foot. The female bird flew down and pecked away at the mesh until her mate was freed. In the dream the fowler set the snare again, and this time caught the female bird. But the male did not come to her rescue and the fowler cut her throat. The lady Dunja took this dream as a sign that all men are faithless, and without any good intent to women."

"Then tell me," said the prince, "how can I ever catch a glimpse of her?"

"There is a chance," said the old woman. "She has a private garden close to the palace, and spends a while in it every month, entering and leaving by a secret door. You must hide in the garden when I tell you she is about to appear, and if she chances to see you, I know her heart will change." The young man thanked the old woman and gave her gold, and she left.

When the wazir was told this story, he said, "I have a notion." And, telling the young men to put on their richest apparel, he took them towards the garden. To the keeper of the gate he handed a hundred pieces of gold, saying, "We are strangers to the city and desire to refresh our spirits in this place of green trees and running waters."

"Make yourselves welcome," said the old man, and he took them through the grounds.

"What is that building?" asked the wazir.

"It is an old summer palace," said the man, "but it is somewhat in need of repair."

"Then," said the wazir, "I wish to do a good deed to pay for the pleasure of this visit. If you permit, I will have some painting done to the walls." And he gave the man a further supply of gold pieces, to bring back some skilled workmen, with a painter among them.

When they arrived, he asked them to repair and whiten the walls of the palace, then he set the artist to make a mural at the end of the hall showing a snare set by a fowler in which a female pigeon was caught. Beside it, he had another picture painted, showing the male bird unable to reach his mate in the snare because he himself was held in the talons of a hawk. When this was done, the wazir and the two young men returned to their house to wait.

Meanwhile, the lady Dunja, after so much disturbance, had a desire to refresh herself by a visit to the garden. When she heard this, the wily old nurse hastened to tell the news to Taj al-Muluk. Quickly Taj al-Muluk returned to the garden and hid in a flowering bush. As he crouched there, the princess and the old woman entered by a secret door and the nurse led her, as if by chance, to the paintings of the birds. The princess stared in amazement.

"This is my dream!" she cried. "But look! The male bird tries to return to free the female, but cannot, for he is caught himself! Perhaps I was wrong to condemn all men as false."

The nurse said, "I told you that long ago. But now let us walk by the water."

Their way went past the flowering bush, and so, for the first time, the prince saw the lady Dunja. So dazzling was her loveliness that he slipped down in a faint. When he recovered, he stepped from the hiding place and so was seen by the lady in her turn. She was struck by his beauty and overcome by a violent love.

"You must arrange that I meet the young man," she told the nurse, "or I will die."

"Go back to the palace," said the old woman, "and you shall have your wish."

At dawn the next day, the old woman came to the prince's house with a parcel of woman's clothes. She dressed him as a young girl, covered his face with a black veil and directed him to walk with a swaying motion. In this guise he followed her into the palace, passing through many corridors until they reached a round hall in which were seven curtained doors.

"Behind the seventh door," said the old woman, "the princess waits." And this was so.

For a whole month the lovers remained together in constant joy, well guarded by the old nurse. Each day the princess emerged at certain times to keep away suspicion; while the prince remained in the secret apartment. But when four weeks had passed without a word of news, the wazir and Aziz feared that he must be dead, and sadly made their journey home.

When King Sulaiman heard the terrible tidings, he gave a loud cry and fell to the ground. But soon he rose and ordered a state of war through his dominions. Swiftly an army was gathered together covering the earth as far as the eye could reach, to wreak vegeance for the loss of his son. Then the forces began to move towards the Islands of Camphor and Crystal.

Meanwhile, there, in the king's court, the corporation of jewellers came one morning to pay their annual homage and brought with them a golden casket set with gems and filled with rarest emeralds, rubies and diamonds. The king was pleased to accept the gift and told the chief eunuch to take it to his daughter. But when the eunuch reached the lady's private pavilion, he found the old nurse asleep before the bedroom door, while the curtains were still closed. Fearing some mischance, he stepped within and saw the princess in the arms of a young man! Without disturbing the sleepers, the eunuch quickly returned to the king, to whisper in his ear what he had seen.

The king, devoured with rage, had the young man brought before him. He asked his name, and how he had penetrated the inmost parts of the palace.

"O noble king," said the young man, "if you intend my death, I must warn you that you and all your land will be destroyed. For my father is the mighty monarch, Sulaiman, who sought your daughter for me in marriage, and I am his only son."

As the king hesitated, his wazir said, "My lord, the man is an imposter; all delay means further shame for the kingdom." So Taj al-Muluk was taken to the place of execution and bound. The royal executioner raised his sword and waited for the sign to bring it down. Then a great sound made him pause. The horizon was filled with a vast advancing force. Ambassadors came ahead, led by the same wazir who had come to the king with gifts. Now he brought this message from the great Sulaiman: that if the prince were alive and well, all would be well with the King of the Isles of Camphor and Crystal. But if the prince was dead then the whole kingdom would be razed to the ground.

The king sent for his swiftest runners. "Go fast to the place of execution!" he cried. And when the executioner saw them, he laid down his sword. The young man's bonds were cut and he was given fresh clothes and led into the court where the king begged his forgiveness and at once agreed to the wedding with his daughter. Then he ordered provisions and pay to be given to the armies at his door. And then came news of the arrival of King Sulaiman himself.

After greeting his father with utmost ecstasy the Prince Taj al-Muluk said to him, "Sir, I have a request. It is my desire that we should reward my loyal and valued friend, Aziz, and let him return to his family."

And so, Aziz departed after the wedding ceremony of the prince and princess; the singing and feasting through the land continued for a month, but the happiness of the pair, each day a round of delights, endured for a long lifetime.

THE TALE OF THE MOORISH SORCERER

A TALE IS TOLD – WHY should it not be true? – of a king and queen, in olden days, who had no child.

One day a Moor came to the palace and said to the king, "If I mend this trouble for you, will you give me the first of your sons?"

"Certainly," said the king. The Moor held out his hand; in the open palm were two sweets, one green, one red.

"The green is for you," he said, "the red is for your wife. Eat them, and Allah will do what he will do." Straightaway he was gone.

The king ate the green sweet, the queen ate the red, and presently she gave birth to a boy. The father named him Muhammad, and he grew up clever and wise, with a love of learning and a very sweet voice. A year later, a second son was born, and the father named him Ali. He grew up awkward and stupid. Finally, a third son arrived. Mahmud was his name, and he was an idiot.

Ten years passed, and who should turn up at the palace but the Moor.

"I have come for my boy," he said.

"Wait," said the king, and went off to whisper with the queen.

"Never!" said she. "He will *not* have Muhammad. Give him Ali the awkward."

The Moor went off with the boy Ali, and they walked and walked through the burning heat until noon.

Then he said, "Are you hungry or thirsty?"

"What a question!" said the boy. "How could I be anything else after half a day without food or drink."

"Humph!" said the Moor. He turned round and took the boy back to his father, saying, "That is not my son. Let me see the three together and I will know my own." So the king made them stand in line and the Moor at once picked out Muhammad, the one who loved learning, and also had a very sweet voice.

They walked for half a day, then the Moor asked, "Are you hungry? Are you thirsty?"

"If you are hungry or thirsty," said the boy, "then I too am hungry and thirsty."

The Moor embraced him, saying, "O wise and learned one, you are indeed my son." When they reached Morocco, he took the boy into a garden and gave him food and drink. Then he handed him a book of magic lore, written in strange words.

"Read this!" he ordered. But the boy could not understand it at all. The Moor was enraged.

"By Gog and Magog and the wheeling stars," he cried, "if you do not know this by heart in thirty days, I shall cut off your right arm." And he left the boy in the garden.

For twenty-nine days Muhammad studied the pages, but found no way of learning what they said, or even which way up to hold the book.

In despair he said aloud, "If this is to be my last day, I would rather spend it exploring the garden than poring over this detestable thing." So he began to stroll through the grass and flowers until he reached a grove of rustling trees. Hanging from one of them by her hair was a young girl, and he hastened to set her free.

She embraced him, saying, "I am a princess. The Moor hung me here because I learnt his book of spells by heart."

"Indeed," said Muhammad, "I am a king's son. That Moorish sorcerer gave me thirty days to learn his book, but I cannot make head or tail of it. Today is the final day."

The girl smiled. "Do not worry," she said. "I will teach you. But when the Moor comes, you must pretend that you still cannot read a word. Now sit down here." They sat down side by side, with the book between them, and soon the young prince had learnt it all.

"Now," said she, "hang me up as I was before." Muhammad did as she asked.

At the end of the thirtieth day the Moor appeared.

"Well, quick-learner," he said, "I have come to hear you recite your task."

"Sir, how can I?" said the boy. "I cannot read a word of it." The Moor promptly cut off the boy's right arm.

"I grant you another thirty days," he said. "But if by then you have got no further – chop! you will lose your head." Then he left. At once Muhammad went to the girl, carrying his right arm under his left.

When he had let her down from the tree, she kissed him many times, saying, "Here are three leaves of a rare and special plant. The Moor has been seeking it for forty years, to complete his knowledge of magic. Hanging here, I saw it

under my feet, among the grass and tree roots. Apply the leaves to the severed parts of your arm, my love." The boy did so, and at once he was whole again.

Then the girl turned a page of the spell-book, read some words, and rubbed one of the magic leaves. She had scarcely finished speaking when the earth opened and two fine camels rose out. They knelt down; the princess mounted one, the prince the other.

"Now," said the girl, "we will each return to our parents. Then you may come to my father's kingdom and ask for my hand in marriage. But remember one thing; keep the camel's halter, for that's where the magic lies."

Muhammad rode to his home like the wind. Once there, he handed over his camel to the chief eunuch, saying, "You may sell him in the camel market, but bring me back the halter." The eunuch at once went off to the market and a hashish-seller offered to buy. They bargained a while, and then the man said, "Put in the halter as a makeweight and I'll take the beast." The eunuch thought he was doing well. So much for him.

The hashish-seller took off the halter, led the camel to the front of his shop and set a bowl of water before it, to entertain his customers. But the camel placed its forefeet in the bowl, threw up its hind legs, dived head first into the water, and vanished utterly. The hashish-seller ran about screeching, the halter still in his hand. The merchants laughed; they thought he had hashish-madness.

But where all this time was the Moor? He was biting his fingers with rage at the disappearance of the pair. "By Gog and Magog," he thundered, "I will catch them, even if they have reached the fourteenth planet." Off he sped to Muhammad's city, and in the market place he heard the hashish-eater crying out about a camel. The halter, he perceived, was still in the man's hand.

"My poor fellow," he said, "let me help you. He who does a generous deed, wins favours in the hereafter. Now, just as a token, you give me that halter in your hand, and I will repay what you gave for the camel, with an extra hundred dinars." The man was overjoyed – and so was the Moor.

Now this halter had many powers, and one was this. The Moor held it out towards the palace and Muhammad was irresistibly drawn towards it. His head passed through the loop, and he became a camel, kneeling before the sorcerer. The moor mounted his steed and urged it towards the home of the princess. But when they paused at the palace walls, Muhammad caught the halter in his teeth, snapped it through and escaped. Using the power of the magic cord, he turned himself into a pomegranate and hung himself on a flowering tree in the royal garden.

The Moor asked for an audience with the king, the young girl's father. After suitably humble greetings, he said, "O king of the ages, I come to beg you for a pomegranate. My wife is pregnant and calls for one night and day, yet none can be found in any garden other than yours."

"But surely," said the monarch, "there are no fruits at this season, only the early flowers."

The Moor replied, "O ruler of all time, if there is no pomegranate in your garden, you may cut off my head."

The king called his chief gardener. "Tell me yes or no," he said. "Is there a ripe pomegranate in the grounds?"

"O master," said the man, "it cannot be; this is not the season."

"As I thought," said the king. "Stranger, your head is forfeit."

But the Moor cried out, "O mighty king, mysterious are the ways of Allah. Before I lose my head, I beg you to send your gardener to look among the pomegranate flowers."

"As you wish," said the king, "though you merely delay your end for another few minutes." The gardener went off, and returned with a large pomegranate, like none that had never been seen before.

The king was amazed. He wished to keep the unusual fruit – but should it rightly go to the wife of the stranger? He called his wazir, and put the question before him.

The wazir thought for a while, then said, "If the pomegranate had not been found, would you have cut off the stranger's head?"

"I would indeed," said the king.

The wazir gave his verdict: "Then justice demands the fruit be given to him."

So the monarch held out the pomegranate, but the Moor had scarcely touched it before it burst asunder, and all the grains were scattered on the floor. Uttering curses, the sorcerer picked them up one by one until he came to the last grain, which was hiding in a little hole near the base of the throne. Now this grain was the one which held the vital essence of Muhammad. As the vile magician bent down, a dagger came out of the hole and stabbed him to the heart. That was the end of him.

And there stood Prince Muhammad, graceful as a sapling tree, a pleasure to the eye. He kissed the earth between the monarch's hands, and when he rose, who should be there but the princess, smiling and radiant.

"Dear father," she said to the king, "this is the youth who rescued me when I was hung by the hair from a tree by that sorcerer there."

"Since that's the case," said the king, "you cannot do less than marry him."

The wedding was joyfully celebrated, and the prince and princess lived together in sweet content ever after. Who can foresee the ways of Allah?

64   *from Kamar al-Zaman and Princess Budur*

THE WONDROUS TALE OF KAMAR AL-ZAMAN AND THE PRINCESS BUDUR, MOON OF MOONS

ONCE, IN FAR-OFF TIMES, there lived a Sultan of great wealth and power who ruled the land of Khalidan; Shahruman was his name. But though he had four wives, each one a king's daughter, and more than sixty concubines, he had not a single child to inherit his throne. As the years passed, the problem troubled him more and more; at last he called his chief wazir and asked what he should do.

The wazir sat silent for a time, then said, "Most noble king, I suggest that you order a feast for the poor and needy, hand out some generous gifts and then – with your special desire in mind – offer suitable prayers to the Almighty."

"You speak wisely," said the king. "This shall be done at once." And he awarded the wazir a robe of honour. Sure enough, nine months later, his youngest wife gave birth to a son.

Even as an infant, this boy was a moon of beauty, and so he was named Kamar al-Zaman, Moon of the Age. By the time he was fifteen, he caused both women and men to swoon with love. His eyes, black as plums, might have been the eyes of angels. His cheeks were full-blown roses. His crisp locks were as black as midnight. His waist was as pliant as bamboo and fine as a stem. Poets and singers in thousands tried to capture all this beauty in word and song, and ended in despair. As for the king, he loved the boy so dearly that he could not bear to be parted from him, night or day. But he began to fear that he might not live to see the young prince with his wife or sons of his own. Life was perhaps too pleasurable for the boy; why should he take on these burdens? So the king sent for his son and the prince stood respectfully with lowered eyes before him.

"My son," said the king, "I wish to see you married in my lifetime; it would be good to make plans now."

But at these words the boy changed colour.

"My father," he said, "I have no liking for women of any kind. I detest them all. Besides, they are dangerous. You must be aware how every tale, every legend speaks of their wickedness, greed and deceit. In fact, I will never marry, even to please my loved and honoured father. If I am forced into marriage, I shall take my own life straightaway."

The king's face grew dark as thunder, but he loved the boy, and kept his wrath to himself; indeed, for a whole year he said no more on the matter. Then he called the prince and asked him if he were ready now for marriage.

"It will give me so much joy," he said, "to see you with wife and sons."

The prince replied, "I have thought much about the subject and I can tell you absolutely that never in my life will I consent. I find women foolish, shameless and disgusting. I would die sooner than marry."

Sadly, the king called for his wazir, and said to him, "Only a fool would wish for children; they bring nothing but grief and disappointment. Kamar al-Zaman is more opposed to marriage than before. What should I do now?'

The wazir was for a long time silent. Then he said, "O lord of the age, be patient one more year. Then, instead of speaking to your son in private, call together all the chief men of the kingdom, ministers, merchants, high officials, and announce to the assembly that the prince's marriage is to be arranged straightaway. In the face of this congregation, he will not dare oppose you."

The king rejoiced at this excellent notion and gave the wazir a fair robe of honour.

The year passed, and then the monarch summoned the lords of his empire, the leading warriors, ministers, counsellors, merchants, men of great wealth, all the high dignitaries; they filled his mighty hall. Then he sent for the prince.

In he came, radiant as a star, his hair black as midnight, his forehead white as the moon, his cheeks like two anemones. He kissed the ground three times before his father, then modestly stood before him, his hands clasped behind his back. But when the king announced the approaching marriage of his son to a royal princess, a frantic rage and fury seized the youth, and wild words left his lips.

"O man of great age and little sense! Twice before have I told you that I would sooner die than be linked with a woman; the very name of woman is loathsome to me." And he stood and faced his father defiantly.

The king felt that he could swoon with grief and shock. Yet anger gave him strength. He called for his guards in a terrible voice and ordered them to imprison the prince in an ancient haunted tower near the palace. But the servants favoured the boy; they swept out the prison room and brought in rugs, a couch, a lantern and other comforts.

The hours that followed were heavy ones for father as well as son. The king, already regretting his harshness, was ready to free the boy; but the wazir advised him against this.

"To do that would certainly cause a scandal, and mark your royal self as weak in kingly power. Wait for fifteen days; the prince will be more than ready to change his mind by then."

The king agreed, but tossed all night upon his bed.

Meanwhile, shut in the tower room, the prince was regretting that he had vexed his elderly father so.

"Women are the cause of all misfortunes!" he murmured to himself.

When darkness fell, he called for water, washed, recited the evening prayer, bound his head with a blue silk turban, lay down on his couch and slept. Little did he guess that, before the night was out, an event would change his life beyond imagining.

Now it happened that the tower where he was held had been built in ancient times, but had long been abandoned by humans. At the back was a well, the dwelling place of a young Efreet called Maimounah, daughter of the mighty king of the subterranean Jinn, a monarch famed for his power and virtue. That midnight she rose from the well, as was her custom, flying into the upper air to gather news from heaven and other gossip. As she passed the top of the tower, she was amazed to see a light in a place forgotten for centuries. Pausing in her flight, she swerved aside and lightly passed through the locked and guarded door to where the prince was sleeping. She folded her wings and looked about her. A young man lay on a couch, a lantern at his head casting a light upon his face. The Efreet saw that he was of exquisite beauty. She gazed as if held by a spell; for a whole hour she did not move.

Then she said, "Blessed be Allah, creator of all loveliness. But how can the parents of this rare creature shut him away in this mouldering place, gnawed away by time? Do they not know of the frightful ruin-haunting Jinn? For there are evil spirits as well as good ones like myself. By Allah, I will take this youth under my protection." She kissed the boy on his lips, his cheeks, his eyelids and his forehead. This done, she soared away.

She was high in the air, approaching the lowest heaven, when she heard behind her a furious beating of wings. Wheeling round, she recognised the Efreet Dahnash, a Jinnee well-known for playing all kinds of low tricks. His reputation was shocking but he was, however, famous for his speed in flight. Maimounah feared that this scoundrel might see the light in the tower and work some mischief on the beauteous youth. So she pounced upon him like a hawk.

But before she could dash him to the ground, he cried out: "Oh,

Maimounah, royal Efreet, daughter of the king, I conjure you by the sacred seal of Sulaiman to do me no harm. I am not planning any naughtiness."

"You are using a mighty name," said Maimounah. "But I will not free you until you tell me where you have been at this late hour, and where you are heading for now. Don't try to deceive me. If you speak less than the truth, by even as much as a grain of sand, I will tear out your wing feathers and break your bones."

"Wait!" said the Jinnee. "I have something stranger than strange to relate. But swear first that, when my tale is told, you will give me a talisman to preserve me from bands of hostile Jinn, of earth, of air, of sea."

Maimounah replied, for she was deeply curious, "I swear upon the stone of the sacred seal of Sulaiman. Now speak!"

So the Jinnee began his tale.

"I come this night from the Interior Islands, beyond the furthest borders of China, a kingdom ruled by the mighty Ghayyur. In all my wanderings I have seen nothing to match the strength of his armies, the fairness of his women and the wonders of his realm. But all are as nothing compared with the beauty of his only daughter, Budur. No words can bring you the ecstasy of actually seeing this marvel. I will tell you only that her hair is as dark as the hour of separation and farewell; her face shines like the hour of reunion, after a long parting. Her cheeks are twin anemones; her nose is a sword; her mouth a dark plum, running with juice; her hips are two great ripe melons; her waist a stalk. I swoon to describe her any further.

"Now King Ghayyur is of mighty powers and vast dominion; he is fearless in battle, merciless to his foes. But the love of his life is his daughter, Budur; he is for ever looking for some new gift, some new way to keep her amused. He has had seven marvellous palaces built, each one of a different material. The first is all of crystal, the second of transparent alabaster, the third of porcelain, the fourth a mosaic of rare stones, the fifth of silver, the sixth of gold, the seventh of diamonds. Each is a treasure-house of gifts, surprises, discoveries, of gardens and waterfalls; each has the taste of a dream, which the dreamer hopes will never come to an end. She moves each year to a different palace, so that the wonder never has time to fade.

"All the neighbouring kings sought her hand in marriage, but each time she told the king, her father: 'I am queen and mistress of myself and no man shall rule over me. Moreover, the very thought of men fills me with disgust.' Yet suitors continued to come and the father tried each time to change her mind. At last she said, 'If ever you speak again of marriage, I will take a sword and pass it through my body; I would sooner die than belong to a man.'

"This time, the king was filled with fear and ordered his daughter to be kept in the care of ten old women, one of them her old nurse. She was not to be left alone for an instant, whether by night or day. One of these guardians always sleeps across the door of her room. And so have matters been for a year."

"But locked doors are no defence against spirits," the Jinnee continued, "and now I will tell you that, every night, I gaze on her as she sleeps, sometimes kissing her gently between the eyes. I love her too much to do her injury. I don't expect you to believe my story. But if you were to see this miracle of loveliness, you would understand." Overcome by the memory, he stopped, as if in a state of trance.

Maimounah had listened in silence. Now she gave a scornful laugh and struck him with her wing.

"Enough of this nonsense!" she cried. "Your damsel sounds like rubbish. If you were to see the beauty of a youth I have discovered this very night, you would beat yourself for your ridiculous praise of that wretched girl."

Trembling, for he feared her wrath, the Jinnee replied, "Dear mistress, I know nothing of your young friend and, unless I see him for myself, how can I judge his worth against the worth of the Princess Budur? Where can I find him? Where is he hiding?"

"Cease prattling, scoundrel!" cried Maimounah. "He has the same problem as your princess, he refuses to think of marriage. As punishment for this refusal, he is shut away in an ancient tower which is my personal dwelling. Don't imagine that you will catch a glimpse without my permission; I would not trust you as guard to a holy man. But just to prove that your judgement is of no more worth than a whiff of dust, I will take you to see my enchanting boy, and will glance thereafter at your girl. If my discovery is finer than yours, you will pay me a large forfeit. If the reverse, which is impossible, I shall do the same. Now let us waste no more time in words. We will start with my candidate, since the tower which holds him is just underneath us now."

They promptly made a downward dive through the air and slid into the locked and guarded room where the prince lay on his couch.

"Now look, devil," said Maimounah, "and admit that you have lost."

Dahnash looked – then hastily turned away, for his eyes were dazzled. He looked again and stood transfixed in silence while the minutes passed. Then he spoke.

"Mistress," he said, "I understand why you make your claim for this youth. Yet, if there can be a perfect likeness of male and female, barring a few differences, my princess and your prince were made in the same mould. It was used for these two alone, and then broken."

70

Hearing these words, Maimounah burnt with rage; she struck the Jinnee so violent a blow with her wing that one of his horns snapped off.

"Go at once to the palace of this Budur," she screeched, "and bring the creature back with you. I will not make the journey for so contemptible a being. We will then put them side by side, and you will see the truth."

Grumbling, the Jinnee picked up his horn and put it back, then sped off into the night at his customary lightning speed. He returned in an hour with the sleeping girl.

"You have taken long enough," said Maimounah. "Were you about some villainy on the way? Well, lay your candidate by the side of mine."

When this was done, the spirits both gazed down. What the Jinnee had said was true; one was almost the mirror of the other. But neither judge wished to give way.

"You must admit," Maimounah said, "that, all in all, my beloved prince is the lovelier."

"I would judge differently," said Dahnash, "but I am quite prepared to utter a little lie if it keeps your temper smooth."

Maimounah uttered a shriek. Then she said in scornful tones, "There is no sense or reason in the mind of the fool. The only way to bring this trifling to an end is to call in an outside judge."

"As you will," said Dahnash.

Maimounah stamped on the ground, and out of it rose an enormous Jinnee, horned, clawed, with a three-forked tail, hideous beyond belief. Seeing Maimounah, he kissed the ground before her.

"Mistress," said the fearsome creature, "what service do you ask of Kashkash, your lowly slave?"

"Good Kashkash," she replied, "I wish you to judge between the accursed Dahnash and myself. Which of the two sleepers on that couch is the more beautiful?"

Kashkash gazed at the sleeping pair. His eyes grew round; mutterings left his enormous lips.

At last he said, "By Allah, from the outward view there is no shade of difference. Both reach a pinnacle of beauty, allowing of course for the few details of gender, and the choice here varies with each beholder. But there is one way of settling the matter."

"And what is that?" said Maimounah.

"Simply this," said Kashkash. "Wake each candidate in turn, and study the response of each to other. The one most affected with passion is of course the loser. We three – need I say? – remain invisible."

"Your plan shall be tried without delay," said Maimounah.

"Agreed," said Dahnash, who promptly changed himself into a flea and bit the youth Kamar al-Zaman in the neck.

The sleeper woke – and found beside him a being of unfamiliar shape, surely a female, yet wonderfully pleasing. He clasped her in his arms, kissing her on her lips, and begged her to wake; but he could not break the spell of sleep laid on her by the Jinnee.

Then he thought to himself: "I suspect that my father has placed this damsel here, and even now may be watching through a hole in the wall. If I take further pleasure in her company tonight, he will taunt me tomorrow, saying that I am a fraud and a hypocrite, who falsely claimed to have no taste for women. But I will tell him that I have chosen a wife at last – this lovely damsel at my side – and that he must arrange the marriage immediately. Then I may honourably rejoice in her company."

He took a priceless ring from his smallest finger and placed it on one of hers, saying, "This shall be a sign and token of our union." Then a deep sleep overcame him once again.

It was now the turn of Maimounah to become a flea and wake the princess Budur with a bite. She did this with a mocking relish. The girl woke with a start – and saw that she was not alone: a youth of extraordinary beauty lay fast asleep at her side. Fear gave way to amazement, then to passionate love.

"This must be a plot devised by my father to punish my pride," she murmured. "Perhaps this is one of the suitors I have so long rejected. Well, he shall be my husband, come what may."

She tried to wake the lovely boy, but the spell of sleep was not yet due to be broken. However, she clasped him in her arms with such abandon that the watchers began to see that the damsel would be winner and loser both. Suddenly she perceived the prince's ring on her finger.

"This must be a token of our alliance," she said, "given to me while I was sleeping. Well, I will give one of mine in exchange." And she placed a priceless ring on the young man's smallest finger. Now, clasping him closely to her, she fell deeply asleep.

The spirits all agreed that, by the rules of their contest, the damsel had lost the contest for Dahnash.

But Maimounah said generously, "I shall not claim the forfeit, Dahnash. And I shall grant you the safe conduct pass to protect you from spirits of earth, air and sea. But first you must return this girl to her father's palace. I propose to take an interest in her, for she has great possibilities. Kashkash, you will help to transport her. You have done well, and shall be chief of my messengers."

72

At daybreak the young prince woke and looked about him for his partner of the night. She was nowhere to be seen.

He shouted to the slave at the door, "Answer, accursed one. Where is the damsel who passed the night on this couch?"

"What damsel?" asked the astonished slave. "No one has entered or departed. I was on guard at the door from dusk to dawn."

"Liar and scoundrel!" cried the prince. He threw the unlucky slave to the ground and beat him, until his clothes were soaked in blood and he was almost dead.

Then he tied the man to a rope and lowered him into the freezing well, saying, "Tell the truth. Where is the damsel?"

"Pull me up and I will tell you," said the shivering slave. But when he reached the surface he staggered out and made his way to the king.

King Shahruman was at that moment with his wazir, lamenting his harshness to his son. The wazir, however, was advising him to leave him in the tower for the full fifteen days. They were astonished to see the prince's slave come tottering in, covered with blood, his clothes in rags.

"O, our lord the Sultan," gasped the wretched fellow. "Your son, my master, has been afflicted with madness. He declares that a damsel passed the night with him on his couch, and that he cannot live without her. He has beaten and tortured me because there is no sign of any such visit, nor any damsel at all."

The wazir scurried off to the tower, scolding the slave as they went. He opened the door in fear, expecting a madman's blow. But what did he see? The prince was sitting calmly on his couch, piously reading the Koran.

The wazir sighed with relief, and said, "This accursed slave came to your father swearing that you were mad, and had told him matters not fit to repeat to you."

"What were these matters?" asked the prince.

"That you had spent the night with a damsel, on this couch; that you had then demanded to know where she had gone, and insisted on her return. He should be whipped to death for such falsehoods."

The prince replied, "Your joke has gone far enough, you evil old man. Unless you restore to me my divine companion, or tell me where my father has hidden her, you will have double the punishment of this filthy fellow here."

The wazir stepped back in terror, saying, "In the name of Allah, I beg you to clear your mind of this dream, for your words have the taint of madness."

"Say you so, foul wretch!" cried the prince, and he seized the wazir by the

beard, and kicked and beat him furiously.

At length the old man thought of a stratagem: "A lie told to a madman is no lie. If only a lie will save my life, a lie will have to be told to this insane youth."

Aloud, he said, "O cease your blows, I beg you. Your father forbade me, on pain of death, to reveal where he had hidden the damsel. But if you let me go, I will beg your father to release you from the tower and arrange for you to marry the damsel of your heart."

"Go now to the king, my father," said the prince, "and return at once with his answer."

When King Shahruman saw his wazir he was shocked by his battered appearance.

"Some dreadful thing has happened to you! Who has done this mischief?"

"Some dreadful thing has happened to your son, O king," said the wazir. "It is he who has treated me so. He has totally lost his wits."

The king turned purple with rage. "O foulest of wazirs!" he cried. "If this news is true, you will be nailed to the highest tower of the city, for you alone have brought this thing about. I go now to test your tale for myself."

He hastened off to the prince's room, the anxious wazir following. Seeing his father, the young man rose to his feet and made the correct greetings. The king gave a terrible glance at the wazir.

"No sign of madness here," he hissed at the old man. Then he turned back to his son. "Tell me, what is today?"

"It is Saturday," answered the youth.

"And tomorrow?"

"Sunday, followed by Monday, Tuesday and the rest."

Asked to give the names of the months, he promptly did so.

"You see," said the king, "The only madness here is in yourself, you wicked old man."

To his son he said, "You would not believe the ridiculous tale that the wazir and the pitch-black slave have been spreading around. They actually declared that you told them a story of spending the night with a damsel on this very couch. Tell them before me that they are evil liars."

"Father," said the prince, "I have no taste for your jokes. I know that you sent the damsel to cure my pride and I tell you now that I desire nothing more than to obey you, and to make this marvellous girl my wife. So passionately do I long for her that I cannot even speak of her calmly."

The king was greatly disturbed. "Perhaps it is true that you are mad," he said. "All this talk of marriage has confused your senses; you cannot distinguish dreams from fact."

The prince replied, "My father, I can prove to you that the damsel was no dream. The ring on my smallest finger was placed there during the night. And I, in turn, gave her a ring of mine. Father, find this girl or I die."

The father looked at the ring and knew that here was a mystery outside his power to solve. He took the boy back to the palace, and for weeks they lived together, away from all comers, the prince grieving for his lost girl, the king grieving for his son's plight. He ordered a palace to be built by the sea, for greater solitude. And there the prince made and recited endless verses of love.

And what, meanwhile, of the Princess Budur? It was almost dawn when the Jinnee placed her back on her own bed. At the first ray of morning, she woke, still smiling from the night's adventures, held out her arms, and found – nothing. She was alone! Where was her beautiful companion of the night? She uttered a terrible cry and all the old women came running to her side.

"Mistress, what troubles you?" asked her nurse.

"You know very well what troubles me," said the damsel. "What has become of the beautiful youth with eyes like midnight and cheeks like red anemones? Where has he gone? He lay with me all night long, until near morning, when I was overcome by sleep."

The old women raised their hands in horror.

"By Allah," said the nurse. "Do not tease us with these dangerous jokes; if your father heard your naughty words, what would become of us all!"

"This is no joke," said the girl. "A youth of the utmost loveliness did indeed pass the night in my arms, and I in his. Where is he? What have you done with him?"

"This is indeed the voice of madness!" said the old nurse.

And all the old women cried, "Indeed, by Allah!"

The damsel could endure no more. She seized a sword from the wall and rushed at her aged guardians. They shrieked and fled, then breathlessly rushed to the king's royal bedchamber.

"O noble master," said the nurse, "your daughter has lost her reason. She

would have killed us if we had not escaped."

The king, in gown and slippers, rushed to his daughter's room. But what did he see? A smiling girl who ran to welcome him.

"Ah dear father," she said, "how glad I am that you have come. These women have no sense or understanding. You chose the young man well, and indeed cured my refusal to marry. But where is he now, my beautiful partner? Do, I beg you, hasten the wedding ceremony that we may never be parted again."

Her father could scarcely believe his ears. What a disaster! His only daughter, utterly deranged! He gave orders that she should be closely guarded in case she tried to injure herself. Then he called together all the doctors, magicians, astrologers and other such wise men of the kingdom and made an announcement: whoever should cure the princess Budur of her malady would have her as his wife, and be next heir to the throne. But whosoever tried and failed would have his head cut off and set on the spikes of the palace wall. By the time some forty heads adorned the gates, the flow of candidates stopped. No one seemed to want to take the risk.

Now the princess had a foster-brother, son of her old nurse. His name was Mazawar; he had read much and travelled far and had studied the magic arts and secret sciences. Returning now from a long journey, he saw the heads on the spikes and learned the news of his foster-sister's malady. She had been a close friend of his childhood and he decided to help. He asked his mother if she could arrange a secret meeting with her charge and the old woman dressed him in women's clothes to smuggle him past the eunuch guarding the princess's door.

The Princess Budur rejoiced to see her foster-brother.

"You of all people," she said, "will know that I am not mad." And she told her strange tale.

"I smell magic here," said Mazawar. "But be assured that I will track down the mystery."

He left, starting that same day on a long strange journey. Everywhere he went he heard the same tale about the Princess Budur's madness, brought about by bewitchment or by dream. But at last he came to a great city by the

from Kamar al-Zaman and Princess Budur

sea, named Tarab, where the name of Budur was not known at all. What everyone spoke of now was the madness of the king's son, Kamar al-Zaman, in the island realm of Khalidan. This seemed so like his sister's story that he knew where his road now lay.

"How far are these islands?" he enquired.

"They lie to the east, six months by land, one month by water," he was told.

"Then I go by sea," he said and found a boat setting sail that day for Khalidan.

The voyage started well, with a fair wind; but on the last day of the month a mighty storm drove the ship on to rocks and he was cast into the swirling waves. He caught hold of a spar of wood and was swept ashore on to a narrow strip of land, which led to the palace where the wazir, who had come to bring news of the kingdom, was looking out of a window at the waves beneath and saw the half-drowned man. He sent slaves to bring him in, and give him food and clothes. Then the stranger was brought before him. He seemed a young man of quality by his looks, and a scholar by his conversation, learned in science and medicine.

"Fate has sent you," said the wazir. "Our prince lies here, sick in mind and body, awaiting a true healer." And he told the story of the dream which had confounded the prince's reason.

Mazawar listened patiently, as he had done to his sister Budur. The tales had a strange likeness.

"Take me to the prince," he said at last. "I think I know of a cure for his sickness."

"But," the wazir warned him, "tread with care, for the father heeds only the son and the son heeds only himself. And to cross them can mean death."

"I have no fear," said Mazawar.

And such was his charm that both father and son were roused from their gloom when he stood before them. As for Mazawar, one glance at the prince had revealed the truth, as lightning shows the edge of a precipice. The prince was the mirror likeness of the Princess Budur.

"Blessed be Allah," Mazawar said aloud, "who has made a damsel to match this prince in beauty, his perfect likeness in fact and story too."

The youth on the bed listened with rapt attention.

"I beg you, father," he said, "to leave me alone with this physician."

The king was ready to humour any whim of his son, and went outside the door, beckoning to the wazir to join him.

Then Mazawar whispered to the prince, "Allah has brought me here to give you news of your beloved damsel. She is the Princess Budur, daughter of King

Ghayyur. She is also my foster-sister and I know your tale to be true."

The young man who had lain for so long, too weak to move, now rose to his feet.

"Let us set out at once," he cried.

"The distance is far," said Mazawar, "and you must prepare. Meanwhile, call in the king, your father, and show that you are restored."

At that moment the king and the wazir, restless at waiting, entered the room and saw the change in the prince with amazement and delight. Celebrations were held throughout the realm; jewels and gifts were showered on the young astrologer. But as the days passed, the prince grew more and more impatient to leave and seek his Budur. Yet the journey was one of many months, and he knew his father could never endure so long a separation.

"What shall I do?" he asked Mazawar. "How can I go without offending my father?"

"I have foreseen this problem," Mazawar replied, "and I have devised a plan. First, you must tell the king that you wish to go hunting, to give you strength after being enclosed so long in a sickroom. Then, when we have reached the cross-roads, we will kill a horse and mingle some of your clothing with the blood and bones. The king will think that you have been killed by robbers and that I have fled. His grief will be great – but this will make him all the more joyful when he hears that you are alive and well and married to the princess Budur."

"An excellent plan!" cried the prince.

Mazawar's scheme worked just as he had foretold and the two young men started on their journey. After many months, they reached King Ghayyur's kingdom, and entered the capital city. Mazawar now made the prince put on an astrologer's gown, ornamented with magic signs and talismans; he also gave him a set of magician's instruments, made of gold and precious stones, and took him to the palace gate. The grim heads still mouldered on the spikes, but Mazawar told the prince to have no fear. Then he proclaimed to north, south, east and west, that a master wizard and healer had arrived who could cure all ills, even the malady of the Princess Budur.

So great was the crowd attracted by the handsome young magician and his daring claims, that the king himself came to the window. He sent for the young man to be brought into his presence.

"You say, my child, that you can restore my daughter's reason. You know, of course, the conditions. I should be very grieved to see your head on a spike, but the rules cannot be changed. On the other hand, I would be happy enough if you were my son-in-law. Are you prepared to take the chance?"

"O noble king," said the prince, "I know the risk, but I also know the power of my gifts. I beg that you will let me start the cure without delay."

At this, the king ordered his chief eunuch to take the young magician to the princess.

As soon as they were outside the princess's apartment, the prince said, "I wish you to take this package to the princess; it is the first stage of the treatment. Say that it comes from one who knows what no one else knows but she. I shall meanwhile stand behind the curtain and watch the effect."

He handed the eunuch a folded paper containing the ring that she had placed on his smallest finger. Wrapped round it was a written note, saying that it came from the Prince Kamar al-Zaman, who had lain beside her all one magic night, and had been devoured by love for her ever since.

The eunuch went to the princess and handed the package and the message, adding that it had come from a young astrologer much like herself in looks. The damsel was intrigued. She opened the package, found the ring and the note and uttered a cry of joy.

"Where is this young man to be found?" she exclaimed. "Bring him to me."

The prince stepped forward, threw off his astrologer's gown and they kissed and clasped each other without a pause. They were still embracing when the king himself appeared, to see if the evil spell had been destroyed. When the king heard the full story he called it a marvel, and ordered the royal scribes to write it down, so that it could be read and told for generations to come, through future centuries. Meanwhile, he commanded general rejoicing though the realm and the killing of thousands of animals to provide rich feasting. Messengers were also despatched to the prince's father, to tell him that his son was alive and well, and was marrying the only daughter of a great monarch.

The throne in time passed to Kamar al-Zaman, who lived long in joy and delight with his queen, the lady Budur: a scourge to all western invaders of his city by the sea, but ever just and generous to his own. And so ends the wonderful tale of Kamar al-Zaman and the Princess Budur, Moon of Moons.

THE AMAZING TALE OF THE UNENDING TREASURE

MANY AMAZING TALES ARE TOLD of the Khalifah Harun al-Rashid, of all the great princes of the east the most magnificent. But no tale is more strange than the one which touches upon his single weakness – Allah alone has none! And what was that? He would boast that no man gave more splendid gifts, or gave more bountifully.

"Now who in the mortal world," he would say, "has richer treasures to draw upon?"

The wazir Jafar felt that this lack of delicacy was unworthy of his master's greatness and at last took courage to answer him. Kissing the ground three times between the Khalifah's hands, he said, "O Ruler of the Faithful, monarch of monarchs, pardon your slave that he dares to set before you the words of an ancient philosopher, that the riches of this world and the qualities of the soul are only lent to man by Allah; he who is greatly endowed with both has yet no cause for pride."

He paused; but since the Khalifah did not at once reply, Jafar continued: "I must not hide the truth. Master of masters, you are not the only one whom Allah has granted treasure matched only in dream, and also a giver's hand to match that treasure. There is a young man in the city of Basrah, Abu al-Kasim by name, no prince but a mere private citizen, who yet lives in greater magnificence than the most powerful emperor. Even the mighty ruler of the Faithful, highest of all living men, is not so bountiful nor so unceasing a giver of great gifts."

The eyes of Harun flamed when he heard these words; his neck swelled; his face became red and purple.

"Woe upon you, dog of wazirs!" he cried. "Do you not know that such a lie means death?"

"I swear to you by all that is most holy," said the wazir, "that I speak the truth. When I was last in Basrah I was myself in the house of Abu al-Kasim, and witnessed this wonder for myself. And so I dare to maintain that this

young man is the very emperor of givers in our time. If you doubt my word, put it to the test; send a secret emissary to investigate."

Speechless with rage and shock, the Khalifah signed to his guards to seize Jafar and place him under arrest. Then, as the wazir was being taken to the cells, he hurried to the apartment of his queen, Zubaidah, and threw himself on the couch, his faced knotted with anger.

Zubaidah asked him no questions but handed him a glass of rose-scented water, saying, "May this refresh your spirit! And may Allah be with you always".

"It is the accursed Jafar who will not be with me always," replied the Khalifah. And he told her what had passed between them." Zubaidah had her own thoughts on the matter but was too wise to seem to disagree. Subtly, she suggested that to prove the case against Jafar, someone should indeed be sent to the young man's house in Basrah. Until then, the wazir's final punishment should wait. Harun, calmed as always by her talking, saw reason in her words.

"True," he said, "Jafar is the son of an old and faithful servant, and I will not proceed without proper evidence. And as I can trust no eyes but my own, I will go to Basrah and observe this Abu al-Kasim for myself." Always a lover of disguises, he dressed as a merchant and started forth at once. Allah brought him to Basrah without mishap, and he stopped at the chief inn of the city.

There he asked the doorkeeper, "Do you know of a young man in these parts, Abu al-Kasim by name, who is rumoured to give more greatly than great kings, or so they say?"

The old man raised his eyes to heaven, wagged his head and declared, "Is there one man here who has not been helped by him? If I had a hundred mouths and a hundred tongues in each, and the gift of golden words in every tongue, I could not begin to give the measure of that young man's munificence." Before he could say more, he was called by a new arrival, and the disguised Harun retired for the night, wondering much.

In the morning he rose early and, looking about him, strolled towards the market place. There he asked one of the shopkeepers to direct him to the dwelling of Abu al-Kasim.

"You must have come from afar," said the man. "The house of Abu al-Kasim is better known here than the royal palace itself." He called to one of his boy slaves and sent him to serve as guide. Harun was led to a noble mansion, built of many-hued marble, with great doors of green jade. A group of young slaves were playing in the courtyard, and Harun beckoned one towards him, telling the boy to inform his master that a stranger had journeyed from Baghdad to Basrah solely to see him. The slave sensed an unusual authority in

from The Unending Treasure

the visitor and ran to give the message. At once Abu al-Kasim came into the courtyard to receive his guest, then, taking him by the hand, he led him into a hall of dazzling splendour and seated him at his side.

Harun gazed about him. The great couch on which they sat was draped in cloth of gold, soft as silk, with wonderful embroideries. Twelve beautiful white boy slaves brought them fragrant wines in cups of rarest crystal set with rubies. Then twelve white slave girls, as exquisite as the boys, brought in porcelain dishes of fruit and large golden goblets of sherbet cooled with snow. All these things were so seductive to the eye, the taste, the mind that Harun was forced to admit to himself that, in his own palace, with all the choice in the world, he had never known such delicacies. This thought continued as the roasted meats, fragrant with rarest herbs, were served in golden dishes, then preserves of roses and violets, and pastries, light as air.

Musicians entered, singers and lute players, thrilling his inmost core with their subtle melodies, causing him to say to himself, "Music sounds in my own palace from sweet voices and plucked strings; in my service too is the greatest of known musicians, Ishak of Mosul, from whom no secret of the craft is hidden. Yet here in the home of a private citizen I find a concert that would be a marvel even in Paradise."

While Harun mused upon these mysteries, Abu al-Kasim quietly left the hall and returned with an amber wand in one hand and a little tree in the other. It was no ordinary tree; the trunk was of silver, the leaves were emerald, and the fruit was crimson rubies. Perched on the top was a golden peacock, marvellously made. As soon as Abu al-Kasim tapped the bird's head with the wand, it stretched its wings, spread its tail and began to pirouette round and round. As it moved, it wafted scent and incense from tiny holes in its sides, until the delicious odours filled the entire hall. Harun wished to study this marvel and put out his hand. But before he could even touch the bird, the young man took it up and carried it away. Harun's anger rose.

"Is this how a proper host behaves?" he said to himself. "This Abu al-Kasim must have feared that I would ask for the toy. So much for his generosity!"

As these thoughts ran through his head, Abu al-Kasim came back, this time leading a little boy slave of radiant beauty. The child was dressed in a robe of gold brocade embroidered with rare pearls; in his hand was a cup carved from a single ruby, filled with purple wine. He kissed the ground between the Khalifah's hands, then offered him the cup. The Khalifah drank and handed it back – but, lo! it was still full to the brim. Again he emptied it – and again it was brim-full.

"How does this miracle come about?" asked the Khalifah.

"Simple enough," said his host. "It is the work of an ancient craftsman who had mastered certain secrets of the earth." Then he took the child's hand and hurried him out of the hall, still bearing the magic cup.

Harun found this hard to endure. "How vulgar and ill-bred is this young man, who shows his fine possessions, then quickly snatches them away as if I might be a thief! Jafar shall suffer for this." But as he looked up he saw before him the young man with yet another treasure, a little slave girl of a beauty beyond imagining. The robe that she wore seemed totally made of diamonds; thus, the very least of her lithe movements dazzled the watcher's eye. In her hand was a lute of aloe-wood and ivory, and she began to play.

So greatly was Harun enthralled that he cried out, "O fortunate youth to own this miracle!" But at once the young man hastened the lovely child away.

Now Harun decided to stay no longer. When his host returned, he rose to his feet and said, with bitter sarcasm, "O most generous Abu al-Kasim, I have no wish to trespass further on your great hospitality. Allow me now to go." The young man escorted him courteously to the gate and Harun strolled back to the inn, murmuring to himself, "Jafar shall learn the penalty for lying. He shall! He shall!"

But what was this? At the gate of the inn, awaiting his coming, was a crescent-shaped group of young slaves, one horn of the curve made of black slaves, the other of white. In the centre were three exquisite prizes: the lute-playing girl in her dazzling diamond robe, with the pretty boy holding his ever-filled ruby cup on her right, and a no less lovely boy clasping the emerald tree and the peacock on her left. All prostrated themselves before Harun, then the girl presented him with a silken scroll from Abu al-Kasim, begging his guest to accept these few unworthy tokens of homage and gratitude for the visit, which had brought honour and joy to the house. Harun read the scroll, then stood amazed.

"How have I misjudged this noble and excellent young man," he cried. "And you too, good Jafar, you have rightly humbled my pride. But how is it possible that a mere citizen can give away treasures that an emperor could not rival? I must at all costs solve this mystery'. So saying, he left his gifts in the courtyard of the inn, went back to the mansion and sought out Abu al-Kasim.

"O most honoured host, of the noble heart and golden hand," he said, "Allah be with you always. But how can I, a mere merchant, accept such prodigious gifts? If I may do so without offence, I would ask if I might return them, leaving only the greatest gift of all, the knowledge of your matchless generosity. For you are the very king of givers!"

The young man answered sadly, "Honoured stranger, have my poor gifts displeased you by their paltry nature? Why else would you reject my offering, made, I assure you, in no insulting spirit!"

Troubled at this, Harun replied, "O prince of hosts, may Allah close my lips for ever if I should pain one whose guest I have been. I feared only that you, a young man, might ruin yourself, for – however great your treasure may be – it cannot be endless."

"Noble friend and master," said the youth, "your scruple has given me the joy of a new visit, and I am glad to set your mind at rest. Indeed, I will tell you a tale so strange that centuries later, listeners still will marvel." So saying, he led his guest into a quiet hall where a ravishing odour of incense rose from many small braziers and directed him to sit on a couch draped in a cloth of gold; underfoot was a silken carpet of melting softness, woven with designs that could have been living flowers. Then, taking his place beside his guest, the young man began his story.

"Honoured guest, I must tell you first that I am the son of Abd al-Aziz, the great jeweller of Cairo. Although he was a native of that city, like his ancestors before him, the Sultan of Egypt's greed and ill-will obliged him to flee, and he settled in Basrah, marrying the only daughter of the wealthiest merchant here. I was the only child of the marriage, and so, on my father's death, I inherited vast possessions. But being young and heedless I lived so extravagantly that in two years, all was spent. I felt that it was better to be poor among strangers than where I had once been prince among my kind. So, I sold what was left of my property and joined a merchants' caravan; by way of Mosul and Damascus, and a pilgrimage to Mecca, I arrived at last in Cairo, home of my ancestors. I thought of my father. How ashamed he would be to see me now, his son a beggar where he himself had been a lord among merchants.

But as I wandered sadly by the Nile, behind the Sultan's palace, I was shaken from my sorrow by the sight of a girl's face at a window. Then the vision disappeared. I waited, but to no avail. The next day I came again; the hours passed, but I saw nothing. The day after that, however, I perceived a little trembling of the curtain, and a glimpse of two dark eyes. On the evening of the third day, the curtain parted and a face as fair as stars and moon revealed itself. I bent to the ground, then rose, gazed upward and murmured words to convey my love, my longing and desire.

An expression of fear came over the damsel's face. She looked to the right and left, then whispered hastily, "Return at midnight. But now depart!" Then curtain and window closed. All trace had gone.

I felt delirious with joy, and, seeking out the poor man's hammam or bathing place, I spent the next few hours preparing myself for the meeting.

Then, in the midnight dark, I glided through the streets to the palace window. A silken ladder was hanging down the wall; I climbed it silently, and found myself in an unlit empty room. Beyond was another, also empty and dark. I advanced to a third, and there a lamp was glowing. In its tender light I saw a silver bed; on it lay the lovely girl herself. She smiled, leaned on her elbow, and in a voice sweeter than syrup of roses, told me to lie beside her. Presently she asked who I might be and how I had come to pass her window. Tears came to her lustrous eyes as I told my tale.

Then she said, "O Abu al-Kasim, beautiful stranger who is now no stranger, I am the lady Labibah, the Sultan's favourite wife. But jealous rivals surround me; what is more, I have no joy from my husband. It seemed to me, from my window, that you would bring that joy. Now I know that my thought and hope were true."

At that moment the door shook with a violent knocking and Labibah leapt to her feet in terror.

"We are lost!" she said. "Only the Sultan has the key and the right to enter here." I tried to scramble under the bed, but the door burst open; the room filled with eunuchs; at least twenty hands dragged me forth and cast me out of the window into the Nile. As I fell, I saw the body of the damsel, thrown from a neighbouring window, sink in the flowing waters. Fate decreed that I did not drown; but though I searched and dived repeatedly, I could not find the body of the lovely girl, doomed by my recklessness. Racked with remorse, I left the land of Egypt and did not rest until I had reached Baghdad. In my belt I found a single dinar; with this I purchased sweetmeats, sweet-smelling herbs and rose conserve, placed them in a wicker basket, and in the fashion of a pedlar, hawked them about the market. But unlike the other pedlars, I sang about the excellence of my wares instead of shouting the usual market cries. This pleased the passers-by and brought me trade.

One day, a venerable old man who owned the largest shop in the market, called me towards him and asked my name.

"Dear master," I replied, "to speak of myself will open wounds which only time can heal." He purchased one or two trifles, put ten dinars into my hand, kissed me as a father kisses a son, and went back to his shop. The next day he sought me out again, bought some incense, and so persuasively begged me to tell my story that I yielded.

He listened gravely, then declared, "My son, your trials are over. You lost a father who gave you wealth and love. Now you have found another, even wealthier, with a love for you no less great. Abu al-Kasim, I adopt you as my child. I have no other. Cast away your wicker basket; tomorrow we shall leave for Basrah, which is my city, and we shall live there in comfort and joy until Allah chooses to call the one or the other."

And so we moved to Basrah, where I devoted myself to pleasing the good old man. Those were happy days. But after a year a sickness overcame my guardian, one for which the doctors could find no cure.

At last he called me close to his bedside, saying, "My son, you have given me a year of joy; few men have as much. Now I am leaving you a treasure which will make you richer than all the kings of the earth; it has belonged to my people since the beginning of time, though where it came from I have never known. As for where it lies, each father passes on the secret to his son. This secret I am about to reveal to you. Bend down." I did so, and he whispered the directions in my ear. Then he added, "Seek happiness before all things. And do not fear to give with open hands. You will never exhaust the treasure of my line."

After the death of this good man, when all the fitting ceremonies were performed, I settled in his great house, entertaining each stranger as if he were a king. The path has not been without a few stones.

The chief of police visited me, and after chatting of this and that, observed, "It is of course not my place to ask a young man of quality to account for his sudden riches. So we will talk of other matters. Strangely, my family's cow has ceased to give milk just when the price of bread has doubled."

"O prince of detectives," I said, "how much would it cost to replace the cow and supplement the extra price of bread?"

"Oh, a mere ten gold dinars a day, my lord," said the man.

"Surely more than that," said I. "Let it be a hundred dinars a day. Call each month; my treasurer will give you this trifling sum."

Two other officials approached me in the same way but with different stories. To one I offered a thousand dinars a day to distribute among the poor and afflicted – that, I think, was the phrase we used. The other was the wali of Basrah.

He called me to his presence, saying (after mutual courtesies), "If a young man were to show me some virtuous use of wealth, I alone in my calling would not reproach that youth for any seeming extravagances."

"Indeed," I cried, "you are sent by Allah! I have been seeking some holy man to distribute a trifle of two thousand dinars a day from my humble pittance to those who walk in religious poverty." The wali at once replied that he would be delighted to oblige.

Since then I have punctually paid this extortionate blackmail and have been left in peace to live as I will, handing out treasure with both hands from my inexhaustible store."

The Khalifah sat silent for a moment, overwhelmed by the thought of his host's possessions. Recalling that he was still in his merchant's guise, he spoke at last.

"Dear master, there can be no lack at all in your happiness. Judging by the exquisite young slaves you have given to me, you must have your choice of the world in youth and beauty."

"Many beautiful women are in my house," said the young man sadly, "but they mean nothing. My heart still weeps for one who was cast into the Nile, as I have told you. I would give all my wealth to bring back my lost Labibah."

As soon as Harun returned to Baghdad, his first act was to have Jafar released from prison and to present him with the two delightful boys. Then, having told his tale, he asked the wazir's advice.

"O wise Jafar," he said, "what can I give this man that will seem worthy? For even I cannot match the splendour of his gifts."

"I have a suggestion," said the wazir. "You can make him King of Basrah." The Khalifah rejoiced, and sent Jafar to bring back Abu al-Kasim in princely fashion, while the coronation ceremony was prepared. When the young man arrived at Harun's palace, he found himself in the presence of none other than the supposed merchant. The Khalifah embraced him as a son, and they spoke long. While they were being served with sherbets and with fruits, the Khalifah sent for a young slave, whom he had just bought, to come and sing for them. But no sooner had the guest looked on the damsel's face than he uttered a piercing cry and fell swooning to the floor. The slave girl was Labibah! A fisherman had rescued her from the Nile and sold her to a dealer. Because of her gifts and beauty the man had kept her hidden until he could offer her to the Khalifah himself.

And so did Abu al-Kasim, King of Basrah, find his love again, and she became his queen. They lived in delight and joy for many a year until they were visited in their turn by the Sure-Comer, the unseen Builder of Tombs, whom no man can avoid.

ISHAK'S WINTER EVENING

THIS STRANGE AND MARVELLOUS TALE was told by Ishak of Mosul, singer of all singers at the great court of Harun al-Rashid.

"That winter night I sat in my home alone while the winds howled like warring demons, and the black clouds poured down rain like the emptying of giant waterskins. I warmed my hands at the copper brazier, but I felt no cheer, since — because of the darkness, mud and downfall — I could neither go forth nor expect any friend to call.

In a half-dream I thought of a delightful girl at the palace and murmured aloud, "O would that the lovely Saidah were here, and would sing for me. Then all my cares would fly." Hardly had I spoken when I heard a knocking at the door; it had an urgent sound, and I hurried to open it. "Some traveller seeks shelter," I reflected, There, standing outside, was none other than the longed-for Saidah! But in what a state! She seemed to have left the palace in haste, for her green silk tunic and the light cloth of gold over her head had given her no protection from the storm. Rain dripped from her hair and clothes; her feet were splashed with mud.

"Sweet damsel," I said, "why have you honoured me with this visit on such a night?"

She answered in a dream-like voice, "Your messenger told me that your need was great. I had no choice but to come without delay."

I knew that I had sent no messenger, but I did not wish to question the curious ways of Fate, so I answered, "Praise be to Allah who saw my grief and brought me joy. So greatly did I yearn towards you that if you had not come to me, I would have taken the road to you." Then I ordered my slave to bring hot water and essence of roses and silken robes. I washed Saidah's feet with my own hands and gave her the new attire, and we shared a feast of delicate sugar cakes and fruits and cups of sweetest wine. Then I offered to sing to her a song I had just composed, as yet unheard at the palace.

Now, usually I require many pleadings before I consent to sing. But the girl said, "Dear Ishak, do not be offended, but even the best of your songs is not to my taste tonight."

"Then, dear mistress," I said, "will you sing for me instead? Without music, all joy is incomplete."

"Truly, you are right," she answered. "But this evening, I know not why, the voice I wish to hear is neither yours nor mine. It must come from the street, from some rough wanderer, some homeless beggar even. One such may be passing even now. Beloved Ishak, humour my fancy; open the door and see."

I was certain that no one would be abroad in this bitter night. Still, I opened the door, pushing hard against the wind. To my surprise I saw an old beggar, leaning on a stick, grumbling to himself.

I just made out the words: "What an infernal noise! How can I be heard against the storm? And if the poor blind singer can't be heard, how can he earn his bread? He must die of hunger. Aie, aie, aie." Murmuring in this fashion he began to tap his stick as if to resume his journey.

"Wait, good uncle!" I cried. "You say that you are a singer. Come within and join our company. You will shelter from the storm; we shall have your songs."

"If you wish," he said. "But you must lead me in." When he was seated I brought him food, which he ate with great delicacy, using the tips of his fingers. Then, after drinking several cups of wine, he asked whose house he was in; what was the name of his host?

"I am Ishak of Mosul," I replied. He did not seem impressed.

"Yes, I have heard of you," he said. "I am told that you have a fine singing voice. May I take the privilege of a guest and ask to hear it?"

Naturally, I was delighted. I took up my lute, and as I plucked its strings I sang with all the skill within me. Then, with a modest smile, I waited for the praise.

But the beggar only nodded and said, in a condescending way, "Yes, Ishak, you could be called quite an accomplished singer and a tolerable musician altogether." I was so piqued that I cast the lute aside. But remembering my place as host I quelled my angry words.

The old man broke the silence, saying, "Is there no other here to play or sing? The night is lost without music."

"There is a young slave girl here whom some think gifted," I replied.

"Tell her to sing that I may hear," said the beggar. Saidah was at first unwilling, but then she took the lute and sang more beautifully than she could ever have done before.

But her song was not yet ended when the beggar held up his hand, saying,

"Enough. You still have much to learn."

Saidah was enraged and would have run from the room if I had not knelt at her feet and begged her to remain. Had not I too, a master of my craft, been rebuffed?

Then I turned to the old man saying, "Honoured stranger, we have done our best, as Allah knows. More is not possible. Now it is your turn to show your skill."

The beggar smiled and said, "Bring me a lute which no hand yet has played." I took a new lute from its wrappings and put it in his hands. He lightly touched the strings with a sharpened goose feather and began to play in a manner that was quite unknown to me. Almost at once I realised that in my house was surely the greatest musician of our time, almost supernatural in his powers. Then, in a voice that thrilled the very core of my being, he began to sing. What was more, the words dealt with that very night's events: the storm, my solitude, my wish, the arrival of the girl. I could find no words to express my wonder, awe and fear. It was the beggar-singer himself who spoke.

"In an hour or two," he said, "the storm will have worn through its anger. The dawn will bring back travellers, and I can resume my trade. If I might sleep in some corner until then, I will count you a very prince of hosts."

At once I went to fetch a candle to light him to my guest chamber. Less than a minute later I returned, but where was the beggar? Where was the fair Saidah? The door was still locked on the inside, the windows were still closed; my guests were nowhere within the house; there were no footprints in the mud without.

Some to whom I have told this tale said that it was Allah rebuking my vanity. But I am inclined to think that it was Iblis, the Wicked One, who played sport with me that night. Somewhat to my regret it has not happened again."

THE TALE OF SINDBAD THE SAILOR

LONG AGO, IN BAGHDAD, IN the reign of the mighty Harun al-Rashid, there lived a poor labouring man called Sindbad, known as Sindbad the Porter, for he earned his bread by carrying loads for hire. One day when the heat was great, and his burden more than usually heavy, he paused at the gate of a handsome house where a bench was set for wayfarers; the ground was swept and sprinkled with water, and a cool breeze blew through the leafy shade. Sweet sounds came from within, plucked strings, and ravishing voices linked in song, and all around the melodious noise of birds. Dazed with pleasure, he became bold and peered through the scrollwork of the gate. There he saw a great garden with sparkling fountains and bright flowers; everywhere were richly attired guests, attended by slaves and servants whose beauty and elegance made them also a pleasure to look upon. Odours of exquisite foods rose towards him: savoury roasted meats with herbs, sweet and fragrant wines.

Hardly knowing what he did, he cried out: "Glory be to Allah, whose ways I do not question. Yet the reason remains a mystery, why he makes one man high and lofty, such as the master of this mansion, living in honoured ease and comfort, while another he makes poor and burdened, toiling long hours in the day's heat for meagre and wretched pay. But I do not complain. The ways of Allah are the ways of Allah!"

It was the porter's custom to sing as he worked, and he rapidly turned these thoughts into verses, which he sang to his own melody, and this relieved his mind. After a few minutes' silence he was about to take up his load again when he saw a pretty little slave boy, elegantly dressed, stepping towards him, holding out his hand.

"Come," said the child, "my master has heard your words, and wishes to see you." The porter was filled with fear, but dared not refuse to go. So, leaving his load with the doorkeeper, he followed the slave-child into the great house. He found himself in a noble mansion, pleasant to all the senses. In the central hall was a company of guests, lords and ministers, scholars and sages, and others arranged by rank. Delicate foods were set about; roasted lamb on silver platters, sweetmeats and rare fruits, conserves of roses and violets. Slaves of the finest kind, fair to the eye, of subtle skills, sang haunting songs to the lute, or moved about to do service to the guests.

"Surely this must be the palace of some ruling Jinnee," thought the porter, "or of some mighty king."

The page led him forward to the end of the hall, where the guests had left a space. There, on a sumptuous couch sat an old man with a grave distinguished face, looking at the assembly with an air benign and calm. The porter stood bemused; if only he could escape! But he rallied his thoughts sufficiently to make the proper greetings, then stood with lowered head, awaiting – he knew not what.

Yet the old man simply said, "You are very welcome, stranger. Be seated, if you will," and he beckoned him to sit down by his side. Then he called for food and drink to be brought to his guest, and waited until he was satisfied. "Now," said the host, "do you permit me to ask you your name and the nature of your work?"

"Master," replied the other, "I am called Sindbad, known as Sindbad the Porter, because I live by carrying loads for hire. The loads are heavy and the pay is light. That is why I spoke as I did at your door, and I beg you, in the name of Allah, to forgive my unseemly words."

The old man smiled, saying, "Then you are not only my guest but my namesake, for I too am Sindbad, known as Sindbad the Sailor, from the number and the strangeness of my voyages. But what first wakened my interest were the verses which you sang outside my gate. I invited you here in the hope that you would sing them to me again."

The porter trembled. Did his host wish to punish his boldness?

"O noble master," he said, "I beg you in the name of Allah not to condemn me for my thoughtless words. They rose out of years of toil and poverty, and were not meant as insolence."

"O my brother Sindbad," said the venerable man, "make no apology. It was for sheer pleasure that I desired to hear your song again. Now, will you sing?"

So the porter sang, and the other Sindbad was greatly pleased.

"O my friend and brother," he said, "greatly have I enjoyed the wit and melody, but I have another reason for smiling at your words. You see me as a man of substance in a princely mansion, honoured by the leading men in the land. But I must tell you that all this was earned by terrible hardships and sufferings. Seven voyages have I had, each one bringing me to the very edge of a dreadful death. My survival each time was a miracle, nothing less. But such was the will of Destiny. Listen, and you shall hear – and all my friends here also – how these voyages came about.

My father was a great merchant, and on his death I became heir to money, lands, and wealth in many forms. But at once I began to squander this fortune on luxurious clothes, rich food and wine, parties and other pleasures. One day, in the cold light of morning, I came to my senses. What was left of my inheritance? I soon found the answer – almost nothing. What was my future? Unless I changed my path, and promptly too, I would have to drag out the rest of my days in homeless poverty, a beggar in the streets. Whatever remained to me of property, furnishings, any possessions, I sold at auction; then, with the money, I bought merchandise of various kinds, and had it all laden on to a trading vessel about to leave Baghdad. Then I too joined the ship.

So began my journeyings, taking me to unknown seas, to islands where no human foot has trod. I have been held by a monstrous giant, who crunched up shipwrecked men as if they were chicken legs, and by cannibal people who fattened their human cattle by dreadful means. I have been buried alive; I have been forced to carry for days and weeks an evil being known as the Old Man of the Sea. I have known even stranger perils. How did the hand of Destiny enable me to survive, when others fell away? Listen, and I shall tell you of the voyage that brought me to the terrible Valley of Diamonds.

Everything promised well when I left Baghdad in an excellent trading vessel. A fair wind sped us from the harbour and we sailed for weeks, stopping at any port where we could sell or exchange our goods most profitably. Then we were led by Fate to an island, the most beautiful we had ever encountered, green and fresh, rich in fruits and flowers, watered by sparkling streams, with lofty trees that gave cool shade in the hottest hours of the sun. But not a living human could be seen, so no trading could be done. Yet since we all wished to pass a few hours in this delightful place, the captain cast anchor and we went ashore, stretching our legs, joyfully tasting the luscious fruits and fresh water after our weeks at sea. Strolling a little apart from my fellows I sat down under a tree by a stream and soon was lulled into a pleasant sleep. This must have lasted several hours, for when I woke I looked around for my comrades. Not one was to be seen. Then, far out, I perceived the white sail of our vessel, growing smaller and more distant every moment. No one had noticed my absence and I was left alone in the lovely, desolate place.

I screamed, I cried, I tore my hair, I lay and beat the earth with my fists. But at last some sense returned, and I climbed to the top of a tree to keep clear of any savage creature, man or beast, and also to survey the landscape of my prison. At first, nothing met my gaze but sky and sea, land and rock, and the tree tops close at hand. Then, turning about, I saw at the further end of the island, somewhat hidden by rising ground, a great white shining thing, like an oval dome. Slowly, and with some fear, I climbed down and began to make my way towards it. What could it be? Nearness brought no answer. It had no door nor opening, not a single seam or crack. It was warm to the touch, but hard, not like a plant or creature. And it was vast. I tried to measure it by walking and marking the earth; it was at least a hundred and fifty paces across.

Suddenly, as I stood perplexed, the day turned to night, or so I thought. Then I beheld a great cloud passing over the sun. It was no cloud (I now discovered) but an enormous bird, like none that I had ever known in life or dream. A memory came to me of a legend heard in childhood of an island where a gigantic bird had its resting place, a bird so huge that it could lift an elephant in its beak. Surely this could be none other than the legendary rukh, and the domelike thing its egg. And so it proved, for the bird flew down and settled on the white warm object, stretching its wings on either side so that each one touched an opposing shore. Then it seemed to sleep.

When the bird began its descent I had cast myself flat on the earth in a patch of tall wild grass. I now saw that I was scarcely a hand's reach away from the creature's foot. Had I not known, I would have taken it to be the roots and trunk of a mighty ancient tree. A desperate notion came to me, of a way to leave this place. I took off my turban, tied it around me, and fastened the ends round one of the mighty claws.

"Presently it will fly away," I told myself. "Wherever it goes, it will free me from this island."

The bird remained asleep and motionless all through the night, but I did not dare to close my eyes. At last, at the first rays of dawn, the great thing stirred, rose from the egg, shook itself mightily, uttered a terrible cry – its morning song, no doubt – and soared into the air, lifting me higher and higher, until I thought we would reach Heaven itself. Then, with a shocking suddenness, it dropped, taking my breath away, and alighted on a bare rocky crag. Hastily, with shaking fingers, I untied the cloth and moved into a narrow crevice which would hide me from my unwitting carrier, and from which I could watch unseen. The bird looked down, swooped to pick up a vast black coil in its talons, and vanished into the sky.

I looked about – and what I saw filled me with terror and despair. I was in a deep valley, bounded on all sides by sheer precipitous cliffs. Nothing grew on the sharp and glittering ground – and this was not surprising, for every stone was a diamond. There they lay, in heaps, of every size. My fear gave way to wonder, and I bent down to look, to touch, to gather a handful. Then a thrill of horror ran through all my being. The whole of the valley floor appeared to writhe. It was covered with huge black snakes, thick as tree trunks; any one could have swallowed a mighty elephant. As I later realised, they were making for their dens within the cliffs. Night brought them forth, these guardians of the stones, but by day they feared the rukhs, who came to feed.

All thought of diamonds, all thought of food and drink even, flew from my mind. All I desired was a hiding place from the hideous serpents. At last I found a cave, empty it seemed, except for a curious lump of stone. Once inside, I piled up bits of rock to close the entrance and looked about for a comfortable resting place. Then, my heart almost stopped through shock – the large black stone in the centre of the cave was a serpent coiled about her eggs. My head swam, and I fell to the ground, unconscious. When I came to, streaks of morning light were coming through the cracks in my built-up door. The serpent had not left her eggs; I was still alive, undevoured. As quietly as I could, I shifted the rocks from the opening and tottered into the daylight.

As I stood there wondering where to turn, something fell with a heavy thud almost at my feet. I looked. It was part of a dead sheep. Then another memory came to me, of a tale told by travellers who had reached the diamond valley, and had found a way of gathering the stones while keeping clear of the dreadful guardians. Their method was to cut a sheep into quarters and throw these into the valley from the greatest possible height so that the diamonds were embedded in the flesh. Presently a rukh would swoop down and carry off the meat to its nest in the hills. At once the waiting men would utter loud cries, and wave their arms, and beat the air with sticks until the bird flew off. Then the men would pick out the diamonds and leave the birds their meat.

Reflecting on this legend, I saw a possible way of escape, though a desperate one. First I went about searching for the largest and most perfect of the diamonds, until I had filled every pocket and hem of clothing. Then I again unrolled my turban, lay on my back and fastened myself securely to the lump of sheep nearby. Quite soon a great shadow fell over me, and I felt myself lifted into the air; above me were claws and talons so immense that they could belong to none but the rukh. The flight was fast; in a matter of minutes we had reached the creature's nest.

The bird began to rip up the food, and the sharp beak tore me too. Luckily, a great clamour filled the air, of banging, shouting, whistling. The bird paused and then flew off; when it was well away I unfastened my bonds and stood up on the ledge. A merchant hurried to the spot; seeing me with bloodstained clothes and damaged face, he looked aghast. But as I made no hostile move, he turned the meat over to seek the diamonds. There were none. He gave a great cry of despair.

Then he turned to me with a dawning hate, saying, "Who, or what are you? How have you come here, evil being, stealer of my goods?"

"Worthy merchant, have no fear," I said. "I am no thief, nor am I a Jinnee, or any kind of spirit. I am a man like yourself, a merchant also, but one who has passed through happenings strange beyond imagining. How I came to be here is a tale of wonder which I will relate to you. But first, to prove my honour and goodwill, I ask you to accept these diamonds, which I gathered with my own hands from the valley where no human can have been and stayed alive."

Then I took some of the finest stones from my pocket and gave them to the man. His eyes opened wide, for the diamonds were of a size and beauty beyond any that he had known. He called blessings on my head, thanked me again and again, until I begged him to say no more.

"A single one of these," he exclaimed, "is enough to keep me in wealth for the rest of my days. Even in the courts of kings your diamonds have no match." He called together the other merchants to hear my tale, and at last, seeing my weariness, they gave me food and drink and a tent where I might sleep. When I was fully rested they took me to the seashore where I boarded a ship that brought me in time to Baghdad. There I was joyfully greeted by friends and relatives, who long had thought me dead.

"And that is sufficient for this day," said Sindbad the Voyager. "Tomorrow, if Allah wills, I will tell you more. Tonight we have had our fill." And indeed, the company, which had listened amazed, still sat as if spellbound. Then he sent for a hundred golden dinars and gave them to Sindbad the Porter, requesting him to return the following day, to be his guest as before and to hear more of the wondrous voyages.

*   *   *   *

The day arrived when Sindbad the Sailor told the story of his last voyage to Sindbad the Porter, and to all the assembled guests.

"You must know, my friends, that a time came when the desire for adventure left me entirely. Moreover, I had become the richest man in Baghdad, and also had known events and marvels enough to keep the Khalifah himself entertained for a lifetime. One day, however, the Khalifah summoned me on other matters.

"My friend," he said, "I wish you to carry a letter and a few gifts to the King of Sarandib; you know better than any man where that land lies, and it will give him pleasure to see you again. Make ready to start today."

I felt the world darken, for I desired never again to leave Baghdad. But I could not refuse. The gifts I had to deliver were numerous and magnificent: a great jewelled bed of scarlet velvet, a hundred robes of rarest silk, a pair of marvellous Arab horses, a white carnelian vase of remote antiquity, gold beyond counting, and much else. After two months' sailing our vessel reached Sarandib, and I duly presented the letter and presents to the king. He urged me to stay, but I was anxious to return, so we embarked again on the same ship, now laden with further gifts, and started back to Basrah.

At first the wind favoured us, but a day came when a terrible storm rocked the vessel. The captain climbed the mast and looked about for a long time. When he descended his face was yellow and ravaged with despair.

"Pray to Allah," he murmured. "Say your farewells. There is little hope that we may survive. A false wind and evil tides have thrown us into the last seas of the world." He then opened his sea-chest and took from it a linen bag containing a grey powder. He sniffed at this, then drew forth a small book and studied the pages.

"Yes," he said, "it is as I feared. The land to which we are driving is the Clime of Kings, where our lord Sulaiman lies buried. Monsters and terrible serpents inhabit the coast, and the sea is full of great creatures which can swallow a whole ship at a gulp."

As we stood frozen with horror at this account, a mighty wave seemed to cleave the sea to its floor. The waters boiled; the noise was deafening, and a monster, vast as a mountain, rose from the depths followed by two even larger and more dreadful to behold. The third and largest opened its frightful mouth and drew in our ship with all that were within. Fate decreed that I had just time to leap into the sea; then, holding fast to a plank from the doomed vessel, I endured many hours on the tossing waters until I was suddenly cast on a firm shore.

I found myself on an island, covered with fruit trees and watered by a fast-running river. The idea came to me to construct a raft and let myself be borne along by the current.

"If I am saved by this method," I thought, "it is well. If I perish, I shall be quit of danger and suffering for ever, and this will also be well." So I collected some of the larger branches of a tree (I did not then know it was sandalwood) and bound them together with the stems of climbing plants. Then I took on plenty of fruit for the journey and embarked. What I had not foreseen was the river's force and speed; I was seized with vertigo and almost lost my senses. When my head began to clear I saw that my raft was hurtling through boiling

from Sindbad the Sailor

foam towards a yawning fall of water, sheer as a precipice.

I closed my eyes, certain that my end had come. Suddenly, at the very edge of the abyss, the raft seemed to halt; it had been caught in a vast net held by men on the bank. I was dragged on to dry land where I lay giddy and shivering. Then an old man with a white beard advanced towards me; he made courteous greeting, and covered me with a warm cloak. When I felt able to stand, he took my arm and led me to his own house. First, I was given a perfumed bath, then exquisite food was brought to me, delicately served. Finally, I was taken to a beautifully furnished room, where slaves brought me all that I might desire.

For three days I received these kindnesses and was asked no questions. On the fourth, however, when my strength seemed fully restored, the old man sat beside me and said, after courteous greeting, "O guest, I give thanks to Allah that he enabled me to save you from the precipice. Now, if you are ready, I would ask you to tell me who you are, whence you are come, and for what purpose."

"O most noble and generous of hosts," I said. "The words that would convey my thanks have not yet been invented in any language. I am called Sindbad the Sailor, because of the many strange voyages I have made upon the seas." Thereupon I related the whole history of my life and journeys, up to that very moment. The old man listened as if spellbound, and when I had done he sat for an hour, unable to speak a word.

At last he said, "These are wonders that I must ponder on. Now, dear guest, I have some advice for you. Sell your merchandise without delay. Many are anxious to buy, for not only is it of excellent quality but it is a great rarity in this place." What could he mean? Here was I, a castaway without even rags of my own to cover me.

But having learnt both caution and cunning, I hid my surprise and said, "That may well be."

"To ease you of burdens," continued the old man, "I will have the goods taken to the market place. If a fitting offer is made, we will accept it; if not, your valuable property can stay in my storehouse until the right purchaser is found."

Though more perplexed than ever, I replied, "O most honoured host, whatever seems good to you, is good for me also. I have no thought which is not yours." When we arrived at the market place, I was amazed. There was my raft, surrounded by merchants and dealers who were respectfully examining it, and murmuring words of admiration.

"By Allah," said one, "what marvellous sandalwood! Never have I seen its like." Now I understood what I possessed, and arranged my face into a suitably proud and reserved expression.

The sale began with an offer of a thousand gold dinars.

"Two thousand," said another.

"Three thousand," said a third. After ten thousand there was silence.

"I will not sell for that!" I said. But the old man advised me to accept.

"If you like," he added, "I myself will offer an extra hundred dinars, and buy the lot for ten thousand one hundred."

"Whatever you say is my wish," I told the good old man. The wood was taken back to the storehouse, while the money was given to me and placed by my host in a strong locked box.

As we sat that evening over our meal the old man said, "My child, there is a favour I would ask of you."

"It is already granted, whatever it may be," I said.

"It is this," said he. "My years are many but I have no son. I have, though, a beautiful daughter who will inherit great riches when I die. If you will consent to remain with us I will give you this girl in marriage, and you will be heir both to my high position and my wealth." For a moment I was silent, but he read my thoughts. "You will not lose by accepting," he said. "Only during my lifetime need you stay in this country. When I am gone you are free to go with your wife, my daughter, to your own land and people."

"Venerable father," I said, "I am more than willing for you to direct my destiny. When I have tried to do so myself, mischief has always followed. I am honoured to marry your daughter, and will do so gladly."

So the ceremony and feasting were arranged. I was delighted to find that my bride was not only beautiful and sweet-natured, but possessed a great store of jewels, silks, ornaments and other such treasures worth thousands and thousands of gold pieces. We lived together for many years in sport and joy.

After the death of my worthy father-in-law I inherited all his power and wealth; his slaves became my slaves and his goods my goods, and the leading merchants named me their chief in his place. Because of this I had occasion to notice the customs and manners of the land more closely than I had ever done before. And so I became aware that the men of this kingdom underwent a strange experience every year in spring. First came a physical change lasting a day and a night. Then they emerged with wings on their shoulders, enabling them to fly as if they were birds. During this time of flight they endlessly soared about, so that only women and children were left on the ground below, for these did not have the gift of wings. I felt shame at being the only flightless male; it was a sad thing that Sindbad the Sailor should not also be Sindbad of the air. But no one would or could reveal to me how I too might fly.

One day I took aside a certain merchant whom I had helped in various ways and, after much pleading, persuaded him to let me cling to his body when next he flew aloft. Up we went, higher and higher, until I could hear the angels singing their holy songs under the vault of Heaven.

This music stirred in me so devout an emotion that I cried out, "Praise be to Allah! Let all creatures glorify his Name!"

Hardly had I uttered these words, when my winged carrier fell through the air like a thunderbolt, cursing frightfully. My brain whirled with the dizzy speed of descent and I fainted away in terror. By fortunate chance we landed on a mountain top, where I came to just in time to see the winged man taking off again, with a glance of devilish hate in my direction.

I knew not what to do, and cried aloud, "There is no power save Allah! Whatever misfortune happens to me, I must have deserved!"

Then, as I sat in despair on a ledge of rock, trying to plan some way of escape, I saw two young boys approaching. They were of superhuman beauty and each held a red-gold wand in his hand. I rose to my feet and greeted them, and they greeted me in return.

"Tell me, you marvellous beings," I said, "who are you? What brings you here?"

"We are lovers of the true God," they replied. Then one of them pointed out a path I had not seen, gave me his golden wand, and the two disappeared, hand in hand.

I took the wand and started on my way. Suddenly the path was blocked by a gigantic serpent, which had almost swallowed a man; only the head hung out of the creature's jaws.

The head cried out to me, "O stranger, save me from this serpent and you will never repent of your goodness." I ran behind the snake, dealt it a blow with the golden wand, and at once it died. Then I helped the man to emerge from the coiling tomb.

I looked at him. He was none other than the flyer who had nearly been the cause of my death.

Gently I said, "Was that the way for a friend to behave to a friend?"

"First," said the man, "I must thank you for saving me. Then I must tell you something you do not know. My fall was caused by your unfortunate mention of that Name. It has the same effect on all of us, and we never speak it."

"I spoke in all innocence," I said, "and I promise not to repeat my blunder if only you will take me back to my home." The flyer lifted me on to his back and in a flash of time I was on the terrace of my own house.

My long absence had filled my wife with fear; now, after giving thanks to

Allah, she declared, "We must no longer dwell among these people, for they are the kin of devils."

"How then," I asked, "did your father come to be living among them?"

"My father was not one of them," she said. "He did not behave as they behave; he did not lead their life. As he is dead we have no reason to stay in this wicked city, so let us leave. But first you must sell whatever property you possess. With the money, you may buy fine merchandise and, by trading as we go, we will be well equipped to return to your people in Baghdad. There we can live in peace and happiness." This was sound advice. I sold my property piece by piece and gained a hundred dinars for each one laid out by my father-in-law. Then I bought fair merchandise, hired a vessel, and with my wife made an excellent trading voyage to Basrah. From there, we went upstream and entered the city of Baghdad. I found that I had been away for twenty-seven years.

And now, at last, I put my affairs in order, distributed my remaining merchandise and sat in my home to receive the joyful visits of my friends. I vowed that never again would I leave Baghdad, and this vow I have kept. The hand of Allah has kept me alive in so many desperate situations; I have no wish to try its power too far."

When Sindbad the Sailor had finished his tale, he turned to Sindbad the Porter, saying, "Now my friend, you have heard of the labours and hardships that I have undergone. Would you not say that your life as a porter has been more tranquil than mine as a voyager?" Sindbad the Porter kissed the hands of his host and begged him to forgive his ill-timed song.

Then Sindbad the Sailor gave a great feast to his guests, lasting thirty nights, and he appointed Sindbad the Porter to be his major-domo, always at his side. The two Sindbads lived thereafter in utmost friendship and harmony until they were visited by that which ends the days of king and beggar alike. Glory be to Allah who dies not!

THE MAGIC TALE
OF THE EBONY HORSE

ONCE, FAR OFF IN ANTIQUE time, the Persians were ruled by a mighty king named Sabur. He was as widely known for his great benevolence and charity to the poor as for his strictness of justice. He also had an especial love for astronomy, geometry, and all mechanical sciences. This monarch had one daughter, a flower of beauty, and one son, the Prince Kamar al-Akmar, the very moon of loveliness.

Each year the king held two great festivals, one in the spring, the other in the autumn. Then, all the palace gates were opened, alms were freely handed out, pardons were announced, new officials appointed, and people came from all ends of the vast empire to do homage to their ruler, bringing him gifts of slaves, eunuchs, and other items of value. During one of the spring festivals, as the king sat in state to receive such visitors, a learned man arrived at the court, a master of arcane studies, secret arts and hidden mysteries.

He approached the king, and after due homage had brought before him a horse, made of a rare black ebony, inlaid with gold and gems; the very saddle and bridle were of a richness and worth that an emperor might marvel at.

"O sage," said the king, "what is the special mystery of this fine steed?"

"O lord of lords," answered the man, "its special power is this. Whoever mounts the horse may ride through the air, wherever he will, covering in a single day a journey that would take at least a year on the fastest steed of earth."

Amazed, the king exclaimed, "As Allah lives, if what you say is true, I will fulfil the most hidden inward wish within your heart."

Then the sage showed the action of his gift. The horse rose high in the air with its maker on its back; then, after tracing a vast circle in the sky, it gently came to earth again at the king's feet.

Almost delirious with joy, the king declared, "O sage, master of hidden skills, name your desire and it shall be fulfilled."

"Great king," replied the sage, "I would wed your daughter and so become your son-in-law. Such is my chosen wish."

At once the king replied, "Your desire is granted." And he ordered the marriage contract to be prepared.

Now it so happened that the daughter was concealed behind a curtain in the hall and had noted all that had taken place. Fairest of all the maidens in that land, in motion like a young gazelle, the moon was not more light and radiant than this delicate girl. But the spouse awaiting her (for so she saw from the curtained nook) appeared to be at least a hundred years old, toothless and moth-eaten, his scant hairs dyed, his face a yellow map of wrinkles; his head waggled; his feet stumbled; he was a thing of horror. When she beheld this monstrous sight the young girl ran to her room, fell face down on the ground and screamed and wept. Her cries were heard by her brother, the Prince Kamar al-Akmar, who had just returned from hunting. He loved her dearly and entered her room to find the cause of her grief.

"What is troubling you?" he said. "Tell me quickly. Hide nothing from me."

"Dear brother," she replied, "our father has promised me in marriage to a vile old man, a hideous sorcerer who has given him a flying horse as a gift. I am resolved to flee from the palace and if I am prevented I shall take my life."

"Leave this to me," said the prince. "Dry your tears and wait here quietly. All will be well, I assure you." Then he hastened to his father, saying, "What is this news I hear of my little sister being given in marriage to an old sorcerer? She is near to death with grief. What gift, what offering can have made you do this dreadful wrong?"

The king replied, "My son, if you but saw the amazing ebony horse that the sage has given me, you would understand."

"Then let me see this wonder," said the prince. They went to the courtyard and slaves brought forth the horse. The young man lightly leapt on its back but nothing happened.

The king turned to the sage, saying, "Explain to my son how to make it rise, and surely he will help you to achieve your wish."

The sorcerer hated the prince for his interference and told him only half what he should know. He pointed to a tiny peg on the right of the pommel, saying, "Twirl that, and you will rise."

The prince boldly twirled the peg and soared into the air so swiftly and to such a height that no trace of him could be seen from below. Minutes passed, then hours – and still the prince did not return.

In great agitation the king said to the sorcerer, "What has happened? How can we bring him back?"

"Great master," said the other, "I can do nothing. Alas for the arrogance of youth! Your son would not give me time to explain the method of descent. I fear he is gone for ever." The king was inflamed with anger. In his rage he ordered his slaves to beat the wily sage and to cast him into the darkest dungeon cell. Then he tore off his crown and pulled out his hair and beard in handfuls, loudly bewailing the loss of his son. The whole palace was darkened; mourning filled the land.

But where *was* the missing prince? When the horse rose up he was filled with joy, but soon this turned into fear; for unless the flight could be halted they would go straight into the burning heart of the sun. What bitter remorse he felt for his rashness!

"I see now," he reflected, "that this was the work of the sorcerer, because I tried to prevent him taking my sister. Now I am lost for ever. But wait! Since he has ridden the steed himself and returned, there must be a means of descent." He felt about and at last found a tiny screw like the head of a pin on the left hand side of the saddle. "The answer must be here!" he cried, and he pressed it down. At once the upward movement stopped; for a moment man and horse hung motionless, then they began a rapid downward flight, yet they touched the earth as softly as a bird.

Now that the prince understood the workings of the horse, he began to savour the pleasure of riding through the sky, seeing from above whole lands and oceans, all the pattern of deserts, forests, cities, lakes and waterways. One city pleased him especially with its graceful buildings, orchards, parks, and gardens. As he circled about it, he saw that the sun was sinking; soon the dark would come. Looking about for a resting place he saw a great palace flanked by towers and battlements. He carefully steered the horse on to the palace roof and stayed there quietly until all seemed asleep within. Then, leaving the horse above, he went down the stairs in search of food and drink. He found himself in a great courtyard, paved with white marble and lucent alabaster, softly reflecting the rays of the moon and giving walls and towers an unearthly beauty.

Where should he turn? Suddenly he perceived a point of light within the palace. Noiselessly he searched about, and found that it came from a lamp before a curtained door. Beneath it, fast asleep, lay a huge black eunuch, ugly as a Jinnee, and snoring thunderously. Near his head was a bag of provisions; by his side was a sword whose hilt glittered in the lamplight.

The prince uttered a prayer to Allah, "May the fellow not wake!" Then he took the bag of food, and satisfied his hunger. He drew the sleeper's sword from the sheath, and with new courage began to venture further. Drawing aside the curtain he beheld a door, which opened into a room of radiant whiteness, hung with silks, glittering with jewels. And there, on a carved white bed, adorned with amethysts, emeralds and pearls in the form of flowers, was an exquisite young maiden. She was lovelier than the rising moon; her forehead was a white rose; her cheeks were two anemones. Feeling as if he were in a dream, the young man bent and kissed the sleeping girl.

She woke with a start. "Who are you?" she said.

"I am a prince in my own land, but here I am your slave."

"Are you perchance the king's son of Hind who sought me in marriage yesterday, but was rejected by my father because of his ugliness? No, you cannot be; you are not ugly – no indeed, you are the sun and moon of beauty and you have won my heart entirely." Then they embraced and lay in each other's arms, tenderly voicing their love in a thousand different ways. And so the sweet hours passed.

Presently, their whisperings woke the handmaidens. They looked at the couch with alarm.

"O lady," cried one, "who is this young man?"

"I do not know," said the princess. "I found him at my side when I woke from sleep. I think he is the prince who went to my father yesterday to ask for my hand in marriage."

But the girls, in great fear for themselves, cried out, "As Allah lives, this is not that one, for he was hideous, and this young man is a vision of loveliness." Then they woke the eunuch at the door, saying, "You are supposed to guard this room. And yet you let strange men enter while you sleep!" The eunuch jumped to his feet in terror, the more so when he felt for his sword and found it gone. Trembling, he entered the room to see the intruder for himself. There on the couch with his fair mistress was a handsome youth.

"Are you a Jinnee or a man?" stammered the eunuch?

"Miserable wretch!" replied the young man. "How dare you confound a royal prince with an Efreet or a Jinnee! I am the king's son-in-law; his daughter is my bride."

Hearing this, the eunuch ran to the king, uttering loud cries, tearing his hair and clothes.

"What disaster brings you here?" the king demanded. "Speak quickly, for you fill my heart with dread.

"O king," replied the eunuch, "a Jinnee in the body of a royal prince is lying in close embrace with your daughter. Hasten! or he will have vanished." The king's face swelled with rage, and he ran like a madman to the princess's room. He found the attendant girls crouching outside the door, pale and trembling.

"O king," they cried, "we do not know what happened while we slept, but when we woke a young man of perfect beauty was with our mistress. When we asked who he was and what he did in our room, he told us that the princess was his bride, that you yourself had given him to her in marriage. But he is so gentle, so agreeable, so perfect in manner and clearly so nobly born that you cannot think ill of him."

The king's anger abated somewhat at this and he cautiously peered through the curtain. But what he saw inflamed him once again, for there was his daughter lying beside a young man, each whispering sugary nothings to the other. He strode into the room, brandishing his sword, his face contorted with rage. At once the young prince leapt to his feet, raised the sword he had taken from the slave, and uttered a terrible war-cry. The king quickly saw that he was no match for the stranger, so sheathed his sword and began to converse with him. Soon he was well convinced that the youth was as worthy a son-in-law as he was likely to find. Yet if the facts of the night became known, with his own seeming connivance, his royal honour and power might be at stake.

"You have two ways of solving this problem," said the prince. "You can engage me in single combat, in the sight of all. If you are beaten you will have to yield me your throne as well as your daughter – and that is quite a risk. Or, you can send against me your entire force of horse and foot and slaves. By the way, how many are there?"

"I have some forty thousand warriors," said the king, "that is, without counting my slaves and my slaves' slaves – perhaps another forty thousand or so."

"A trifle," went on the prince. "Have them drawn up at dawn. Say to them, 'This man desires to marry my daughter. I have said that, if he overthrows you singlehanded, the princess is his.' Then, if I am slain, your honour is safe. If the victory is mine, however, you will have a son-in-law whom the mightiest kings will envy."

Dazed by the youth's assurance, the king agreed to the plan. He ordered the finest horse to be brought from his stables, fully equipped for battle.

"If this steed is for me," said the prince, "I have no need of it. The horse on which I arrived last night is the only one I shall ride."

"As you will," said the king. "Where is it stabled?"

"On the roof of your palace," said the prince.

"How can this be?" said the king. But he sent his men to investigate. What they found was a horse, indeed – but one made of gleaming ebony, and they set it before the king. The monarch was perplexed.

"Is this your chosen steed?" he asked.

"It is indeed," said the youth, "but I will not mount until your forces are drawn up in battle order."

As the men waited they began to doubt their chances against so sure an opponent. But what befell was beyond their imagining. The young man mounted his strange black steed, then horse and rider rose straight up from the ground, circled over the waiting ranks, and disappeared from sight. The soldiers scattered in all directions, terrified at the sight. As for the king, he felt both shocked and betrayed.

"Catch him! Catch him!" he cried out. But who can catch a soaring bird?

As soon as the prince reached his home he found his father's palace in a state of grief and mourning, every part strewn with ashes. Was one of the royal family dead? He made his way to the private rooms of the palace, where he found his father, mother and sister, pale and hollow-cheeked, weeping and lamenting. But when they saw the prince, grief turned to joy; feasts were held through the land, prisoners were pardoned; gold was handed out. At the request of the prince the sorcerer, too, was released. But no more was said to the old man about marriage to the young princess. This made him bitter and venomous; he waited a chance of vengeance on the youth who had stolen his horse and ruined his careful plans.

Yet the prince's mind and heart were still with the faraway damsel. One day, hearing a lute-player singing a haunting song of parted lovers, he could wait no longer. He climbed to the roof, leapt on to the horse's back, flew through the sky to the city of Sana and made his way to the room of the princess. But behind the curtain were mournful sounds, that came from his dear damsel. Sometimes she recited verses of anguished love; sometimes her women spoke to her.

"Dear mistress," one was saying, "why do you waste your tears on one who has long forgotten you?"

"Be silent, fool," was her reply. "Do you think that sweetest prince could ever forget the passion of our love?" Then she was torn with cries again. The prince felt pierced to the very core; his heart seemed to break within him. He lifted the curtain and found the damsel lying pale and desolate on her bed.

"Sweet girl," he said, "I have come. So no more tears – neither yours nor mine." They wound their arms about one another, and told of their love and anguish.

"If you had stayed away longer," said the girl, "you would have found me dead."

"Are you willing to leave your home and come with me?" said the prince.

"I am indeed," said the princess. She put together some precious jewels, bracelets, rings and other ornaments and went forth with the prince. Her maidens watched, but none dared hinder her going. The prince placed her behind him on the ebony horse, bound her to him with swathes of cloth, and up they soared into the air. The maidens uttered piercing cries which woke the king and queen and brought them to the terrace.

"O king's son," cried the monarch, "have pity on a father and a mother! Do not take away our only daughter!"

The prince turned to the damsel, saying, "Desire of my soul, do you wish to return? It is not too late."

But she replied, "All I wish is to be with you, even though I love my father and mother."

By morning they had reached the prince's city and landed in a royal garden outside the city walls. In it was a domed summer pavilion.

"I must leave you here for a short time," said the prince. "I go to tell my father of your coming; he will wish to arrange a proper welcome. Very soon I shall send a messenger to collect you." They embraced many times, and he left.

The king almost died of joy when his son appeared again. But the prince gave him little time for scolding or embracing.

"Dear father," he declared, "guess what rare treasure I have brought back."

"As Allah lives, I cannot guess," said the father.

"Rejoice," said the son," for I have brought back the daughter of the king of Sana, the most gifted and lovely girl in all the eastern world. I have left her in our summer garden just outside the city in order that you may prepare a fitting welcome."

"Whatever you desire shall be done," said the king. He ordered the streets to be decorated, and placed himself at the head of a magnificent procession, led by armoured cavaliers, with banners flying, to the sound of fife and drum. But the prince himself, unable to bear a minute's delay, leapt on one of his father's swiftest steeds and sped back to the pavilion where he had left his fair princess.

She was nowhere to be seen. And gone, too, was the ebony horse.

The young man ran around like a madman, beating his face, tearing his hair and clothes. But when he had calmed a little, the thought came to him that she could not have ridden off by choice, for she did not even understand the workings of the horse. Only one knew its secret – the sorcerer!

The prince ran to the keepers of the gate, saying, "Has anyone passed through in the last hour?"

"As Allah lives," said the man, "no one has entered but the Persian sage, who came to gather herbs. He must still be there, for he has not yet returned."

The prince rushed back to stop the procession and to tell his father the dreadful news.

"I shall not return until I have found the damsel, and have brought her back on the horse. Farewell!" Then he rode away.

But what had taken place in the garden? Destiny had arranged that the Persian sage had come there that very morning to gather herbs and samples for his mysterious usages. What did he see but his own lost ebony horse! And just within the pavilion, lying at ease on a couch was a girl of peerless beauty – surely too of royal birth from her attire and manner. So! using the magic horse, the prince had brought back this prize! A frightful joy filled the sorcerer. Advancing to the lady and making proper obeisances, he announced that he was a messenger to bring her to the queen.

Aghast at his hideousness, the damsel murmured, "Could not the prince have found a less ugly messenger?"

Though mortified by this, the sage replied, "There is no lack of pretty slave boys at the palace. But with me, the prince need have no cause for jealousy. Indeed, as proof, he has asked me to bring you on his own flying steed." He lifted her on to the horse, climbed into the saddle – and they rose up high in the air leaving the city far behind.

"Old man!" cried the girl. "Why do you disobey your master's orders?"

"I have no master but myself," said the sorcerer. "Your prince is a stupid blubber-brain and a thief besides. Forget that rubbish-bag. I am immensely rich, with magic powers. You will be far better off with me."

The princess wept and screamed, but what could she do? At last they came down in a bright green meadow, with sparkling streams and flowering trees. It bordered a fair city whose king had just ridden forth to take the morning air.

Seeing the strange black horse and the ill-matched man and maid, he asked, "How does a hideous old man like you come to be with so lovely a girl?"

"O king," said the sorcerer, "I am a merchant and this is my cousin and my wife."

But the princess said, "He is a stranger to me, an evil sorcerer who has carried me off against my will." The king ordered his slaves to beat the vile old man and cast him into a dungeon, which they did most heartily. But he had the girl and the horse (whose powers he did not guess) brought to his own palace.

Meanwhile the prince pursued his search, through land after land, but to no avail. But chance at last took him into a tavern where he heard one merchant telling another the latest piece of gossip. Had he heard that the king of the next great city had found in a field a great black wooden horse with the strangest pair of riders: a disgusting old greybeard, at least a hundred years old, and a young girl of matchless beauty? The girl was now at the palace, but she was crazed in the head.

The prince did not waste a moment. When he reached the city gates it was already dark, so the guards brought him into the prison for the night. But they found the youth so charming and well-mannered that, instead of locking him in a cell, they asked him to share their meal in their own quarters.

"Where are you from, young stranger?" he was asked.

"From Persia," he replied. At this there was a mighty laugh.

"We have a Persian locked up here who must be the ugliest old fellow in the world, as well as the greatest liar. He spins us yarns about being a learned sage with magic powers. The king found him in a field with a black wooden horse and a fair young girl – a real beauty. He wants to marry her, but she has gone mad and no one knows how to cure her. As for the horse, that's stored in the treasure house, for it's nicely made."

At once the prince saw how to solve his problem. When morning came and the warders took him before the king (for that was the custom with strangers), he declared, "Gracious monarch, I am a Persian; my special craft and mystery is the healing of the sick, especially those crazed in mind, possessed, maybe by a Jinnee. To increase my knowledge I travel continually; where I find a patient needing help, I heal that one."

The king's heart leapt with hope. "I have one such in my palace – a damsel greatly disturbed in mind and sense, whom all physicians have so far failed to mend." And he told the stranger how she had been found.

The prince then said, "Some clue may lie in this ebony horse you speak of; is it possible for me to examine the creature?"

"Indeed it is," said the king, and the horse was brought to the courtyard. The prince saw that it was whole and sound, then asked to be taken to the damsel.

"I think I see where the evil lies," he said.

The princess moaned and writhed as the young man entered the room, but when he spoke a few words in her ear, she gave a cry of joy. Quickly he explained his presence, and told her to be calm and even affectionate to the king when next he visited her.

Then he returned to the monarch, saying, "Great master, I think that I have driven the Jinnee from the maiden. But he may return, for his base is the wooden horse. Now I would have both maiden and horse brought together in a

from The Ebony Horse

quiet place where I can exorcize the evil thing for all time. First, the damsel must be placed on the horse. I shall light fires of fumigation all around, then I too will mount the creature. You will see movement and struggle even, but have no fear. The demon must be rendered powerless before the maiden is free."

The horse was brought, the fires were lit, but once the prince had his damsel on the steed, he twirled the peg and they sailed away, vanishing in the clouds. The unhappy king waited long for their return, but in vain. At last he called to mind the old man in the cells, and had him brought forth.

"Treacherous toadstool!" cried the king. "Why did you not reveal to me the secret of that steed? You are responsible for my loss, both of the girl herself and of the jewels and treasures of mine that she has taken with her." He gave orders, and the court executioner briskly smote off the old man's head. So much for the sorcerer.

But the prince and princess flew without pause to the prince's home. Once again he found the palace in mourning, but rejoicing soon took its place. The marriage was announced; feasts and celebrations were held throughout the land for a full month. Nor was the father of the princess overlooked. Gifts of great price were sent to him, together with a long epistle from the prince describing all the events that had followed the arrival of the ebony horse. The king of Sana sent back presents no less valuable, and a message of rejoicing in the marriage. Many and delightful now were the years of this fortunate pair, first as prince and princess, later as king and queen of that country, until the time came for them to join those great and small, rich and poor, who have already gone. Allah alone chooses the moment. As for the ebony horse, it is said that the old king had it destroyed for fear of future accident, but this may only be legend.

FRIEND SO-AND-SO, FRIEND SUCH-AND-SUCH

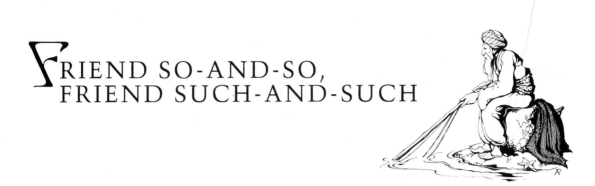

LONG, LONG AGO THERE LIVED in a city edged by the salt sea a fisherman, happily married to a very beautiful wife. But though he rose early and worked hard, he never earned more than would feed them for that one day. So that when he fell ill, there was no food in the house.

Next morning, his wife said, "If you cannot fish, we shall starve. If you can rise up now, I will carry your net and basket, and you can tell me what to do." The fisherman agreed, and slowly led the way to a stretch of shore at the foot of the Sultan's palace; it was known as a rich place for fishing. His wife came after, with basket and with net.

Now at that moment the Sultan was at his window, gazing out at the sea. Suddenly he saw the fisherman's beautiful wife, and was seized with a longing to possess her. He called his Grand Wazir and asked for his advice.

"Shall I order the guards to kill the fisherman? Then I can marry the widow."

The wazir answered, "You cannot lawfully have the man put to death without a reason. Let me think. Ah, I have it. You know of course that the audience hall of the palace covers exactly an acre. I shall summon the fisherman and say that you command him, on pain of death, to cover the whole floor with a single piece of carpet. Since to do this is impossible, he can be disposed of without anyone suspecting a motive."

"Good, good," said the Sultan, rubbing his hands together.

So the wazir sent for the fisherman, and had him brought into the hall.

"O fisherman," he said, "our master, the king, requires you to cover this floor with a carpet, woven in a single piece. He allows you three days, and if you fail to produce the carpet, you shall be burnt in the fire. Write an agreement and seal it with your seal."

"What is all this?" said the fisherman. "I am not a man of carpets; I am a man of fish. Ask for any kind, size, colour of fish and I shall oblige, but – carpets? As Allah lives, I don't know them, and they don't know me. Fish, by all means. Carpets – no, no, no."

"Enough of your saucy words!" said the wazir. "The king has commanded this thing."

"Then seal it yourself," said the fisherman, and he ran from the palace in a great rage.

"Why are you so angry?" asked his wife.

"Be quiet, woman," he replied. "We have no time to waste. Bundle our clothes together, for we must flee from this city."

"But why?"

"Because the king means to kill me in three days' time."

"For what reason?" she persisted. So the fisherman told about the carpet.

"Oh, is that all?" she said. "Stop worrying. I will procure your carpet. Now, listen carefully. Go to the well in the garden, the one that is overlooked by a crooked tree. Put your head over the side and say, 'O So-and-so, your dear friend Such-and-such gives you greeting and begs you to send her the spindle which she forgot yesterday. We wish to carpet a room with it.'"

"You must be mad," said the fisherman, "but a desperate man tries anything."

He walked to the well and called down into it, "O So-and-so, your dear friend Such-and-such gives you greeting and begs you to send her the spindle which she forgot yesterday. We wish to carpet a room with it."

Then that which was in the well gave answer: "How could I refuse anything to my dear friend? Here is the spindle. When you have finished with it, bring it back to me." Up came a spindle; the fisherman neatly caught it and took it home.

"Good!" said his wife. "Now go to this tiresome wazir, and ask him for a large nail. Hammer this nail into the floor at one end of the hall, and fasten round it the end of the spindle thread. As you move away, the carpet will unfold itself behind you."

"People will think me mad," said the fisherman.

"Don't argue; do as I say," said the wife.

So the fisherman went with heavy steps to the palace, murmuring to himself, "O most unfortunate man! This is the last day of your life."

The Sultan and the wazir were waiting in the hall when he arrived.

"Well, where is the carpet?" said the Sultan.

"It is in my pocket," said the fisherman.

"Here is a fellow who jokes before his death," said the Sultan, laughing merrily, for soon he would gain his wish.

"Look here," said the fisherman, "you asked for a carpet. There the matter

from Friend So-and-so, Friend Such-and-such

ends. If someone will fetch me a large nail, I can deal with the matter at once, and get on my way."

The wazir, still smiling, went to get the nail, and whispered to the Sultan's executioner, who was standing near the door, "As soon as you see that the fellow has no carpet, cut off his head without further orders."

The fisherman took the nail, hammered it in at the end of the hall, and fastened the thread to it. Then he took up the spindle, saying, "Spin my death; that's all you can do." But wait! a magnificent carpet began to flow out, covering the whole space of the floor with a weaving of marvellous beauty. The king and the wazir looked at each other in stunned silence. Then they whispered together.

Finally the wazir said, "Well, you've certainly done this task, and the king is satisfied. But he has another demand – easy enough for so smart a fellow as you. He requires you to bring him a little boy not more than eight days old, who shall tell him a story which is nothing but lies from beginning to end."

"Is that all?" said the fisherman bitterly. "That won't be difficult if you are so good as to bring me all today's new-born children of the Jinn."

"We do not want your jokes," said the wazir. "We think them in bad taste. You are allowed eight days to find the child, or your head will roll before our eyes in this very room. Write out an agreement and sign it with your seal."

"I know nothing about seals," said the fisherman, "nor of lying infants either. Fish – now that's another matter, I believe you want an excuse to get rid of me. Well, it may not be so easy."

He went home, and called out to his wife. "Hurry," he said. "Bundle our goods together – we must flee. I told you this before."

"But what happened about the carpet? Did the spindle work?"

"Oh yes, but now they want a little boy, less than eight days old, who will tell the Sultan a tale made of lies from beginning to end. They've given me eight days to find the creature."

"Don't worry," said his wife. "There's always a remedy."

But the eight days passed, and the fisherman still had no idea what to do. On the ninth morning he turned to his wife, saying, "Have you forgotten my problem? If you can do nothing, my life will end today."

"Don't worry so much," said the woman. "Go to the well beneath the twisted tree, give back the spindle with some grateful words, then add, 'O So-and-so, your dear friend Such-and-such begs you to lend her the boy who was born yesterday, for we need him in a certain matter.'" The fisherman went off grumbling that a two-day-old child would know even less than an eight-day one.

However, he returned the spindle and gave the message, adding, "And for Allah's sake be quick, for my head is just about to leave my shoulders!"

That which was in the well called up in answer, "Take the child and return it when the task is done." Up rose a swathed bundle which – Allah be praised! – he managed to catch before it fell back again.

As he made his way homeward, he thought to himself, "Even if this were an infant Jinnee, how could it speak, much less know enough truth to lie?" Aloud, he said, "Talk to me, child; I want to know if this is indeed the day of my death." The infant responded in the manner of its kind; it uttered tuneless wails and howls, and did that which soaked its wrappings, not sparing either the garments of the fisherman. The man was not pleased.

He said to his wife, "This infant has no wisdom; it utters nothing but noise, and it has ruined my clothes."

"Never mind about that," said his wife. "Just do what I tell you. When you reach the palace, be sure to demand three cushions for the child. Put one at each side of him and one at the back. And for good measure, utter a few prayers. They cost nothing and won't be wasted. Now be off."

When the wazir saw the fisherman arrive with the swaddled bundle, he swayed from side to side with laughter. Then he poked the child with a finger, but it did not speak, merely making the tuneless noise which all infants use as a voice.

The wazir ran to the king, crying joyfully, "The man has brought a newborn infant, and all it does is wail! Soon you will have your wish." Then the Sultan and the wazir made their way to the great hall, where the court had assembled, and the fisherman was called forth.

"First," said he, "I must have three cushions. Then you will hear what you will hear." The cushions were brought; the child was placed on a couch, and the fisherman used them as the wife had said to prop the child in an upright position. The king peered down.

"Is this thing the infant which is supposed to tell us a story made of lies?" he asked.

But before the fisherman could answer, the day-old child remarked, "Greeting, O king and company."

"Greeting to you," replied the astonished king. "Have you a story for us without a grain of truth?"

"Listen," said the child. "Once, when I was a young man, I bought a water melon for a hundred gold dinars because I was thirsty, and the fruit was cheap and plentiful. I cut it open and saw inside a tiny city. At once I stepped within, one leg at a time. For many hours I wandered through the shops and houses in the fruit. At last I stopped at a date tree, growing on a mountain top, each date at least a yard long. I climbed into the tree to gather some, but found it full of peasants sewing seeds of corn, and others harvesting, so quickly did the grain grow. I saw a train of little cocks and little hens; hand in hand, they were going off to get married. A donkey offered me a sesame cake, saying, 'Think before you eat.' I broke it in half and saw within the king and his wazir, busily whispering plots. They leapt out of the cake; I followed them briskly, and we all arrived this morning where you see us now."

"Enough!" cried the king. "O sheikh and crown of liars! There can't be a grain of truth in anything you have said."

The child replied, "I can speak truth as well. Shall I tell the court the reason why you persecute the fisherman? You wish to kill him because you saw his beautiful wife and you wish to possess her. Is this worthy of a mighty king? I swear by Allah that if you do not leave the man and his wife in peace from now onward, I shall wipe you out so thoroughly – you and your wazir too – that not even the flies will find a trace of your remains."

Having said these awful words, the infant turned to the fisherman. "Now, uncle", he demanded, "take me away from here." The people all stood back and made a path as the man and infant left, no one daring to speak. The child was returned to the well, with words of grateful thanks, and the fisherman and his delightful wife lived merrily together, untouched by harm, for years beyond this story.

THE TALE OF ABU KIR AND ABU SIR

A TALE IS TOLD THAT once, long ago, in Alexandria, there lived two neighbouring shopkeepers, a dyer called Abu Kir and a barber named Abu Sir. Abu Kir the dyer was a cheat and a scoundrel, treacherous, mean and greedy. When his dishonesty finally drove away all customers and suppliers, he sat down before the shop of Abu Sir, complained that fortune had served him badly, and that he soon would starve to death. The barber, though poor himself, with a family to keep, was a kindly man. He took the dyer into his own home, and freely gave him food and drink and other necessities.

But as the weeks passed, and the dyer made no effort to help or to leave, the barber grew increasingly troubled by his own poverty. Customers were few and poor; his family's needs were many. He spoke of this to the dyer.

"Brother," said Abu Kir, "the answer is simple. We must leave this city, where we are not valued, and find new lands where our gifts will be appreciated." He spoke with such enthusiasm that Abu Sir agreed to go. He wrapped his tools in an old patched cloth, settled his few small debts, and, with Abu Kir, embarked on a ship just about to sail.

"Now," said the dyer, "to prove that we are brothers, let us agree that we put our profits into a common fund to be divided when we return to Alexandria. We will also have an undertaking that whichever of us finds work shall provide for the other if he cannot earn for himself."

They had set out with neither money, food nor drink. But Allah willed that, among the passengers and crew, one hundred and forty in all, there was no other barber. So as soon as they were at sea, Abu Sir threw a ragged cloth over his shoulder, took his bag of equipment, and walked around, offering his services. Instead of money, he asked for a little food, some bread perhaps, and water. Soon he had acquired rolls of bread, cheese, cucumbers, olives, slices of water melon, and even fish. He took these back to the dyer, who promptly shovelled all the food he could grab with both hands into his mouth, his face red, his eyes bulging. Chumping and crunching, soon he had swallowed the lot. And so he continued, day after day, the barber earning the food and the dyer gobbling it. But the cheerful and helpful Abu Sir had become a favourite with the captain, and was often invited to dine at his table.

On the morning of the twenty-first day the ship reached land, and dyer and barber stepped ashore into an unknown city. Here they rented a small room in an inn, Abu Sir paying for both. Each day he went out to find work, always bringing back food for his gross companion who stuffed it all down and then went back to his couch. The effect of the voyage, he always explained, had left him too weak to work.

So passed forty days. Then the barber fell ill and for nearly a week lay as if unconscious. Quite soon the dyer began to feel hungry; reluctantly, he got to his feet and looked around for food. There was nothing, for he had eaten it all. So he went through the clothes of his sick companion, found his careful savings, and went out to spend the money. First he made for a pastrycook's where he ate a whole plateful of sweet cakes washed down by sherbet flavoured with musk and amber. After more delicacies of this kind, he strolled into the market to buy new clothes. One thing struck him; all the people, buyers and sellers, rich and poor, were dressed either in blue or white; no other colour was to be seen. Very strange! He looked about until he found a dyer's shop and peered within. The vats held nothing but blue!

Overcome with curiosity, Abu Kir took a white handkerchief from his robe and said to the dyer, "O master of the craft, what colour may I have this dyed?"

The man replied, "Why, blue of course, worthy stranger. What other?"

"May I not have it red? or yellow? or violet?" said Abu Kir. The man was bewildered.

"What are these?" he said. "I have no knowledge of them." Then Abu Kir named all the many colours that he knew in his craft, but they meant nothing at all to the man.

"Are all the city's dyers like yourself?" asked Abu Kir. "For I see only blue and white clothing."

"There are forty of us in the city," said the man. "We are a close guild, and pass down our secret skills from father to son. But none of us knows of any colour other than blue – light blue, dark blue, indigo."

"O master dyer," said Abu Kir, "I too am of your trade, but I know of a range of colours beyond your imagining. If you care to employ me, I will teach you mysteries that will make you the wonder of your guild."

But the man said, "We are forbidden to employ strangers. Nor may you open a dyer's business yourself." And however much Abu Kir looked for work about the city, he met the same response. This did not please him at all. Rage made him reckless, and he boldly presented himself before the king of that place.

"O monarch of time," he said, "I am a stranger and a dyer by trade. But I can get no work here. And yet I can transform a cloth into any one of a hundred shades, of rose red, violet, emerald green, gold of lemons, gold of the setting sun, the dark, the light, the bright the pale, whatsoever you will. O most generous of kings, how can I use my craft in your great city?" The king was so excited by the sound of these wondrous colours that he ordered a magnificent dyeworks to be built for Abu Kir on a place of the dyer's choice. A robe of honour and a great purse of gold were given to him, also a horse of rarest breed, a mansion like a palace, and multitudes of slaves. Abu Kir selected a site in the heart of the chief market, and watched complacently from his horse while all the shops were torn down by his orders. Soon the dyer was the richest man in the city, and former masters of the guild, now homeless and workless, were beggars in the streets.

But what of Abu Sir, the barber, left robbed and near to death by the dyer for whom he had done so much? After several days the doorkeeper of the inn, seeing nothing of his lodgers, became anxious.

"Have they left without paying?" he asked himself. "Have they met with disaster? With death? Or something other?" So he entered the room and found the barber scarcely alive, without either food or water.

In a faint voice the sick man said, "I beg you, friend, to take from my purse and buy me something for my thirst." The doorkeeper found only an empty wallet, and realised that the barber had been robbed and deserted by his own companion.

"Allah sees all," he said, "and judges men by their works. I will undertake your care until you recover." For two months he tended the barber until he was fully recovered and able to rise.

"Only Allah can truly reward your goodness," said Abu Sir. "But whatever I am able to do when fortune turns, that I shall do for you, O my benefactor." Then each called the blessing of Allah upon the other and Abu Sir, with his bundle of instruments, left the inn.

Chance led his steps to the great dyeing establishment of Abu Kir. Looking within the shop, the barber beheld Abu Kir, fat and fine, in sumptuous robes, stretched on a soft couch while four white slaves and four black slaves fanned him endlessly.

"Now," thought Abu Sir, "he will rejoice to see me and help me in my need."

But no sooner did the evil dyer perceive his old companion than he leapt to his feet saying, "Thief and wretch! Away! Are you trying to disgrace me?" Then he ordered his slaves to beat the unfortunate barber, a hundred blows on his back, a hundred on his front, then to cast him into the street.

When Abu Sir was able to move at last, he looked about for a hammam or bathing place where he might wash his wounds and clean himself of the taint of his long illness. But no one in the city had ever heard of such a thing.

"We go to the sea," they told him, "even the king does so."

"Is that possible?" the barber asked himself. "Then I will seek an audience with this king." And he made his way to the palace.

"O monarch of the centuries," he said, "I come, a stranger, to your city, yet nowhere can I find what is the chief adornment and delight of other great cities."

"What is that?" said the king. "Tell me more."

"I speak of a hammam or bathing place," said Abu Sir. "The nearest thing to paradise on earth, some call it. I am a barber by trade, and know the working skills as well as the joys." And he went on to describe them.

The king felt that he could not wait to experience such delights. He ordered a hammam to be constructed under the barber's directions. And in the shortest possible time there it was, built of rarest marble and transparent alabaster, with musical fountains and rose-scented waters of every degree of drowsy heat or refreshing cold, with beautiful attendant slaves, and burning nard as incense, and sherbet with sliced snow – something for all the senses.

The king declared, "By Allah, my city was no city before this place was built. You must charge a thousand dinars to each user."

But Abu Sir said, "O most noble king, some are rich and some are poor. May we not leave the price according to the means and soul of the client?"

"This is well spoken," said the king.

So the hammam became the wonder and pride of the city, with no set payment but what was in the purse, and the heart of the bather to give. And Abu Sir was known and loved throughout for his good will. This was to save his life, as we shall later learn. For a certain sea captain, who, through some mishap, found himself without money, was given a bath of highest quality for nothing, then refreshed with sherbets and honourably escorted to the door by Abu Sir himself.

"You will not regret your goodness," said the captain. "Allah alone can see tomorrow's need."

Now when the evil dyer heard of the marvellous hammam he at once decided to savour its pleasures for himself. So he rode out, a train of slaves clearing the way before and after with long sticks. But who was that at the

from Abu Kir and Abu Sir

desk in the vestibule? None other than his former companion Abu Sir, whom he had treated so cruelly, and indeed thought dead. But the barber was plump and smiling, and richly clad.

"Well, well, my friend," said the wily dyer. "Where have you been? What became of you? I have been searching for you everywhere since I became established in this city."

"O Abu Kir," said the barber, "have you forgotten how you received me when I came to visit you? The vile abuse? The beatings?"

"No! Surely that was not you!" said the dyer. "I took that yellow-faced skeleton to be a common thief. What an absurd mistake! Well, well, well. But now let all those misunderstandings be forgotten; they were written, after all, in the Book of Destiny."

"Allah will pardon you, if it is his will," said the kindly barber. "For my part I invite you in to have a refreshing bath, without payment, and I will serve you myself as a token."

And this was done. But forgiveness can become another name for folly. As he took his bath the dyer planned a new way of destroying Abu Sir.

"Only one thing is lacking here," he said. "When you need to remove a hair from your client's limbs, what do you use – a tweezer, which is slow and causes discomfort. Now I know of a paste made of yellow arsenic and lime – add a pinch of this powder also – and musk to sweeten the smell; it works as a miracle. The king will be delighted with this method."

Abu Sir thanked him for the recipe and the powder and they parted. At once the dyer hastened to the palace.

"O king of the centuries," he said, "I come to bring a warning. Allah be praised that he has enabled me to save you from the traitor Abu Sir!"

"What are you telling me?" said the astonished king.

"O lord of time," said the dyer, "he has prepared a poisonous paste to remove hair, but it burns the skin like fire. The man is a spy, working for the king of the Christians, and he now intends to use the noxious stuff for your destruction."

"This is grave news," said the king, "but keep it to yourself. I will go at once with my Grand Wazir to put it to the test."

When they arrived at the hammam, Abu Sir greeted them with proper courtesy, then told of his new discovery.

"Try it first on the wazir," said the king. But as soon as the wazir felt the paste on his skin, he leapt into the air with a shriek.

At once the king called to his slaves, saying, "Arrest the man Abu Sir!" And he sent for the captain of the port and ordered him to tie the prisoner in a sack of quicklime and throw him into the sea beneath the palace windows – a double death by drowning and by burning.

"I hear and obey," said the captain. But he was that same one who owed a debt of gratitude to Abu Sir. He filled a sack with quicklime, as if it contained a man; then, during the night, he secretly freed the barber from his dungeon and took him to a small uninhabited island near the coast. Only then did he ask Abu Sir the cause of the king's anger.

When he had learnt the truth of the story he said, "Allah will see that justice is done. Meanwhile this is a safe refuge."

Then he returned to await the king's order to cast the sack in the sea. The king raised his hand to make the signal, but in doing so, his gold ring slipped from his finger and fell into the water just below. Now this ring was the most precious of all his possessions, and the key to his royal power. For it held a magic ray which could shoot out and strike an enemy lifeless, making his head roll from his body. Yet the king dared not speak of his loss, for once it was known, any man might take his place.

Left alone on the island Abu Sir took a fishing net which the captain had left him and cast it into the waves, partly for food, but also to distract his mind from thoughts of the wrongs and injustices done to him. When he drew it in, he found it full of fish of many kinds, mostly unknown to him. He selected a large one, slew it, and found within a curious ring which he slipped upon his finger. At that moment a boat arrived with two cook-boys, asking for the captain, who usually supplied them with the king's fish for the day.

"He went in that direction," said the barber, pointing, as it were, towards the youths. At once their heads leapt from their shoulders and their bodies fell to the ground. They had been struck by the terrible magic ring. Abu Sir was aghast. Then he saw the captain coming towards him. The man has seen the flash of the ring and had guessed what had taken place.

"Brother!" he called. "Do not move your hand or I too will be lost. Stay still until I can reach you." Then he came to Abu Sir and asked how he had come to possess the ring and told him of its powers.

"You are the master now," he said, "and can do what you will, even to the king himself." And he agreed to take the barber straightaway to the palace.

There sat the king with all his wazirs and counsellors about him. When he saw Abu Sir he cried out, "Wretch! How have you risen from the sea? You should be both burned and drowned!"

But Abu Sir replied, "Allah sees all, and justice is in his hands." And he told how he had been secretly rescued, and how he had found the ring. "If I were a criminal I would use this for my own ends. But I have always sought to be an honest man, and I give it back to you. In return I ask only that you tell me on what grounds you ordered that terrible sentence, and I in turn will tell you my true history." So the king revealed that Abu Kir the dyer had accused the barber of being a spy and had hoped to cause the monarch's death by means of the poisoned paste. Then all the treachery, greed and ingratitude shown by Abu Kir came into the barber's mind and he told the king their story from the start.

The king listened as if spellbound. Then he called to the guards, "Bring me the dyer, bareheaded and barefooted, with his hands tied behind his back!" They willingly did so, with kicks and beatings for good measure, for the dyer was not loved.

When he arrived the king said, "I know your shameless story. And everywhere there are witnesses to confirm it. Guards, drag him by the feet through the city, tie him in a sack filled with quicklime, and cast him into the sea."

Then the barber cried, "O king of time, I intercede for this man; he has my forgiveness."

"You have done this too often," said the king, "and it has only encouraged his evil. Besides, you are not the only sufferer, and it is not in your gift to forgive his trespasses against other than yourself." So Abu Kir died the double death that was his destiny.

"Now," said the king to Abu Sir, "name your wish and it shall be fulfilled. "For a start, will you accept the post of Grand Wazir?"

"All I ask," said the barber, "is to return to my own city and my family."

"I would prefer you to stay," said the king, "but what will be will be." And he had a great ship filled with treasures and with male and female slaves. A fair wind sped it safely to Alexandria. On the shore, as they landed, one of the slaves found a sack in which was the body of Abu Kir, which the sea had returned to its native soil. The barber had it buried where it lay, and over it raised a monument, with an engraved inscription advising all to keep from evil ways: "Evil deeds lead to evil harvest, but the sower of good shall reap the good he sowed." It became a place of pilgrimage. And happiness was the lot of Abu Sir to the very end of his days.

THE STRANGE TALE OF LAND ABDALLAH AND SEA ABDALLAH

THERE WAS ONCE A VERY poor fisherman named Abdallah. He had a wife and nine children to keep, and owned nothing but his net. On a good day he would sell his catch in the market and buy different foods for his family, but on most days his catch was small, and hunger filled the home.

A day came when the mother gave birth to a tenth son (all had been sons, thanks to Allah). "O my master," she said to her husband, "we have nothing in the house but want. I beg you to go forth and bring back food for our emptiness."

"I will go straightaway to the sea," he said, "and call upon Allah in the name of this newborn child. Perhaps it will bring luck." So he took his net and cast it into the sea, crying out to Allah as he did so, and after a while drew it in; but it was filled with rubbish, gravel, sand and weed, not a single fish. He moved along and cast again, and a third and a fourth time, but nothing was caught but stones, not a sprat nor minnow. At last, with dragging feet, he started off for home, saying, "What shall I do? What shall I do?"

Suddenly his feet seemed like roots in the ground, and the whole of his being was warmed by a fragrance, the wonderfully savoury smell of baking bread. He had reached the shop of a baker, where many were waiting for the loaves to be taken from the oven. The fisherman stood apart with downcast head, for he had no money to buy. But the baker saw him, and felt his hunger and called across the crowd, "Fisherman, come nearer, here is bread."

The fisherman answered, "I cannot pay you, for I have nothing; but if you will give me bread for my family's need, I will leave you my net in pawn."

The baker said, "If I take your net, I take your shop and your living. Feel no shame. Today I offer you bread; tomorrow or the next day your luck will change and you will bring me fish to the same value." And he gave him bread and ten copper coins, and the fisherman's family rejoiced.

The next day he went again to the sea and cast his net, but caught no fish, and so it happened every day for forty days. But each day the baker beckoned him into his shop and gave him bread and coins, saying, "O my brother, when your fortune changes you will repay me."

At last the fisherman felt that he could not endure this state of grief and shame. "Today is the end," he said. "If I fail once more I must seek some other way of life." Then he cast his net, and presently felt a heaviness in it. There was a movement also and with trembling hands he laboured to bring it in. And there, caught in the meshes, was a being like a human man, but where his legs should have been was the tail of a fish.

The fisherman looked with dread at his prisoner. This surely must be an Efreet, one of those whom the lord Sulaiman long ago shut as a punishment into a copper jar and cast into the sea. And, the metal being worn thin by the years, the naughty spirit must have escaped and crept into his net.

He cried out, "Mercy, mercy, O Efreet of Sulaiman!" And he turned to flee.

But the being called to him, "Wait, wait, fisherman; have no fear. I am a son of Adam like yourself."

"Then you are no Efreet and no Jinnee?" said the fisherman.

"No, indeed, I am one of the children of the sea, believers in Allah, living below the waves as you do on earth, and as the birds live in the air. I was about my affairs when the net came over me. But since the will of Fate made me your captive, I have not torn your net and escaped as I might have done. Instead, I have a proposal. You shall free me from your net, and together we make a pact of friendship. Each day at the same time we shall meet at this spot and exchange the treasures of earth and sea. You have fruits in plenty, grapes and figs, peaches and pomegranates, plums and dates and watermelons. We have abundance of jewels – emeralds, jacinths, chrysolites, sapphires, amethysts, coral, pearl – I cannot name them all. When I have emptied the basket of fruit that you bring, I shall fill it with these jewels in return."

The fisherman marvelled much at this, but readily agreed. Having helped the merman from the net he asked, "What is your name? I must know how to call you from the waves."

"I am Abdallah of the Sea. Now tell me your own."

"I also am Abdallah," said the fisherman.

Then said the merman, "You are Land Abdallah and I am Sea Abdallah, and so we are twice brothers. Now I will bring you a token of our pact." He vanished into the water, and the fisherman wondered if he had been deceived.

"Why did I let him escape?" he grumbled. "I might have displayed this man-fish to the city folk, and received good money." But even as he was thinking these unworthy thoughts the merman reappeared, both his hands filled with shining jewels.

"Forgive me for bringing so few, brother of the land," he said, "but I have no basket. When you bring your own you shall have it heaped to the brim. Now, remember our pact. Come each day, just before sunrise, and we can exchange our gifts." Then he dived into the waves.

The fisherman set off joyfully, as fast as he could, and made for the baker's shop. "O my brother!" he called out. "Good fortune has come to me at last! Tell me how much I owe to you."

The baker replied, "I keep no such accounts. Give me what you can spare and take what bread you require, as before. The need is more important than the money."

But then the fisherman took out the jewels and divided them into two equal piles, saying, "This is rightly yours." The baker was amazed. Together they went to the market and purchased meat and fruit and many sorts of vegetables and took them to the fisherman's home, where the family rejoiced, and feasted through the night.

At dawn the following day the fisherman filled a basket with the choicest of the fruits – figs, grapes, peaches, pomegranates – and went to the appointed place on the shore.

"O Abdallah of the Sea," he called out, "come fast, for your friend is waiting." At once the merman rose from the waves with a beaming face. He took the basket of fruits and slid below, returning in a very few minutes with the same basket, but now brimming over with emeralds, sapphires, all manner of sparkling gems. Then, after greetings had passed between them, the fisherman left the beach with his dazzling load, which shone through the dark of dawn, even though it was covered with strands of seaweed.

First he went to the baker's shop, plunged his hand in the basket, and three times brought it out full of jewels; these he gave to the good man, who had already cooked for him, hot and fragrant, forty of the finest spicy cakes. Then, when he reached his own home, he chose the finest specimens of each kind and colour, wrapped them in soft cotton, and went to the jewel market, where he sought out the chief of the jewel merchants. The man looked at the gems with amazement.

"These are of the rarest quality," he said at last. "Have you more?"

"Yes indeed, I have a basketful."

The merchant went aside and told his servants, "Arrest this man. These must be the queen's stolen jewels, and he must be the thief."

So the servants beat Abdallah and tied his hands behind him, and the merchant led him to the palace and brought him before the king. The king said to his wazir, "Have these jewels taken to the queen and ask if they are her own

lost gems." But the queen replied that the missing treasures had already been found in her own apartment. Moreover, these jewels were of a finer quality than any she possessed. Indeed, if the man were willing to sell them, she begged the king to purchase them for her daughter, their only child, Princess Umm es-So-od, which means Bringer of Prosperity. When the king heard this message he was seized with rage against the merchant for ill-treating an innocent man.

"May Allah ever withhold his blessings from you!" he cried, and drove him forth with shame. Then he turned to Abdallah, saying, "Tell me the truth. How did these jewels come to you?"

"O king of the ages," replied Abdallah, "I have at home a fish basket full of such gems; they are the gift of my friend, Abdallah of the Sea." And he told of their daily pact.

When the king heard the tale he marvelled, saying, "O fisherman, wonderful are the ways of Allah! But great wealth should go with rank and station, and you must now live in a mansion befitting your new riches. Therefore I propose to marry you to my only daughter, also to appoint you my wazir, to give you knowledge of state matters, for you will inherit the kingdom after my death." Then he ordered his attendant to lead the fisherman to the bath, and bathe him and clothe him in royal robes. His old wife and ten children were also brought to the palace, in a palanquin carried by ten black slaves, and were bathed and dressed in silks and treated with honour, and the wife was made Chief Counsellor to the Queen. And the wedding was promptly celebrated between the fisherman and the young princess. The city was lit with torches; feasts were held in every street, and music from a thousand instruments filled the festive air.

On the following day the king woke early, just before dawn. Looking from his window, he was amazed to see his new son-in-law leaving the palace, carrying on his head a basket of fruits.

He called to him, "O my son-in-law, what are you doing at this hour? Why do you carry this burden like a labourer?"

The other answered, "I go to keep my promise to my friend of friends, Abdallah of the Sea. For if I fail to come he will think me faithless and a liar, puffed up by worldly fortune."

The king said, "You are right to go. Hurry to your friend."

So the fisherman went and again exchanged his fruits for a basket of glittering jewels, and so it happened the next day and the next, and a brotherly affection grew between them. But each time the fisherman passed the shop of the baker, all seemed cold and dead: no man, no loaves, no customers.

from Land Abdallah and Sea Abdallah   *135*

He asked a neighbour, "What has become of the baker?" But none would say. Then he knocked at the baker's door, and the man peered out of the window and saw his friend, and tiptoed fearfully down.

"O fisherman," he said, "I heard that you had been seized for theft, through jealous lies, and I feared that my life might be forfeited too, having had some share of the gems. So I hid within, and let my oven grow cold, for I dared not light it, and all my business went."

"Good friend, you need have no fear," said Abdallah, and he gave him the whole of that day's portion of jewels.

When the king saw the empty basket, he remarked, "It seems that your sea-brother has not kept his covenant." But Abdallah told him of the baker's troubles, and how the worthy man had helped him in his poverty.

The king was much moved, saying, "Send for this baker, and he shall be made my Wazir of the Left as you are my Wazir of the Right. For a man of such excellence no reward is too high." And this was done.

It happened one day when the two Abdallahs met at dawn, according to their custom, that they sat and talked on the sand. And the Sea Abdallah spoke of the beauty of his country, and invited his brother of the land to come below as his guest and discover its wonders. But the Land Abdallah was filled with doubt and fear.

"O my brother," he said, "I am a creature of the earth, and if I let the waves close over my head I will die for want of breath."

"All will be well," said the merman. "I will bring you a special ointment to cover all your body. Then you can sleep and wake and eat and move in the ocean world as easily as if it were your own."

"I will try your ointment," said the fisherman. So the Sea Abdallah dived into the waves and returned with a jar of grease, something like the fat of beef, but the scent was sweet and the colour yellow like gold.

"I place my trust in Allah," said the fisherman. He pulled off his clothes, then covered himself with the ointment and stepped into the sea.

At once he felt in a place of marvels. The water overhead seemed a great emerald canopy. Under his feet were sea-green grasses, never beheld by man. All around him were many kinds of fish, some great, some small, some resembling buffaloes, some camels and some oxen, only they swam and had scales. He saw lofty mountains, whose tops pierced the ocean's ceiling, making the islands known to human men. There were damsels too, with faces like the moon and lustrous eyes and floating tresses, but with tails like fishes' tails. The men too and the children had not legs, but tails. Nowhere could he see any buying and selling, as with people of the land. Then the Sea Abdallah led his guest to a great cavern that seemed hewn from the rock itself.

"This is my home," said the merman. "All the houses of this city are carved from the mountains; there is a special fish with a beak that does this work. Now you must enter, and be made welcome." Then he called out, "Come, my daughter; we have with us a traveller from the land." A girl of melting beauty swam towards them; her face was like the full moon; her floating hair swept the ground; her eyes were those of a doe; her waist a stem of wheat, her hips both round and full; but in place of legs she had a tail. When her father told her to bring food for his guest, she set before him two large fishes, each of them like a lamb. Then the merman sent for his younger children; there were two, each having in his hand a fish, which he was craunching as a human craunches a cucumber. All of them stared at the Land Abdallah, wondering that a man could have no tail. And they put their hands up to their mouths and laughed.

But the Sea Abdallah said, "O my friend, take no notice. The intellects of women and young children are feeble, as in your country also." To the family he said, "Be silent, foolish creatures." And they obeyed.

At the day's end, when the land Abdallah wished to return, the two friends set off for the shore. As they went, they passed a crowd of merpeople, joyfully singing and dancing, with a feast of various fishes spread beside.

So the Land Abdallah asked, "O Abdallah of the Sea, what is this joyful happening? Is it the celebration of a wedding?"

"This is no wedding," said the other; "a person of our kind is dead."

"How can this be?" said the Land Abdallah. "I see no grief, only feasting and merrymaking. When death comes for one of us, we weep and mourn, and tear our clothes for sorrow."

The other was silent, but when they reached the edge of the sea which was also the edge of the land, he said, "After this day we shall not meet again."

"Why should that be?" said the Land Abdallah. "We are sworn brothers. What breaks the bond between us?"

But the merman said, "Each soul is placed on the earth or within the sea by Allah. How can there be any weeping when Allah takes back his own to himself? It is not right that we should meet again, having such diverse ways. But because of the service you once did me, you will have no more poverty for the rest of your days." And he turned away, and vanished into the sea. Nor did he ever return, though for many weeks and months his friend of the land continued to go to the shore at dawn and call the merman's name. But the promise held throughout the life of Abdallah of the Land, no want or misery touching his lot again. Wonderful indeed are the ways of Allah!

THE ADVENTURES OF HASAN OF BASRAH

NEVER WAS SO STRANGE A tale as the one you are about to hear. It was the favourite tale of the king of Persia, who kept the manuscript in a golden box.

Once, long years ago, a youth of singular beauty lived in the city of Basrah; Hasan was his name. An only child, he was greatly spoilt, and soon had wasted away the inheritance left by his father. When all the money was gone, his mother used her own portion to set him up in a goldsmith's shop. Because of his beauty, crowds would gather to watch him at his work, and among these was a Persian with a long white beard and tall white turban. One day this man entered the shop, and after exchange of courtesies he made a curious offer.

"I have no son," he said, "and I am seeking an heir to whom I may pass on the secrets of my craft, which is unique in the world. You seem in every way most fit to take that place. What do you say to this?"

"By Allah," replied the young man, "I will gladly be your son and learn your skills, whatever they may be. When do you wish me to start?"

"Tomorrow," said the Persian. "Expect me here at dawn." And he was gone.

Hasan closed the shop and ran home to tell his mother the good news. But she was horrified.

"The man is a heretic; the skill he speaks of is alchemy, which is an evil magic. If you go with him you are lost."

But the reckless boy would hear nothing against the Persian. The next morning he was in the shop so early that no one else had arrived in the market. But the Persian was already waiting.

"Have you any copper or brass?" he asked, looking around. Hasan produced an old battered dish.

"That will serve," said the man. "Now light your furnace, then cut the dish into pieces, put them in the crucible, then set it on the fire and blow it hot with the bellows." When these things were done, the Persian began to wave his hands over the metal uttering strange harsh sounds. Then he dropped a pinch of powder into the molten brass – and there instead was a lump of

shining gold.

"You may test it if you wish," said the man. Hasan did so. It was the truest gold, the kind most sought by jewellers.

"Now," said the man, "take your tools and follow me to my home." The boy gathered his instruments together and started out. But his mother's words returned to him, and he stopped.

The man laughed. "You seem to doubt my intentions. Very well. The first lesson will take place at your home instead of mine. So you need have no fear."

Hasan asked if he might run ahead to prepare his mother, and having reached home he begged her to make a meal for his new master. The mother was horrified.

"An alchemist and a fire-worshipper! I will set you out some food, but I will not stay in the house while he is there. What's more, I will scrub the room and burn incense when he is gone." So she set out some roast fowl and cucumbers, and several kinds of pastry, and went to take refuge with neighbours.

When the sage arrived, Hasan greeted him joyfully, and they sat down to eat. Between courses, the Persian showed the boy a packet of yellow powder, saying, "A single pinch of this can transmute ten pounds of brass into gold. But the making of it is the work of a lifetime, as you shall learn." While the boy was examining it, the old man slipped a morsel of benj into the pastry that Hasan was about to eat, and at once he fell into deep unconsciousness.

The Persian rose with a cry of triumph. "Now I have you, beautiful Hasan!" He bundled the boy into a wooden box, called in a porter from the street, and had it carried to the seashore, where a ship was waiting. Once the Persian and his box were aboard, the ship put out to sea.

When the mother returned, she was inconsolable. She caused a tomb to be built in her home, and wept over it every day. But Hasan was not dead. The Persian was indeed a magician and a fire-worshipper, and he had abducted many a handsome boy; but Hasan was the prize he long had sought. When the ship reached land, the Persian went ashore with his box. He opened the lid and gave Hasan a reviving draught. The boy opened his eyes and saw that he was on a beach of many-coloured sands, unlike any that he had known.

"Where have you brought me?" he cried.

The Persian laughed. "You are now in my power!" he said. "First you must abjure your faith, and follow what I follow."

"What abomination is that?" said the boy.

The Persian had no need to hurry, so he changed his tactics. "I was only testing your faith, Hasan, and you have come out of it well. My real aim in bringing you here is to have the right conditions for our craft. That lofty mountain there is called Cloud Mountain, and at its peak we can gather those plants that grow above the clouds, and are nowhere else to be found. Then I can teach you further."

Hasan dared not refuse, but said, "How can we climb that mountain? It is as steep as a house."

"Easy enough," said the Persian. He drew from under his cloak a little copper drum, engraved with strange characters, with a cock's skin stretched tightly over the top. He beat on this with his fingers and a great black horse stood before them. The Persian mounted, pulled Hasan behind him, and the horse rose on wings, set them on the mountain-top and vanished.

Then the sorcerer gave an evil laugh. "Now, Hasan, you really are in my power."

But Hasan drew away, saying, "Vile infidel, there is no God but Allah." He hurled himself at the sorcerer, snatched the drum from his hands, and pushed him over the sheer cliff edge. The Persian's body was smashed to pieces on the rocks below, and his soul was gathered into the fires of hell. Such was the end of the fire-worshipper.

Now Hasan looked around. The mountain peak was above the clouds, and the summit seemed like an arid plain, with a shining light in the distance. He began to walk towards this light and presently found that it came from the sun pouring down on a golden palace, with golden domes set upon four great columns of gold. The great door seemed hewn from a single emerald.

"Even if an Efreet lives here, he cannot refuse me shelter," Hasan said to himself, and walked into the front court. There, on a marble bench, sat two young girls playing chess. The younger one looked up and smiled.

"Sister," she said, "this must be one of those unlucky young men whom the sorcerer brings every year to Cloud Mountain. But how did this one escape?"

Hasan threw himself at her feet, saying, "I am indeed one of those, but the magician is no more. His body lies far below."

The girl said, "That news is good. You are most welcome here, and I adopt you as my brother." She took him by the hand and led him into the palace where he was given a bath and clothes of the softest silk. Then they sat down to a meal.

Hasan told his story, and the girls said, "You did well to rid the world of that evildoer."

Then the younger said, "I shall now tell you our own tale. My name is Roseleaf; my sister here is Myrtleberry, and we have five other sisters, Morning Star, Evening Star, Jacynth, Emerald, and Anemone. They are out hunting, but will soon be back. Our father is a Jinnee, a powerful king. He thinks that no one is worthy to marry his daughters, so he keeps us in this pleasant place, which has everything to bring delight but the presence of man. So we are not displeased by your coming."

When the other five girls returned they joined in making the young man welcome. For the seven sisters and their adopted brother, day followed day of utmost pleasure. But one morning a whirlwind of dust arose, a black cloud covered the sun and thunderous noises rolled towards the palace.

"Hide!" cried the girls. "We know those signs. Hide in the pavilion!" Then, as he hid, Roseleaf came to him with a bunch of keys.

"Our father has sent a great escort of the Jinn to take us back on a visit, as he does now and then. While you await our return, live as happily as you can. Here are the keys of all the rooms – but one you must not use on any account, this little key with a turquoise stone. Do not forget." Then she kissed him tenderly and was gone.

Alone in the palace, Hasan felt sad and restless. He began to be tormented by the door he might not enter. One day he could wait no longer. He took the little turquoise key and fitted it in the lock. The door smoothly opened, as if he had been expected. But inside he saw – nothing, a totally empty room. Yet there was something, in a shadowy corner: a ladder of black wood, whose top reached a hole in the ceiling. Hasan began to climb, and in a moment saw that the hole led to an open terrace. All around was the most beautiful landscape ever seen by mortal eyes. A lake, bordered by flowering trees, reflected a mysterious palace, whose domes and turrets seemed to melt into the sky. A glittering platform, a mosaic of silver and gold, sapphire and emerald, with awnings of fine silk, led into the water. The fragrance of flowers, the dissolving colours, the sounds of rustling water and rustling leaves, ravished his senses.

Then, as he stood entranced, a flight of great white birds came down from the sky. They alighted on the border of the lake, slipped out of their feathers – and they were girls, beautiful damsels who sat upon the platform and laughed and dived into the water! The one who seemed to lead them was the loveliest of all.

"I know why Roseleaf forbade me to open the door!" he murmured. "My peace is gone for ever."

Then the girl spoke. "Come, princesses," she said. "It is time to leave. We have far to go before nightfall." They entered their feathered cloaks again and flew off.

Hasan was desolate. For days he could not eat or sleep, and when the sisters returned they found him lying pale and weak on his couch. The sisters were all distressed too, but Roseleaf tended him so kindly and so constantly that at last he told his tale. She was not angry, but she put both hands to her face.

"O sorrow, sorrow," she said. "The girl who has your heart is the daughter of the mightiest king of our kind. He lives in a land encircled by a sea which neither man nor Jinnee can pass. He has seven daughters; the one you saw is the youngest, loveliest and most daring; her name is Splendour. She comes here at each new moon, with other royal maidens. The only way to capture her is by taking her feathered cloak. But beware – do not give it back, however much she pleads. For that will destroy us all, yourself, ourselves, our father too."

This news revived Hasan. The night of the next new moon, he hid behind the platform in the lake and, when the girls were diving into the water, he managed to take the Princess Splendour's cloak. So, when the time came to leave, she alone was left weeping on the shore. Hasan's heart was moved, but he remembered Roseleaf's words, and led the damsel back to the sister's palace, where Roseleaf had prepared a royal welcome. And by telling the princess of Hasan's great love for her, a love which had brought him near to death, by reminding her of Hasan's rare beauty, which made all desire him, Roseleaf calmed her rage and grief. When the sisters returned from hunting and heard the story, they too spoke of her good fortune in winning the love of this delightful youth. And so, at last, Hasan and Splendour were wed in the Jinn fashion.

They lived in utmost joy for forty nights and days. But the next night Hasan saw his mother in a dream, weeping over his tomb. In the morning he told his dream, and the sisters agreed, though sadly, that he and Splendour must leave for his mother's home. But Roseleaf made him promise to return each year to visit them. Then the girls prepared many costly gifts. Finally, for transport, Hasan took out the little cockskin drum, beat on it with his fingers, and two great winged horses sprang from the ground. Swiftly they carried Hasan and his bride to the old mother's house. Then they vanished as they came.

The old woman could hardly believe her eyes when she saw her son and his lovely bride. Night after night she listened to the story of Hasan's adventures. Day after day she spent in making them dishes, bringing them robes and luxuries. At her advice they moved to Baghdad, City of Peace, where they would not be known, and where their new-found wealth would not cause false suspicion and harm. So Hasan purchased a magnificent palace in Baghdad where his family could live in peace and joy. And there the princess gave birth to twin boys, more beautiful than young moons. What tale can ever match the tale of Hasan of Basrah?

THE MIRROR OF VIRGINS

ONCE, LONG AGO, A NEW young Sultan ruled the city of Basrah; his name was Zain. He was a handsome youth, no doubt of that, but dashing and reckless, and soon had cast away all the ancestral wealth of the kingdom in pleasures, especially in the purchase of young women and girls. One day the chief wazir came to him with downcast head, saying that all the coffers of gold were empty; nothing was left even for the next day's living. Then the old man hurried away, fearing that he might lose his life for bringing such black news.

Despair seized the young Sultan; why had he not set aside a portion in case of need? "O foolish Zain!" he told himself. "There is nothing for you but flight. It is better to be a beggar, serving Allah, than a despised and wretched king." He was about to seek for a staff and some coarse clothing as disguise when Allah brought a memory into his mind. When the old king his father lay dying, he had said to his son, "If Fate should ever turn against you, look in my Hall of Manuscripts. There you will find a talisman to counter all misfortune."

The young man's spirits rose again, and he made his way through many strange corridors until at last he reached the Hall of Manuscripts. Impatiently he turned up papers and registers, searching under and over, riffling through the great annals of the reign – but nothing like a precious stone, nothing of gold or silver even, met his sight. He began to stamp with rage, crushing important documents underfoot. Suddenly, beneath the fallen papers, he felt a hard metallic object on the floor. He knelt down; it was a red copper casket. He raised the lid with shaking fingers – but what a disappointment! Nothing was inside but a small roll of parchment, sealed with his father's seal. Still, he opened the document and there he read these words: "O my son, take a pickaxe and go to the cellar under the eastern wall of the palace; then dig, and trust to Allah."

"So I am to be a labourer, not a beggar," murmured the young man. "But such is my father's will, and I must obey." He returned to the surface, looked among the gardener's tools, found a pickaxe, and climbed down into the cellar. Once inside he began to tap the floor until he came on a place with a hollow sound.

"Ah," thought he, "this must be where the treasure is hidden." He started to dig, but without result. His anger grew with every blow – and then, the last despairing crash revealed a slab of smooth white stone. After several vain attempts and many curses he managed to prise it up, and found that it concealed a trap-door with a metal lock. No key was to be seen, but he smashed the lock with the pickaxe. What he saw made him utter a cry of amazement.

Just beneath his feet were the uppermost steps of a great white marble staircase which rose from a vast square hall of glittering crystal and finest porcelain. The ceiling and the supporting columns were of sky blue lapis lazuli. Zain climbed down into the hall, and saw in the centre four tables made of shining stone, each table holding ten great urns, some carved from porphyry, some from alabaster. He peered within, one after another, and found that every alabaster urn was filled to the brim with gold dust, while every urn of porphyry flowed over with golden coins. In a frenzy of joy he ran his fingers through the gold and threw it over himself like a shower.

"Only trust in Allah and all will be well!" he cried. And his head filled with plans to resume his life of pleasure with this new source of wealth.

But the thought then came to him: had he yet found the talisman, the special treasure of treasures? Gazing around, he saw in a corner a small copper box, not unlike the one in the Hall of Manuscripts. It opened easily; only one thing lay inside – a jewelled key. But to which lock? He searched around and at last, in a panel of the wall, found a small keyhole. He fitted the key and turned; a door swung back and revealed a second hall, even more striking than the first.

The walls were a lucent green; he might have been in the heart of an emerald. And, arranged in a circle in this silent place, were the carved figures of six most beautiful girls, each on a golden pedestal. A strange light came from the girls; moving closer, Zain saw that each was made from a single diamond. Then he perceived that within the ring of sparkling statues was a seventh golden pedestal. But on it was no diamond girl, only a piece of silk on which these words were embroidered:

My son, these diamond girls were gained by hard and strange adventures. But there is a seventh, a thousand times more beautiful. Death has prevented me from acquiring this marvel. But if you wish to take on the task and complete the quest, you must go to the city of Cairo. There you will find a former slave of mine, my faithful old Mubarek. He alone knows the secret, and will set you on the path that leads to that wonder of wonders, the missing seventh girl. The blessings of Allah be upon you and your journey.

The young Sultan marvelled at these words, and planned to start the quest without delay. But first he carried a quantity of the gold to his own apartments. In the morning he informed his wazirs and ministers that he was leaving at once for Egypt; during his absence the old wazir would govern in his place. Then he left without ceremony, taking only a small band of chosen slaves.

As soon as he reached Cairo he set out to find Mubarek. After much enquiring he learnt that the former slave was now a very rich merchant, living in a palace whose gates were always open to the poor and to needy travellers. When Zain approached, the old man rose courteously from his silken couch, and greeted him as he did all travellers, offering any help that he could give.

"O my generous host," said Zain, "my father, now departed, was the Sultan of Basrah. I come to ask your help in finding his faithful slave, Mubarek."

At once the old man cast himself at the feet of Zain, saying, "O son of my master! This palace is your palace, and I am yours!"

Zain begged the good old man to rise and return to his couch. Then he said, "O my host, you are no slave but a free man. Now I will tell you the strange and wondrous reason for my visit." And he told of the parchment, the hall with the diamond girls, and the message woven in silk.

Mubarek listened carefully, then replied, "O my lord, I do indeed know where the seventh maiden may be found, and will guide you there; but I must warn you that the way holds frightful dangers, in which nothing may be what it seems, even to the very end."

"I am ready for all dangers," said the young man. "I cannot rest until I have found this seventh girl, this wonder beyond all wonders."

"Then, my lord, I must inform you that this prize, this rarity, is in the palace of the Old Man of the Three Isles, a secret region which only those who know the words of a certain spell may enter. I am one of the few who know the spell, one of the few permitted to pass to and from the Isles. Even so, it is a journey of fearful peril."

"Be that as it may," said Zain, "I cannot wait to start." So, after their slaves had prepared supplies, the two set out.

For many a day and night they rode, over grassy plain and desert sand, by stark rock and raging river, the landscape growing more and more strange as they advanced. At last they reached a wide green prairie, which seemed to stretch beyond the horizon, without sign of human life.

Then Mubarek turned to the slaves, saying, "You will wait here and guard the horses; we will soon return." To Zain he said, "My lord, we are now on the borders of those forbidden lands which hold your seventh girl. You must not tremble; you must not hesitate. Come!"

They walked through the pathless plain for a long long time, until a great shadow lay in their path. It came from a mountain of dizzying height, which blotted out the horizon with its bulk.

"This we must cross," said Mubarek.

"I cannot see how," said Zain. "Who will give us wings to fly over these terrible cliffs?"

"We have no need of wings," said Mubarek. He took from his robe an ancient book filled with a curious writing, as if made by the feet of ants. Reading from this, he chanted certain verses, rolling his head from side to side all the while. Suddenly the mountain split in the centre, so that through it was a passage just wide enough for one man. Mubarek entered first, leading Zain by the hand to encourage him. Then, at the very moment when both had emerged on the other side, the mountain clapped itself together again; not a crack was left at all.

They were now on the borders of a lake which seemed as endless as the sea, but in the far distance Zain could just perceive three green islands. He stood on the shore, which was fragrant with flowers, melodious with the song of birds, and felt a desire to move no further.

"Beware of drowsiness," said Mubarek, "or you will be rooted here for ever. Only the winds will be of ice, and the only sounds will be the shrieks of storms. Now rouse yourself, for we must reach those islands."

"I see no way to reach them," said the young man, and his heart began to fail him.

"Listen, my lord," said Mubarek. "At any moment a boat will arrive to carry us there. Only, remember what I say. First, you must make no sign of surprise at anything you see. Then, you must not start back, whatever form the boatman takes. Finally, if you say even a single word while we are on board, the boat will carry us both beneath the waves."

Zain said, "I will be silent. I will imprison any surprise within my soul."

Even as he spoke a boat appeared, whether out of the sky or from the heart of the lake he could not tell. It was made of the finest sandalwood, its cordings were of silk and the mast of amber. But the captain was the strangest sight of

all. His body was that of a man, but his head was an elephant's head, with two great ears that reached as far as the ground. He lifted each of the travellers with his trunk and set them down in the boat. Then he raised his mighty ears and spread them out as sails, and the boat sped over the water like a bird. When they reached the nearest island, they were gently lifted off in the boatman's trunk, then boat and boatman vanished into air.

Now Mubarek led the young man along a path paved with gems of every colour until they reached a glittering palace. The walls were made of emeralds, the great door was of solid gold, and all around was a moat.

Here Mubarek halted, saying; "We can go no further unless we utter the magic incantation." He drew from beneath his robes two fine silk prayer rugs, spread them on the ground, sprinkled certain spicy grains upon them, and uttered magic words.

"These rugs," he said, "will carry us into the presence of the Old Man of the Isles. May Allah grant that he is not angry when he comes! If he is displeased by our intrusion, he may well appear as a dreadful monster. If he is glad of our visit, he will seem a courteous old man, a charming host. Whatever shape he takes, you must rise in his honour and bow to the ground. But take care that you never step off your rug. Then you must say, 'O king of kings, we have reached, by many chances, the realm of your high protection. I am your slave, called Zain, Sultan of Basrah, son of a kingly father, known to you in his life, and now carried off by the Angel of Death. I come to ask if you will extend your favour to my father's only son.' Then, if he asks what you desire, you must say, 'O lord of lords, I desire the seventh diamond girl.' Now seat yourself, as I do, on the rug."

No sooner were they seated than the sky was covered with a vast black cloud, from which sprang a great red tongue of fire, followed by peals of thunder. A furious wind blew towards them, lifting them from the ground; a terrible crying filled the air, and the earth trembled as if the last day were approaching.

"These are bad signs," said Zain to himself.

But Mubarek read his thoughts and smiled, saying, "Not at all; the omens are excellent, Allah be thanked."

Suddenly all was calm and still: the rugs had set them down in a great hall in the palace. And there before them was the Old Man of the Isles. He was in venerable human form, but of such radiant beauty that he seemed more like a god. Zain rose to his feet, bowed to the earth, and spoke as Mubarek had advised him.

The old man smiled and said, "I loved the king your father. Each time he came to visit me I gave him a diamond girl. Indeed, it was I who caused him to leave the messages that brought you here. Certainly I will give you the seventh girl, that wonder of wonders, but I ask one thing in exchange."

"As Allah lives," cried Zain. "All that is mine is yours, myself also."

"But what I ask is not so easy to find," said the Old Man. "I would have you bring me a girl of fifteen years who is of the rarest beauty, and who is also a virgin."

"O my lord," said Zain, "nothing could be easier. I know this well."

The old man laughed so heartily that at first he could not speak. At last he said, "My poor young friend, if this is your belief, you must think again. Even the youngest of women have a thousand ways of deceiving men who think them modest and pure."

"In that case, my lord," said Zain, "how am I to tell if the girl is truly a virgin?"

The old man brought forth a mirror, saying, "Here is the answer. Whenever you find a young girl of perfect beauty, with a reputation for purity, look in the mirror. If it clouds over, our search must still continue. But if the girl's likeness shines out clearly, your quest has come to an end. Take great care of the glass; to lose it brings disaster."

He then accompanied his guests to the lake; the elephant-headed man sped them across the water; the mountain opened to let them through, and so they returned to Cairo. But the young man could not rest, so impatient was he to put the magic glass to the test and find his prize.

"My prince," said Mubarek, "there is a manner of doing these things. I know an old woman, of great experience with young damsels, and she will make a plentiful selection of pure and beautiful girls no more than fifteen years old. From these we will choose one. If she is of low birth we will purchase her; if of noble family we will arrange a marriage; you will wed her in name alone. We will then do the same in other cities, and from this group of chosen girls we will make our perfect choice."

"You are the wisest of friends!" said the young man. "Let us start without delay."

The old woman laughed with pleasure at the assignment. "The easiest thing in the world!" she said. "I have on my list more virgin girls, beautiful as the moon, than I can count; many are of noble family too. Your only problem will be which to choose."

In a short time, with the hurried aid of agents, spies and other useful contacts, she conveyed her first group of candidates to the palace, where Zain sat waiting with the mirror. Alas, as each one entered the hall, the mirror clouded over. Shocked though he was at this discovery, Zain thought it prudent not to reveal the truth to the old woman, and he sent for more young damsels. But the glass blurred every time.

Now Zain and Mubarek moved to other great cities, consulted other old women, marriage brokers and slave dealers, but again without success. Together, they conferred.

"Let us try Baghdad, my prince," said Mubarek. "If we do not find our damsel in Allah's own city, we must count ourselves unworthy of the search." So they rented a palace with a great garden in Baghdad, bought a large number of slaves, invited prominent citizens and distributed broken meats to the poor. This show of fortune stung the jealousy of a certain Imam, Abu Bakr by name; he loudly announced in the mosque that the two strangers were robbers, spending in Baghdad the looted wealth of their own city.

When Mubarek heard the slanderous news, he laughed. Then he put five hundred gold coins in a bag, and went to the Imam's house, where he bowed low, and rapidly spoke in this fashion.

"O most gracious Imam, I come from the Amir Zain, who has heard of your great learning and piety and of the high esteem in which you are everywhere held. He presents his homage, and offers this humble purse of five hundred gold pieces, in no way meeting the worth of the receiver. But in future time he hopes to have the privilege of bringing yet more substantial gifts. The goodness of the Imam overwhelms him —" and more words of this kind.

With these greetings in his ears, and the heavy bag of gold in his hands, Abu Bakr changed his sour mouth into a smile, and declared his readiness to serve the Amir Zain in any way that he could. Perhaps, thought Mubarek, the answer lay with this man, and after other exchanges of courtesy, he confided to the Imam the nature of the search.

"O honoured stranger," answered Abu Bakr, "a beauteous virgin of fifteen years is hard indeed to find. But Allah has set me in your path with knowledge of such a girl: Lalifal is her name, daughter of the chief of all the Imams of Baghdad, brought up in seclusion, away from the eyes of men, but said to be the very flower of beauty and virginity."

"Good friend," said Mubarek, "I beg you to approach this young girl's father without an hour's delay, and have him bring her, fully veiled, to the palace."

When the chief Imam heard of the stranger's wealth and possessions, he ordered the mother of Lalifal to prepare the girl and she was brought to the great hall where Zain waited with the mirror. This time, there was no clouding of the glass, and such was the girl's beauty, revealed in the mirror, that Zain knew that his search was done.

A marriage was promptly arranged between Zain and Lalifal, and after days of celebration and feasting throughout the city, the journey was begun to the Three Isles. Mubarek leading, then Lalifal in a camel litter, and Zain at the rear, with a mighty caravan of slaves and gifts. But as month followed month, the young man's love for the maiden burned with increasing flame, and his heart was filled with bitterness that she must soon be handed over to the ancient man.

At length they reached the Isles, where the old sage warmly welcomed them. Zain handed him the mirror, that he might see for himself the girl's purity, but the sage had no need of it; his eyes had their own mirrors.

"You have done well," he declared to Zain. "This damsel is the perfection of beauty, and purity. Now you must tell her that you are divorcing her, that all has ended between you, then you must return to your kingdom. And when you enter the green stone hall, you will find on the golden pedestal, the seventh diamond girl."

Both Zain and Lalifal wept at the parting, but a prince's promise must be kept, and he turned back, deep in gloom. Even after reaching home his dark mood stayed; he would not even visit the hall to see his hard-won prize.

At last Mubarek came to him, saying, "The king your father sent you upon your quest, and Allah kept you safe for your return. Have you the right to refuse to complete the task?"

Zain saw that he had reason, and replied, "Be it so. I will end where I began, in the place of disaster, the room of the diamond girls." And he traced his steps once more to the green hall underground.

Yes, there were the six diamond girls on their pedestals, but they ringed around another, a seventh, brighter than any diamond. It was – yes! – a living girl, none other than Lalifah herself.

At first Zain could not speak for joy, until Lalifah cried: "Alas, I think you were expecting something far more precious."

"Nothing could be more precious," cried Zain. "My father was right when he said that the seventh girl was worth a thousand of the rest."

There was a sound like thunder, a lightning flash, and the Old Man of the Isles appeared before them. With a pleased smile he joined the hands of Zain and Lalifal, saying, "Since your birth, my son, you have been under my protection. It was I who devised this plan with your father, to ensure your perfect happiness. A beautiful virgin girl is worth far more than diamonds; she is the medicine of the soul." Then, as swiftly as he had come, he vanished.

The love of King Zain and Queen Lalifal never lessened throughout their long and prosperous reign. May their constancy and devotion be a lesson to all!

THE TALE OF ALA AL-DIN AND THE WONDERFUL LAMP

THERE WAS ONCE, LONG AGO, in the land of China, a .... with an only son, named Ala al-Din. But unlike his father, the boy was idle and heedless, always playing with other young rascals in the street instead of doing his studies or learning his father's trade. So when the poor man died, his widow had to spin wool and cotton, day and night, to keep the meagre home together.

By now the lad was fifteen, handsome as any young prince, with eyes like midnight pools and a skin of jasmine. One day, while he was loitering with his friends near the market square, a stranger in the robes of a dervish, but dark-skinned like a Moor, stopped and gazed intently at the boy. The man was indeed a powerful sorcerer who came from the heart of Morocco. Presently he drew aside one of the urchins, and asked him various questions.

Armed with this information he went to Ala al-Din, addressed him by name, and asked, "Are you not the tailor's son?"

"I am," said the boy, "but my father is no more." The man began a noisy weeping and took the boy in his arms.

"I am your uncle," he said at last. "I made the long journey from my home only to see my dear brother once again. Woe, woe, woe! I find now that he is dead." He put his face in his hands. "Now you, his son, must take his place in my heart."

He took ten gold dinars from a bag and gave them to the boy, saying, "Give these to your mother with my respectful greetings; say to her that I greatly desire to visit the home of my dear brother's wife and, if Allah wills, I shall come tomorrow evening." Ala al-Din ran home, full of excitement, and told his mother the news, giving her two of the dinars.

"What uncle is this?" she said. "You have no living uncle." Still, the money lulled her doubts, and next day she borrowed some cooking pots from a neighbour – all her own had been sold – and started to prepare a meal for the visitor. But when evening came the Moor arrived with a porter who carried on basket of fruits, sweet cakes and refreshing sherbet drinks.

, when the servant had been dismissed, the stranger cast himself
, kissed the floor of the home, and wept, saying, "Ah, my dear brother!"
t last, when all were seated at the meal, he told a tale of leaving to go on his
travels some thirty years before, of the riches he had acquired, and of his
growing desire to share them with his kindred. Arriving in the city, he
continued, he had known at once that Ala al-Din must be his brother's son.
Now he turned to the boy and asked, "What trade are you learning? What
work do you do to help to keep your mother and your home?"

Ala al-Din hung his head, and the mother answered bitterly, "Trade? work?
By Allah, the boy does nothing but hang about with the vagabonds of the
streets. It is beyond my power to change him and soon I shall be too old to toil
for us both, as I do now."

The Moor looked sternly at the boy, saying, "Come, you are not made to be a
wastrel. Say what path you wish to follow and I will help you as if you were my
son. If you do not wish to be a tailor, are you prepared to be a merchant, selling
fine silks and brocades? If so, once you have learnt the essentials I will open a
shop for you in the market." Then, seeing that the idea appealed to the boy,
who saw himself in bright soft clothes with a silk turban, he added, "Very
well. Tomorrow I shall take you to buy a new outfit and then begin your
training." And so the three ate and drank merrily, and the mother gave thanks
to Allah for sending an unknown relative to help her in her need.

Early next day the boy was already eagerly waiting when the stranger
arrived. First they went to buy clothing. Ala al-Din chose a striped robe of
shining silk, a white turban decorated with gold, a worked belt and boots of
bright red leather. Then they went to the bath house, and in his new attire the
boy looked like a king's son. After that, the Moor pointed out the shops and
their different wares, and manners of selling, and when evening came they

dined with a number of merchants at the inn where the Moor had taken rooms. Then he was taken home, where the mother greeted their return with joy.

"Tomorrow," the stranger told her, "I shall take him to the gardens beyond the city, where the richest merchants walk and talk together. I wish him to see how the wealthy and well-born behave, for up to now he has consorted only with street rabble." Then he embraced Ala al-Din and left.

Next morning, at first light, Ala al-Din rose, impatient to dress himself in his fine new clothes and to go on the expedition. He was restlessly waiting at the door when the Moor arrived, and they started off at once. Soon they had passed through the city gates and into the fine green outer region of handsome houses and parks and palaces and garden-encircled palaces. Ala al-Din was amazed at all he saw. Then they moved on into an open place where no one lived at all. The ground was bare; a mountain loomed in the distance. Ala al-Din was now quite weary and asked if they might rest and eat.

The Moor gave him some fruit, saying, "We still have a little further to go; then we will reach the most marvellous place in the world. You are a man now, not a child, so show your fortitude."

At last, at the end of a barren valley, they reached the foot of the mountain. Here the magician stopped and they sat down. This place of fallen rocks and withered shrubs was the goal he had been seeking, that had brought him from Morocco to the most distant East.

"Now, my son," he said, "you are about to see a garden never yet beheld by human eyes, and of a beauty no human mind could invent. But first you must collect some dry twigs and bring them here." The boy did as he was told. "Good," said the man. "Now keep well behind me." He took out a tinder box, lit the wood, opened a little package and threw a pinch of powder in the flames. A thick and writhing smoke arose; the rocks moved as if in trouble; there was a mighty crash and the earth opened, leaving a great hole like a pit. Down at the bottom Ala al-Din saw a marble slab, with a copper ring at its centre.

The boy was terrified, and picking up the skirts of his long robe he tried to run back to the city. But the Moor gave a mighty bound, seized him and slapped his face.

This was a mistake, he realised, so he said in honeyed tones, "Now, Ala al-Din, I am your father's brother, and you must do what I say. All is for your own advantage. Under that marble slab is a treasure that can make you richer than all the kings on earth. But Destiny has written that only you can grasp that copper ring and lift the stone; only you can enter the place below. If I seemed harsh with you it was only to stop you turning from the marvellous prize that fate has kept for you. Now, jump down, take hold of the ring, recite your name, your father's name and your grandfather's. Then lift."

Ala al-Din obeyed, and the slab rose easily in his hand. Below, he saw a cave in which twelve marble steps led to a red copper door.

"Go down and through that door; it will open at your coming," said the man. "You will find yourself in a great hall, divided into three. In the first you will see four mighty bronze jars filled with liquid gold; in the second, four silver jars filled with gold dust; in the third, four gold jars filled with gold pieces. Pass these by, for if you touch them you will be changed to a block of stone. At the end of the third hall you will find a garden of fruit trees, strange and glittering. Leave these also. Then you will reach a noble staircase of thirty steps, which lead to a terrace. In that terrace, between two columns, is a niche, in which is a little copper lamp. This lamp you must take, and carry it back to me by the exact way you came." He then drew a ring from his finger. "Wear this," he said. "It will guard you from all dangers. Remember, you are about to win treasure beyond all mortal dreams. Now go."

Ala al-Din forgot his fears at once and started down, through the marble door, the three halls, the garden, up the stairs and along the terrace. Yes, there was the lamp. He put it in a pocket of his robe and started back. But in the orchard of glittering trees he paused. Those fruits — what extraordinary colours they were! — transparent red and violet and orange and green and glittering white, shooting out shafts of rainbow radiance. Ala al-Din did not know that the fruits were really jewels — amethysts, emeralds, sapphires, diamonds, rubies, turquoise, topaz, every kind known to man and many unknown. Thinking them toys of coloured glass he stuffed his pockets full, as presents for his friends.

When he reached the top of the steps the Moor cried out impatiently, "Where is the lamp? Give it to me!"

"I cannot until I am outside," said the boy. "It is in my pocket, under all these heavy glass toys. Help me up, and I can give it to you." The Moor thought that Ala al-Din wished to keep the lamp; moreover, he had no intention of letting him leave the cave.

So he cried out in a terrifying voice, "Son of a dog, give me the lamp or die!" Ala al-Din was shaken by the change in the stranger's manner. Moreover, would a genuine uncle have called him "son of a dog"? So he ran back into the cave. And indeed, the man was no relative but a sorcerer who, by certain necromantic skills, had charted the exact place of the treasure cave and the lamp — but had also learnt that Fate had written the name of Ala al-Din upon

the copper ring. He raved and stamped, but by the magic laws of Destiny, he could not go down himself. He could however cause the marble slab to close again, as if over a tomb. This he did, then sped away to his own country. But we shall hear of him again.

When Ala al-Din found himself entombed in the cave he wept and cried, and thought with grief of all his idle days. Clasping his hands in despair, he chanced to rub the ring which the evil enchanter had given him. At once a great black Efreet with flaming eyes rose out of the earth, and said in a voice of thunder:

> Though I rule the wind and wave
> Of this ring I am the slave.
> Master of the ring are you.
> What you bid me, I must do.

"O, free me from this cave then," cried the boy. And there he was free in the open air. The Efreet had vanished – so, indeed, had the Moor. Ala al-Din hastened home, where his mother stopped weeping, and prepared for him all the food she could find. Then he told her his story, and showed her some of the glittering fruit, and the old copper lamp. Then he slept.

In the morning he still felt greatly hungry, but the poor woman had no more food in the house and no money to purchase more.

"We might get something for the old lamp," said the boy. He picked it up and rubbed its dusty surface. Immediately, an immense shape rose out of the air and resolved itself into a huge black Jinnee, almost filling the room. In a voice that rolled and echoed, the being intoned:

> Though I rule the wind and wave
> Of this lamp I am the slave.
> Master of the lamp are you.
> What you bid me, I must do.

The mother fell to the ground in a swoon, but Ala al-Din, who now knew something of spirits, took the lamp and said, "O Jinnee of the lamp, we would have a delicious meal." At once the Jinnee vanished, returning with a great silver tray full of golden vessels, each containing a different savoury dish, fragrant and steaming, with flasks of rarest wine, fruits, sweets and many other delicacies. Ala al-Din roused his mother, and they feasted joyfully.

But in a few days time they once again had neither food nor money to purchase any. The very thought of calling up the spirit again made the old woman shake and tremble, so Ala al-Din had the idea of taking one of the golden dishes to sell. He carried it under his robe to a jeweller, who gave him a handsome price. In this way, the boy and his mother became quite rich. But Ala al-Din took care to sell always in different places that their wealth might not be known. At one of these, having a few of the glittering fruits in his pocket, he showed the pretty toys (as he thought them) to a merchant jeweller whom he had not met before.

The man looked at them gravely, then said, "These are priceless gems. It is far beyond my means to make you an offer." Hearing this, Ala al-Din went home, and hid the precious fruits in a secret box. Wiser than he used to be, he kept the strange discovery to himself.

One day, when he was in the market place, two of the Sultan's heralds came along, clearing the path with long sticks, and calling as they went: "Merchants and citizens, your royal master, lord of the centuries, king of all kings, bids you shut your shops, go to your homes, close all doors, shutter all windows. The pearl of pearls, the Sultan's daughter Badr al-Budur is to pass these streets on her way to the bathing place. Whoever disobeys this decree may graciously have the choice of the sword, the stake or the scaffold. Allah be praised!"

Hearing this, Ala al-Din, not yet cured of all his wilfulness, daringly hid near the great door of the bathing place and so he saw the princess pass, heralded by a train of eunuchs, surrounded by her women, followed by her slaves. There before him was a fifteen-year-old damsel of peerless beauty, like the silver moon among the stars. The youth, who had thought that all women were much like his old mother under the veil, was struck by beauty for the first time in his life. Dazed and weak, he tottered home and fell in a swoon on the floor. His mother managed to rouse him, but for days he could neither eat nor sleep. At last he told her what was in his mind.

"I have seen the king's daughter," he said, "and if I do not win her in marriage, I shall most certainly die." The woman lamented, wringing her hands, repeating that he was mad. But he continued: "I have in my possession riches beyond the dreams of any mortal. Those glittering fruits are not glass toys but gems that cannot be matched on earth. You must help me by joining in the day's petitions to the king. Take this basket of jewels, but wrap it in a shawl or an apron, so people will think your offering is some small and worthless thing. When your turn comes, you must display the gems, then say what I tell you to say."

It was hard to persuade his mother to go to the palace, but at last she agreed. Holding the gems in an old shawl, she waited with downcast eyes and humble looks in the long train of petitioners. But she could not bring herself to speak, and when the allotted time was ended, she returned home. The next day she went again, and again failed to speak. Each day, urged on by her son's despair, she joined the train, but came back as she went. On the tenth day the king became curious about the old woman who came but never uttered any request, and he asked for her to be brought before him. Trembling, she asked if she might see him alone, and he pleasantly agreed, allowing only his Grand Wazir to stay. Then she told him of her son's desperate love for the royal princess.

The king was in a good humour, and after listening, said, "Now tell me what you have hidden in your shawl." But when she unfolded the cloth, so dazzling were the rays of light that flashed from the jewels that the king quickly put his hand over his eyes. Then he began to study the stones with increasing wonder.

"These are the marvel of all time," he exclaimed. "No mortal eye can ever have seen such beauty, even in dreams." He turned to the Grand Wazir. "Would you not think that the young Ala al-Din, who sends this gift, is more worthy of my daughter than any prince?" The wazir was not pleased, for he had hoped to ally his own son with the Princess Badr al-Budur.

So he said, "True, O king of the centuries. But this man, I have reason to know, is the son of a poor tailor who died in poverty. Who knows where these jewels are from? Would it not be wiser to ask for a fitting dowry before you give your daughter?"

"Riches come from Allah," said the king. "But perhaps you are right; prudence is better than haste." Then he turned to the old woman. "Tell your son," he said, "that the marriage will take place when he has sent to the palace forty great dishes of solid gold, filled with the same rare jewel-fruit; these to be borne by forty white girl slaves, each as fair as the moon, and guarded by forty black male slaves, handsome and strong. They must come in magnificent clothes and lay the jewels at my feet."

The old woman hurried home lamenting, but Ala al-Din was not disturbed. He sent her off to the market to buy food, then rubbed the copper lamp. Up rose the Jinnee, took the instructions, and a minute later the whole assembly filled the street outside the door. Then as soon as the old woman returned, Ala al-Din directed her to go straight back to the palace with the eighty slaves and the dowry. The king was at first struck dumb by the magnificence of the gift, by the speed of its arrival, the radiance of the jewels, the beauty of the girls and the evidence of wealth beyond mortal knowledge.

"What man could be more fitted to become our son-in-law?" he said at last. "Indeed, the princess is scarcely worthy of such a prize." And he turned to the old woman, saying, "From this moment, venerable mother, your son is of my royal house and line, and I wait impatiently for his coming."

The old woman hastened home and told her son what had taken place. Ala al-Din listened carefully, then withdrew to his own room where he summoned the slave of the lamp to make him ready to meet the king.

The Jinnee bowed, and there was Ala al-Din, bathed and refreshed, and perfumed, richly robed, on a splendid steed, with attendant slaves casting handfuls of gold, right and left, to the cheering crowds, as the procession made its way to the palace.

When the dazzling young man arrived the king embraced him, saying, "No monarch on earth would not wish to have you as a son-in-law, Ala al-Din. I hope indeed that your slave, the princess, will prove to be worthy of you." And he ordered the marriage contract to be made out, and it was duly signed and witnessed.

Then Ala al-Din said, "Before we meet as husband and wife, I must have a palace fit for my great love – one also that will allow the princess still to be near her father and her home. If you will grant me the open square facing your palace, I will set about building without delay."

"My son, you need not ask," said the king. "Only let it not take too many years, for I would wish to see an heir to my line before I die."

Ala al-Din smiled and went to his own apartment. There, he summoned the Jinnee and ordered a palace to be built, before dawn, of the most precious materials, with gardens and waterways.

At the first ray of morning light Ala al-Din looked out of the window, and there, facing the king's palace, was another, immeasurably nobler and more magnificent, with treasure houses, stables, pleasure gardens, orchards, and all that could be desired to make a life complete.

The Grand Wazir was devoured with rage, and said to the king: "O Sultan of the ages, the princess's husband must have the skills of a sorcerer."

But the king replied, "A man of such wealth and power might very well have a palace built in a night by natural means. Surely you are not jealous?" So the wazir thought it best to be silent, and the wedding feast took place, of a richness and wonder not even seen in dreams.

Ala al-Din did not forget his early poverty. His slaves were ordered to scatter gold each day to the poorer people, and to give the household's broken food to the destitute. He was soon beloved by all, and still more for winning a victory against rebellious tribes in the kingdom. So passed the early years of the marriage, in happiness and prosperity.

But what of the Moor enchanter, who had left the boy in the underground cave to die? For long he had been gnawed with bitterness at his failure to gain the lamp.

One day he sat himself on a square mat within a scarlet circle, sprinkled a special necromancer's sand before him, made certain marks and uttered certain spells, then cried, "O sand of knowledge, light and dark, reveal to me: where is the magic lamp? And did the boy Ala al-Din truly meet his death?" The sand moved, and returned the message that Ala al-Din was alive, he was master of the lamp and was living in a great palace, in honour and splendour, son-in-law of the Emperor of China, and heir to that great throne.

In a furious rage, the sorcerer sped off, by more than human means, to the capital of China. There he learnt that Ala al-Din was away on a hunting expedition and (from another sprinkling of sand) that his lamp had been left in the palace. Overjoyed at this news, he made his way to the coppersmiths' market and bought twelve new shining copper lamps.

He placed them in a basket and went towards the palace, calling, "New lamps for old! New lamps for old!" The people thought that he must be mad, and a crowd of hooting urchins followed him. He took no notice, but stopped just under the palace windows. The Princess Budr al-Budur heard the noise, saw her attendants at the window, and looked out too.

"He must be a madman," she said, and they all laughed merrily.

Then one of the women said, "Mistress, when I was tidying our master's room I saw an old copper lamp on a shelf. Is it your wish that we should take it to the man and see if his offer is as crazy as it seems?" The idea amused them all, and a eunuch was called to try the lamp on the stranger. At once the magician recognised it.

Trembling all over, he held out the basket of new lamps saying, "Take your choice." The eunuch selected the largest and took it to the princess who was well pleased with the exchange. A fine joke, she and her women thought.

But the old lamp was now firmly in the grasp of the sorcerer. Throwing down his remaining stock he ran until he could find a quiet alley, then rubbed the long-sought treasure. At once the Jinnee appeared, obliged to serve whatever master possessed him.

"I command you," said the Moor, "to transport the palace which you built for Ala al-Din back to my home in Morocco, together with all its contents – and myself." And this, in a flash, was done. But with it also went Ala al-Din's wife, Princess Budr al-Budur.

Next day the king went to visit his daughter as was his custom. But no palace was there, only an empty area of raw earth. He wept and tore his beard, and at last called his Grand Wazir. The old man now saw a chance to wreak vengeance on the hated Ala al-Din.

from Farizad of the Rose's Smile

"O king of the centuries!" he said. "Would you not now agree that this is a work of sorcery? Your son-in-law had the palace built in a night, and may well have removed it by the same unhallowed means. He returns today from hunting; shall I meet him, and ask what he knows of this happening?"

"No – have him dragged before me in chains!" thundered the monarch.

The order was passed to the captain of the guard, who rode out with a hundred men. But they did the deed reluctantly, for Ala al-Din was everywhere beloved. And as he was led to the palace, bound with a heavy chain, he was followed by crowds, angrily protesting at his arrest. But the Sultan's rage had mounted. Allowing Ala al-Din no chance to voice his innocence, he sent him at once to the executioner's block.

The executioner murmured to him, "Master, I do only what I must. Allah sees all!" Then he raised his sword. But the crowds began to climb the palace walls.

The king was afraid, and cried out, "Hold! I grant this wretch his life." Then the mob grew calm.

Ala al-Din now was brought to the waste land where his palace had stood; at the sight he almost swooned with horror.

"Vile imposter," said the king. "You may keep your evil palace, but if you do not return my daughter at once, your head will be the price."

Ala al-Din stood in thought. At last he said, "O king of the ages, none may escape his destiny. You have lost your daughter, but I have lost my wife, the very moon of my being. I ask only that you grant forty days for my search, for who knows how far it may take me?"

"I will grant this for my daughter's sake," said the monarch. "But beware of failure!"

So Ala al-Din wandered into the country, not knowing where to turn. At nightfall, by a river, he knelt down to wash his hands. In doing so, he rubbed the ring, whose power he had forgotten. At once the hideous Efreet rose before him.

Ala al-Din sprang to his feet, full of joy, crying out, "O my good friend, most welcome spirit, the blessing of Allah upon you! I pray you bring me back my palace and my wife."

"Master," replied the Jinnee, "that I cannot do. The power of the lamp is greater than that of the ring and I cannot undo its work."

"In that case," said Ala al-Din, "I ask you to carry me to the palace and set me below the window of my wife."

And straightaway, there he was. Allah willed, moreover, that at that moment a slave woman glanced out and uttered a great cry.

"O mistress, come! There is my master Ala al-Din in the garden just below!" The princess had been sunk in grief, but she rushed to see for herself; a slave ran down and opened a secret door, and in a moment wife and husband were clasped in each other's arms. But Ala al-Din knew that they were in mortal danger.

"Tell me," he said, "do you know what became of that copper lamp which I left on a shelf in my room?"

"Dear husband," she replied, "that is the cause of our misery." And she told of the trick by which the Moor had procured it. "Now," she said, "the sorcerer tries each day to win me for his wife, insisting that you have been beheaded as an imposter. So far I have behaved as if I were made of ice and have kept him at a distance. But his patience will not last and I fear that he will use violence. Allah be thanked that you have come."

"Tell me quickly," said Ala al-Din, "where does he keep the lamp?"

"He carries it closely about him wherever he goes."

"That is well," said Ala al-Din. "Now leave me while I devise a plan."

Once alone, he summoned the slave of the ring, saying, "O my friend and helper, are you acquainted with means of inducing a heavy sleep or swoon?"

"That is my special study and skill," replied the spirit.

"Then bring me an ounce of benj of a strength sufficient to kill an elephant." At once the Efreet brought the drug, in a little tube. Ala al-Din now called his wife, and explained his plan.

"You must deceive the Moor into thinking that you are ready to become his wife. Let the women prepare you with fine robes and perfumes; then when he seems convinced that you are about to accept his embraces, you will offer him a glass of wine, as a token, in a gold cup of honour. In the wine you must put this potent drug; it works at once. I shall come forth from my hiding place, and all shall be well."

And so it came about that the magician took the golden glass, drank and fell lifeless to the ground. Then Ala al-Din drew the lamp from within his robes, summoned the Jinnee – and in a flash the palace was back in its former place. Ala al-Din and his princess went at once to the king and told him their strange tale. The king embraced them both, and begged his son-in-law to overlook his recent hasty temper.

Then a great public rejoicing was announced; alms were given to the poor, prisoners were freed; the city was lit all night with coloured fires. All lived happily for long years after, the king and the old mother, Ala al-Din and the princess and their many children, each like the moon in beauty. And when the monarch died at last, Ala al-Din became the Emperor of China.

TALE OF FARIZAD
OF THE ROSE'S SMILE

ONCE IN THE DAYS OF long ago there was a young king of Persia, whose power, goodness, beauty and generous heart made his reign a delight to all his people. Often he would wander through the city in disguise to learn of their thoughts and needs. On one such night, passing a humble house in a poor quarter of the town, he heard the voices of girls and paused to listen.

"As the eldest," said one, "my wish is to marry the Sultan's pastrycook. Those sweets and cakes! I hear that they are the most delicious in the world. Then I could have my fill of them all day long."

The next voice said, "I would prefer to marry the Sultan's cook. Ah, those savoury dishes, whose fragrance comes from the royal kitchen! I could feast on them all day long, and grow fine and fat."

But the third and youngest refused to say her wish, until her sisters decided to wed her to one of the palace grooms. Then she murmured with downcast eyes, "My wish is to marry the king our master. Our sons would be mirrors of himself, in gifts and beauty; our daughter would be a moon of loveliness; her hair would be silver and gold; her mouth a smiling rose."

The king told his wazir to mark the house and next day sent for the three sisters, saying to them, "O young girls, this is the day when wishes of the heart are granted. Nothing is hidden from a true king. You, the eldest, shall marry our pastrycook. You, second sister, shall marry our cook." Then he turned to the third, the fairest of the three. "And you, maiden, are my queen; this palace is your palace." The weddings took place that day. But the two sisters were angered in themselves that they had not wished more highly.

Nine months later the queen gave birth to a boy of princely beauty. By her own wish her two sisters attended the birth, and they were glad to do so, for it gave them the chance they needed to do her harm. They placed the newborn child in a basket and set it afloat on a stream that ran by the palace. Then they told the king that their sister had given birth to a little dead dog, which they brought to him in a cloth.

166

Now the basket did not sink, but sailed along until it caught the eyes of the king's gardener. He pulled it ashore and was amazed to see the newborn boy within.

He took it home to his wife, saying, "Allah has sent us this gift!" And they both rejoiced, for they had no child of their own. They gave it the name Farid.

The king had been struck down with grief at the terrible news, but because of the queen's rare beauty his love revived and a year later she bore another child, a second princely boy. This time the sisters changed it for a little cat, and again pushed the infant down the stream in a basket. Again the gardener found the child and took it to his wife. They gave it the name Faruz.

In time the king forgave his queen, and a year later a third royal child was born. The sisters now placed a mouse in the bed and, as before, sent the infant down the stream. As before, the gardener rescued it and gladly took it home. This child was a girl, and they gave it the name Farizad. The unhappy king and queen knew nothing of the sisters' deceit.

"Allah has cursed me in my marriage!" cried the king. But he could not bear to sentence the queen to death, so he had her shut away in a cell in the depths of the palace. There she passed the days in tears and mourning. But the sisters were delighted and ate well, becoming fatter every day.

Meanwhile the three foundlings grew in grace and beauty, so that everyone who saw them was amazed. But the loveliest of the three was Farizad. Her hair was silver and gold, her mouth a smiling rose, and her family often called her Smile of the Rose. She read much, composed verses, and rode out fearlessly with her brothers; her manners were those of a true princess. When old age made the gardener unable to work as he had done, the king presented him with a fine house set in spacious grounds, a paradise of birds and flowers – all hidden from outside view by a high surrounding wall. In this beautiful place, away from the world, the brothers and sister lived in peace, and when Allah had taken the good old parents, the domain became their own.

One day, as Farizad sat in the garden, a slave came to tell her that an old woman at the gate wished to rest for an hour in the shade. Farizad welcomed the stranger, giving her sherbet drinks and cakes. And so they sat and talked and Farizad asked her guest if the garden pleased her.

The woman was silent for a while, then said: "Dear mistress, I have wandered far over Allah's world, and yet have never seen a place so fair. But I must tell you that it lacks three things whose presence would make it perfect, and fit for one as perfect as yourself."

"Good mother," said the girl, "tell me, what are these things?"

"Dear young mistress," said the old woman, "if the first were in your garden, all the birds of the air would flock to behold it, nightingales, larks, doves, and others scarcely known, and would sing, in homage, melodious notes beyond imagining. This marvel is the Talking Bird, Bulbul al-Hazar. If the second were in your garden, all the lutes and harps in your home would break their strings with envy. This is the Singing Tree, whose leaves make a sound so ravishing that nothing can match its sweetness. If the third were in your garden, every river and fountain, proudest torrent and smallest brook, would rise to do it honour. They would move uphill, cleave a path through cities. It is known as the Golden Water. A single drop is enough to make a fountain of golden springs that never stop rising and falling. Only this Golden Water can quench the thirst of the Talking Bird. Only the Golden Water can refresh the leaves of the Singing Tree."

"Good mother," said Farizad, "these are great marvels, but you have not told me where they may be found."

The old woman shook her head. "Strange and frightful perils lie in that path. But I will tell you this. Whoever seeks them must take the road behind the palace that leads to the Indian mountains. On the twentieth day he must say to one who sits alone, 'Where are the Talking Bird, the Singing Tree and the Golden Water?' And an answer will be given. More I will not say. Now Allah reward you for your goodness to the old and poor." With these words, she vanished.

And now Farizad lived in a waking dream, thinking only of the marvels that her garden lacked. Nothing gave her joy. Her brothers tried to find the cause of her melancholy, until at last she told them of the strange old woman's visit.

"Sister, if these wonders are what you desire, we will set off at once to find them," said Farid.

"This very day," said Faruz. But after a moment's thought they agreed that one should stay to protect their sister.

"As the older," said Farid, "it is my place to go. But take this knife, little sister. As long as the blade stays bright, all is well with me. But if it grows dull or rusty, you will know that I am in trouble, and you must call upon Allah to help me."

"Do not go!" cried Farizad, fearing for his safety. But he had already galloped off on his swiftest steed, on the road to India.

He rode for twenty days and nights, then halted on a grassy plain at the foot of a range of hills. One tree rose from the green, and beneath it sat a very ancient man. He sat there motionless holding his right hand to his forehead with the forefinger pointing upwards, as a sign of holiness.

Farid walked towards him, saying, "Greeting, O holy man, master of wisdom. I come from a far land to find three marvels: the Talking Bird, the Singing Tree and the Golden Water. Where do I go to find them?"

The old man did not answer at once. Then he said, "I know the road you want, but it holds such terrible dangers that I cannot bring myself to send you there. Turn back, my son; ride homeward. Many young men, strong and full of courage, have tried that path, but none has ever returned. Strength can do nothing against the Invisible Ones."

But his words made Farid all the more eager to face the unknown dread. "There is no power but in Allah!" he said. "My fate is my close companion. If I turn from it, it will follow me. I beg you to tell me what you know."

The old man sighed, then put his hand in a bag which hung at his waist, and drew forth a ball of red granite. This he gave to Farid, saying, "Mount your horse and throw this ahead of you. Follow it where it rolls – it will be your guide. Wherever it goes, you must follow. It will stop at the foot of the highest mountain yonder. Dismount, twine the bridle round the ball and start to climb. Do not stop until you reach the topmost peak. You will seem to be hemmed in by great black stones in frightful shapes; vast chasms will lie beneath you; weird sounds will fill your ears that do not come from howling winds or rushing waters – they are the voices of the Invisible Ones. They will shout terrible things, enough to freeze the blood of the bravest man, but you must not listen, nor ever look behind, even for a moment. If you do, you too will become a hideous black stone. If you pass all these tests – and you will be the first to do so – you will find at the top of the mountain a cage; inside is the Talking Bird. You will say, 'Greeting, O Bulbul al-Hazar! Where will I find the Singing Tree? Where is the Golden Water?' And the Talking Bird will reply. That is all I may tell you now. Be it Allah's will to preserve you."

The old man spoke no more. Farid leapt into the saddle and threw down the red granite ball. It began to roll, faster and faster, over hills and hollows, through thorn and briar; nothing could stand in its way. Though his horse could run like the wind and leap like a flash of lightning, it could hardly keep pace. Suddenly, at the foot of a steep rocky path the ball abruptly stopped. Farid dismounted, twined the bridle about the ball, and the animal stood still. Then he began to climb. But every step made him freeze with fear. He seemed hemmed in by black basalt rocks which had the shapes of twisted human bodies. The thought came to him that these were once young men like himself.

"May Allah keep me from joining them!" he murmured. Then a horrible cry came from above; others came from below; the whole air rustled with eerie sounds – the voices of the Invisible Ones.

Some, he thought, were saying, "Why do you come here? What do you want?" Some were saying, "Stop him. Kill him. Stop him. Kill him." Some were saying, "Throw him over the precipice!" But some said, "Ah, he is charming, charming. We have ways of keeping him with us. We have ways . . ." And these were the worst of all.

The climb grew steeper; Farid felt quite enclosed by unseen things. He began to tremble. A piercing cry came from just behind his ear, and he twitched his head around. At once the voices joined in a howl of triumph. Then all was still. Farid was not to be seen. But a new black stone had joined the rest. And at that moment, far below, the horse was turned to stone, and the red ball rolled back and back to the old man under the tree.

In the beautiful garden of her home Farizad took out her brother's knife, which she looked at every day. But now the blade was no longer bright – it was dull, with stains like rust.

She cried out, "O Farid, what has become of you? Why did I let you go?" And she wept and could not be comforted. Faruz made up his mind.

"Sister," he said, "it is Allah's will that I should go to find our brother, and bring you back the marvels that your heart desires." But before he rode off he gave her a string of rarest pearls, saying, "While these pearls run freely, all is well with me. But if they cling together, I will have shared our brother's fate."

On the twentieth day he reached the old man beneath his tree, greeted him courteously, and asked for help in his quest.

The old man sighed. "Your brother forgot the warning, as all have done before him. Their fate is awful beyond imagining. He was a youth of princely courage and beauty. You are his likeness. Let me beg you not to join the legion of lost ones! Turn back, before it is too late!"

But the thought of his brother made Faruz all the more determined, and at last the old man answered what he asked, and gave him the granite ball. As he began to climb the mountain, voices screamed around him, curses, threats, and words of evil flattery, but they could not make him turn.

Suddenly, he heard a desolate call: "Brother, dear brother, do not pass me by!" The voice came from behind. His glance flicked round – and at once he became a lump of basalt stone. Exactly at that moment the pearls in the sister's hand became a tight hard bunch.

She cried out, "O my poor brother, lost through my heedlessness! But I will come to your aid." She disguised herself as a young warrior, and rode off, night and day, until she reached the old man under the tree.

"Saintly father," she said, "I am seeking two young lords of shining beauty who came this way to find the Talking Bird, the Singing Tree and the Golden

Water."

"Sweet mistress Farizad," replied the sage, "I did indeed see them, and told them where the treasures might be found, and I also warned them not to make that journey. Now I fear that the Invisible Ones have caught them, as they have caught all others on that quest."

Farizad said, "You are not deceived by my boy's attire; you even know my name. These things tell me that you are a sage of special power. I come to save my brothers, whatever the danger, and nothing can make me return. I beg you to tell me how to deliver them."

The sage replied, "O Farizad, because you come on an errand of goodness I will set you on your way. But," he continued, "you will never free your brothers until you have gained the treasures. Strength is one kind of weapon, subtlety is another. You must outwit the Terrible Beings. When you reach the mountain, place in each of your ears a wisp of cotton, and climb as the others have done." And he gave her the cotton and the granite ball, and all the counsel that Allah permitted, and she set off.

As soon as she reached the mountain and started up the steep rocky slope the Invisible Ones began to howl. They screeched, they screamed, but all that came to her was a vague humming sound, and she reached the top without a turn of the head. There, in a small flat space was a gold cage set on a gold pedestal, and in it was, at last, the Talking Bird. Farizad took the cotton from her ears. There were no terrible voices; the Invisible Ones had failed. And the only sound came from the Talking Bird.

"Farizad, I rejoice that you have come; I am yours, for all time. Now you must cross to the other side of the mountain, where the great Singing Tree grows. Break off the smallest branch; it is enough. Then, turn to the west. You will see a shaft of sunlight touch a rock of turquoise blue. From that rock flows a stream as fine as a needle; it appears to be liquid gold, yet it is clear as water. Below is a little crystal phial. Fill this with the Golden Water and return to me."

Farizad found the tree and plucked a branch; it sang with a sound of indescribable beauty. Then she filled the little crystal vase and came back to the bird.

"Sweet bird," she said, "tell me how to find my brothers."

"O Farizad," said the bird, "you have come so far without fear, and fearless you must remain at what you see. Start your downward journey. But on every black basalt rock you must sprinkle one drop of the Golden Water. You will have enough. The phial is small, but however much you pour, it will always be full."

So Farizad started the long descent, with her three treasures. Every rock that she touched with the Golden Water resolved itself into a living being, a young man of noble beauty. But the most beautiful of all were her two brothers, the last to be turned into stone. At the foot of the mountain, all the horses of stone became living steeds, and the whole company rode away, with Farizad at the head. As they went, one young man, then another took a branching path away to his own country, until only the three were left. On the twentieth day they reached their home. At once Farizad took the bird Bulbul al-Hazar to the jasmine arbour. At the first note of his marvellous voice all the birds of the air, too many to name and some that none could name, flew round in homage, answering his notes with skilled responses until the air was filled with a matchless harmony.

Then Farizad went to the marble pool with its graceful fountain and dropped in a single drop of the Golden Water. Up rose a marvellous pattern of golden sprays that filled the air with the coolness of a sea cavern and the brightness of stars at night. She placed the little Singing Branch in the earth, and watered it with the Golden Water. In a few moments it had taken root and grown to the size of the parent tree itself. Its rustling leaves gave out a music so beguiling that the waters ceased to murmur, the birds were silent and the breezes paused as if they were bewitched.

It seemed now as if nothing could add to the happiness of Farizad and her brothers. But a day came when the king, out hunting, saw the young men riding in a wood. He was struck by their princely beauty, their grace and noble manner, and asked them whose sons they were.

"O most high king," they said, "we are the sons of your own old gardener, now with Allah. We live in the house which you, in your great goodness, granted him."

"Why have I never seen you?" asked the king.

"O monarch of the centuries," they replied, "we have a young sister; it was our father's wish that we should guard and cherish her, and we have no desire to do otherwise. For every day passed in our home and garden is even more delightful than the last."

The king said, "It is a miracle to find young men of such princely quality living by choice apart from the world, so free from greed and ambition. I desire to know more of you, and shall give myself the joy of visiting you in your home this very evening."

Farizad heard the news with some dismay, for she had no experience of receiving noble guests, let alone the king himself. So she turned to her never-failing source of wisdom, the Talking Bird.

"Sweet Bulbul," she said, "the king is about to honour us with a visit. How shall we entertain him? What dishes shall we serve?"

The bird replied, "Mistress, put out of your head any thoughts of rich and plenteous fare. But tell your cook to prepare a dish of cucumbers stuffed with pearls."

"Bulbul, what do you mean by this? He will think us mad!"

But the bird said only, "Do as I say. Do as I say."

When the king arrived, he asked to stroll through the garden, for it seemed to him a haven of beautiful sounds, cool fountains and refreshing leafy bowers. One by one he was shown the three marvels, and the Talking Bird called out in sweetest voice, "Welcome, king, welcome, welcome!" And all the songbirds welcomed the king in harmony.

"O house of peace!" he cried. "O magical garden! If only I could live for ever here with the beautiful children of my departed servant!" Then, as he sat on a silken couch in the jasmine bower a golden platter was brought to him. On it were the cucumbers stuffed with pearls.

Now the king had a fondness for cucumbers stuffed with rice and nuts, but what was the meaning of this? As he frowned in perplexity, he heard the voice of the Talking Bird.

"O Kusrauh Shah, Kusrauh Shah, why are you surprised? If you can believe that a Queen of Persia could give birth to a dog, a cat and a mouse, then how can you be astonished by a mere dish of pearls?"

The king hid his face in his hands and wept. Had three real children been born to him? Did the evil midwives destroy them long ago? Then the bird spoke again.

"Remove your veil, Farizad, so that your father may see your face." She raised her veil, and her hair of silver and gold fell all around her; she smiled, and her mouth was a smiling rose.

"Now look upon your sons," said the bird. And the king saw in each of them a likeness to himself. So they all rejoiced.

At last the king said, "We must go to the palace and find your mother, and tell her of all these happenings." Then the queen was brought from her lonely prison and joyfully met her daughter and two sons. The two sisters both fell dead from rage when the truth was known. But the king and queen reigned happily for many a year until Allah drew them from the world and their children took their place. Truly, a tale of marvels.

THE WONDROUS TALE OF THE PRINCESS NUR AL-NIHAR AND THE LOVELY JINNYEH

ONCE, IN OLDEN TIME, THERE was a king who had three sons, each of radiant beauty; Ali, Hasan and Husain were their names. No less beautiful was their orphan cousin, Princess Nur al-Nihar, who had grown up with them like a sister since soon after she was born. Always together in studies, sport or play, the four were inseparable. The princess had the eyes of a doe; her mouth was a rose; the narcissus and the anemone met in her delicate face, and her body was as graceful as the waving branch of a young sapling tree.

The king planned to marry her to some high neighbouring prince. But as she grew, the monarch saw that each of his sons had come to love her passionately, and longed to win her in marriage. Here was a problem!

"If I give her to some strange prince," he thought, "my sons will either kill themselves or go off to be killed in some distant war." At last an idea came to him, and he called the young men together.

"My sons," he said, "since you are all equal in my love, I cannot choose which of you should have our little princess. So I offer you this plan. Each of you must set out for a different land, and whoever brings back the rarest marvel wins her hand." The three accepted the challenge cheerfully, and set out on the same day disguised as merchant travellers, their only company a single slave for each. At first they rode together until they reached an inn at the meeting of three roads. There they shared a final meal before parting, and agreed to meet at this same place in exactly a year and a day. Then they would all appear together before the king.

The eldest, Prince Ali, travelled for several months over moor and mountain, desert and grassland, until he reached the kingdom of Bishangarh on the sea coast of India. He engaged rooms for himself and his slave in the chief inn of the city, and after resting awhile went out to explore the place. An endless crowd of pilgrims filled the streets, jostling their way to the temple. Prince Ali saw jugglers and dancing fakirs, and a great procession of elephants, as many as a thousand, painted with vermilion and gold in whirling patterns.

from The Princess Nur al-Nihar

At last he made his way to the market place whose wide and elegant streets all radiated from a central square, in which sparkling water played from a marble fountain. These streets were each devoted to a single craft or trade; they were arched with stone to keep them cool but through the fretted openings daylight came like stars. Everywhere little boys were selling roses and jasmine flowers; their sweet scent filled the air. Yet though the wares around were so rich and varied, the prince could not find among them the marvel that he sought.

As he paused in a sheltering doorway, a man passed by with a little carpet folded over his arm. A few steps away from the prince, he stopped, turned his head to the left, to the right, and called in a ringing voice, "Good people! I offer a bargain! Unique! Here is a carpet, a special prayer carpet – and for no more than thirty thousand gold dinars! A bargain of bargains!"

"What an extraordinary land!" thought Ali. "Thirty thousand gold dinars for a prayer carpet! Is it a joke?" But as the man continued to cry his offer perfectly seriously, the prince beckoned him to come and show his wares. Immediately the man spread out the rug before him. Ali looked at it carefully but it seemed in no way unusual.

"By Allah," he said, "how can this thing be worth that enormous price?"

The man smiled. "Indeed," he said, "I am asking less than its worth. I was told to sell it for not less than forty thousand dinars, but I am starting at a lower sum. I must tell you that this carpet has a rare magic. Whoever sits on it will be carried along, as swift as thought, to any place of his wish. Nothing stands in its way, neither wall, nor tower, nor loftiest mountain. Tempests halt, doors fly open, such is its power. But I see that it is not for you. Now I shall leave this place."

He began to fold up the carpet, but Prince Ali called out urgently, "O carpet-seller, stop, stop! If what you say is true I will pay you forty thousand gold dinars and a further thousand for yourself. But first I must have proof of the miracle."

"First I must see the forty thousand dinars," said the man. "Also the further thousand."

"They are in the place of my lodging, the chief inn of this city," said the prince. "Let us walk there directly."

"The chief inn is at some distance from here," said the man. "But if we seat ourselves on the carpet we need not walk." No sooner were they seated side by side, and the wish made, than the prince found himself in his own apartment with the man beside him, a satisfied smile on his face. He could not even tell whether they had flown over the roofs or along the ground.

Convinced now of the carpet's worth, the prince said to his slave, "Give this excellent fellow forty purses each of a thousand gold dinars, and a further purse for himself." So this was done.

But as he left, the man turned and said, "Master, I must tell you this. When the need is met, the power wanes." And he was gone.

The prince said, "No matter. This wondrous thing will serve the need and win me the lovely Nur al-Nihar." And he rejoiced. Then, when the sale was over and the man had gone, the prince said, "Praise be to Allah! My quest is done. This marvel will surely win me the lovely Nur al-Nihar."

What of the second brother, Prince Hasan, the taker of the middle road? He, after many leagues of lonely travelling, found and joined a caravan of merchants on their way to Persia. They journeyed far, over moor and mountain, desert and fresh green plain, until they reached the city of Shiraz. There, the prince sought out the chief inn of the place, rested there for the night, and went out early next day. The market place was a dazzle of light and colour. The finest silks and other rich stuffs were displayed for sale, as were paintings, carvings, and ornaments of rarest woods and metals. Everywhere merchants were shouting their wares – all but one, who was silent.

This venerable man, with the looks of a sage, was walking slowly and solemnly, holding in his hand an ivory tube as if it had been a king's sceptre. Hasan felt drawn to the man, and was filled with desire to know the meaning of the tube.

When he was only a few steps away from the prince, the man stopped, and cried out in a great voice, "O fortunate purchasers! I have here a bargain! Only thirty thousand gold dinars for this wonder! The maker is dead, and will never make another! Only thirty thousand dinars! A bargain of bargains!" The prince was astonished that so much should be asked for so slight a thing, and he asked a nearby merchant if the man was mad.

"No indeed," said the man, "he is both honest and wise, and is employed only for highly important business. You need not doubt that the tube is worth that price at the very least. Come into my shop and I will bring him here."

So the merchant brought in the man, and said to him, "This honourable stranger cannot understand why you ask thirty thousand dinars for a little tube, and indeed it is a high price. Tell us what is its special quality?"

The old man said, "Your astonishment does not surprise me, but when you know the secret of the tube you will have no more doubts. Indeed, I am ordered to take not less than forty thousand dinars, but I start at a lower sum. Notice the crystal fitted at one end. Whoever holds the tube to his eye and looks through the glass will see whatever he wishes to see, be it anywhere in the world."

"If this is true," said Hasan, "I will give you forty thousand dinars and a further thousand for yourself, but I must test it first." He took the tube and wished – what else would he have wished ! – to see the Princess Nur al-Nihar. At once he saw her in the great baths, laughing among her slaves. So great was his longing for the damsel that he hastened to take the old man back to the inn and pay what he had promised.

As he left, the vendor turned and said, "Master, I must warn you that when the need is met, the power wanes."

This did not trouble Hasan, for, he told himself, "It will win me the princess, and I have no other desire." And he rejoiced in the thought that the prize for the greatest marvel must be his.

And so we come to the youngest, Prince Husain. His road led by many wanderings to the fabled city of Samarkand. On the morning after his arrival he wandered through the market place, watching the streams of people, the buyers and the sellers. Suddenly he saw a man standing apart with a strange fruit in his hand. It seemed to be an apple, but it was as large as a melon, red on one side and gold on the other, wonderful to see. Husain asked the price.

"I am starting the sale at thirty thousand gold dinars," said the man, "but I am not allowed to sell for less than forty thousand."

"You are joking," said Husain.

"You may think so," said the man, "but not when you know the virtue of this fruit. It is the life work of a great physician, and contains the essence of all his knowledge. There is no kind of sickness or disease, plague, fever, leprosy, or the approach of death itself, that cannot be cured by inhaling the wonderful odour of this apple. If you wish for proof, let us look for a sick person in this market place." As they spoke, they saw a porter pass the shop, carrying in a basket on his back an aged man, bent, blind and paralysed. The broker held the apple to the old man's nose and at once he leapt from the basket, straight and young, with bright eager eyes.

"Do you doubt any longer?" asked the broker. The prince hastened to take him to the inn, paid him forty thousand dinars and a thousand for himself.

Just as he left, the old vendor said, "Master, I have to tell you that when the need is met, the power wanes."

But Husain said, "That does not trouble me," and rejoiced to think of the prize that he must win.

And so, on the appointed day the three brothers met and embraced and told of their adventures. Then each brought forth his treasure, anxious to show the marvel he had found. First, as the oldest, Prince Ali unrolled his carpet, seated himself upon it, told his brothers to join him and wish themselves at the other end of the world then, after a few minutes pause, to return. Swifter than thought they were there, and back, and were quite amazed. Then the Prince Hasan brought forth his ivory tube and explained its powers. He handed it to his brother Ali, who declared a wish to see the Princess Nur al-Nihar. But as he looked his face grew pale.

"Brothers!" he cried out. "Our toil has been in vain! Our sweet cousin lies near to death among her weeping women; nothing can save her."

But Prince Husain, the third and youngest, said, "Have no fear. The apple that I bring cures all ills, and turns away death itself. If we ride upon your carpet, no time will be lost."

In a moment they were in the room where the princess lay, surrounded by weeping attendants. Seeing the princes appear as if from nowhere, the women screamed and ran about wildly. But first one, then another recognised the princes and stood still. Now Hasan held the apple to the face of the princess, and as she breathed the fragrant odour she smiled, sat up, and all sickness fled away. The brothers told how each had a part in restoring her, and she thanked each one, rejoicing in their return.

But now came the testing time, when the king would judge the treasures, and the princes learn their fate. The monarch listened to each of his sons, and marvelled at their adventures, and at the three miraculous gifts they had brought. How could he choose between them?

At last he said, "They are all great rarities, and to raise one above the others is not possible. Have we not seen that each played an equal part in saving your fair cousin? So I must set you another contest. Come to the green plain beyond the city, each of you bringing a bow and a single arrow. He whose arrow is found to have gone the furthest will have the princess for his bride."

In the space of an hour they were all assembled: the king, the princes, and members of the palace guard as watchers and witnesses. First the oldest of the sons, Prince Ali, shot his arrow. It went so far that it reached the most distant edge of the plain. Then Prince Hasan took his turn. His arrow sped exactly over that of his brother and landed just beyond. But the arrow of the youngest prince flew on so far that it could not be found, though the search went on until nightfall.

Next morning the three young men were called into the royal presence. "My sons," said the monarch, "I have thought long, and the answer now is clear. You will recall my words: 'He whose arrow is *found* to have gone the furthest . . .' No one knows where Husain's arrow fell, so it must be Allah's will that Hasan wins the hand of our fair princess." The news was announced through the kingdom, and the wedding took place with magnificent feasting

and celebrations. And there we leave the Prince Hasan and his bride.

But what of the other two brothers? Neither went to the wedding or the feasts. Ali the oldest, feeling that hope and happiness were gone, renounced his place as heir to the throne, put on the robes of a dervish and withdrew from the world to study spiritual matters. Prince Husain had other plans. The prize, he felt, should rightly have been his, and to prove this he set out to find the arrow. He followed the direction it had taken, walking for an hour or more, but he saw no sign at all. At last he found the way barred by a pile of rocks. And there was the arrow, which had struck the wall and rebounded. He was amazed. How could it have gone so far and still kept all its force? Here was a mystery!

He began to study the rock to see what impact it had made, and saw on the stone what seemed to be the outline of a door. At his touch it swung open, solid and thick, and without thinking, Husain stepped inside. At once the wall closed behind him; try as he would he could not find even a crack to mark where he had entered. He seemed to be in a dark passage, so he felt his way along until he saw a faint light ahead. The light grew bright; it was daylight! And he stepped into a stretch of fresh green grass, starred with flowers. It circled round a glittering palace, unearthly in its strange magnificence. As he gazed in wonder, a lady came out of the palace followed by a group of damsels. She had the air of a queen, and her beauty was beyond imagining. Her hair fell to the ground like a dark and shining waterfall; her silken robes changed their mysterious colours as she moved.

She stopped before the young man and smiled very courteously, saying, "Welcome Prince Husain!"

The prince bowed low, marvelling that she knew his name.

She read his thoughts, for she said at once, "Wait. Later you will learn what you wish to know." She led him back to the palace, and into a hall cooled by refreshing fountains. Then, sitting beside him on a silken couch, she spoke.

"Charming Prince Husain," she said. "I am a princess of the Jinn, and have known you from your birth. My destiny is linked with yours. It was I who caused the carpet to be sold in Bishangarh, the ivory tube in Shiraz and the magic apple in Samarkand. And because I felt that you deserved a wife more marvellous even than your cousin, I caused your arrow to fly out of reach, and made you follow its course, to come to me, as you have done. If it be your wish, my hand is yours, and untold happiness." The fair spirit lowered her eyelids and waited for Husain to reply.

The enraptured prince perceived how much this lovely girl surpassed his cousin in beauty, mind and riches, and he bowed before her, saying, "Princess of the Jinn, queen of my heart, how can so rare and wondrous a being love a mere human? Do you not risk the anger of your mighty father?" And he kissed the hem of her robes.

But she raised him up, and said, "I am my own mistress, Husain. I allow no spirit of earth or air to direct what I may do. Is it your wish – or not – to marry me and love me all your life?"

He replied, "Beautiful princess, I would give my life for one day in your company, even as your slave."

To this she said, "Then I take you for my husband, and so, by the practice of the Jinn, we are wed."

She took him into a second hall, perfumed with amber and incense unknown to man, and lit with a thousand candles. And they sat down to a wedding feast of rare and subtle delicacies on golden dishes, while the sweet sound of singing voices filled the scented air. When the feast was over they moved to a third and even loftier hall, where, to the sound of unseen music, dancers floated before them, light as air, drifting at last, like dreams, or waving flowers, up a crystal staircase that led to the bridal room. So Husain came to know that to have for wife a princess of the Jinn brings joy beyond human imagining. Day after day his love increased. But when six months had passed, he felt a desire to see his royal father, and let him know that he was alive, and blessed by fortune. Seeing how much his heart was moved, the lovely spirit gave him a magnificent horse and an escort of twenty armed riders, and many handsome gifts.

"Go, in Allah's name," she said. "But remember, tell no one that you are married to a daughter of the Jinn, nor where we dwell, nor the way to reach this place. Our love is so strong that I know you will return." The prince readily gave his word.

When Husain reached his father's palace the king was overjoyed. He had feared that disappointment had driven his son to madness or to death. The prince spoke of the happiness he had found, explaining that he had sworn an oath not to reveal where he now lived. But he promised to visit his father every month. Three days later he set out for home, and his joy was as great as his bride's to be together again. Each month thereafter he kept his vow and returned to see the king. But the chief wazir and certain advisers were jealous of the young man's seeming wealth and grandeur, and they cunningly worked to set the father's mind against his son.

"O king of the centuries," they said, "do you think your son has forgotten your judgement on the arrow? He did not renounce the world like his brother. Why is he not travel-stained? He must be planning rebellion from a place within the city."

The king was perplexed, not knowing what to think. So he sent for an old woman who dabbled in sorcery, and asked her to wait near the rocky wall which bounded the plain of the arrow contest. For Husain had said that where the arrow had fallen, he had found his destiny. The old hag hid and watched and saw the whole train of horses and riders vanish through the stone. But she could find no door, for the entrance was visible only to men who pleased the Jinn princess, and from all women it was hidden. Still, the sorceress thought of a stratagem. The next month when Husain returned from the court he found near the rock a poor old woman moaning upon the ground. The goodhearted prince asked his attendants to carry her within for care and treatment.

Once inside, the wicked one nosed around, and when it was time to announce herself cured, she asked to see the mistress of the palace to give her thanks. This done, she scurried back to the king with a full account of all that she had seen. The evil counsellors advised the king to imprison Husain for life, but the old woman suggested that he should first obtain as much as he could of the riches in his son's possession. The king agreed, and asked the prince if he could bring a token of his goodwill – a marquee tent, perhaps, to use when hunting or at war.

The prince told his wife of the wish, and she who had seen well enough through the old woman's wiles, replied, "By Allah, I am only sorry that he asks for such a trifle. But leave it to me; I will arrange the gift."

She summoned her treasure-guardian, a Jinnee of extraordinary appearance. Only a foot and a half in height, he had a beard thirty feet long, and his head was twice the size of his body. His strength was that of fifty human men, and he liked to carry a huge iron bar in case of need. The princess told him to take the finest tent from the treasure house, fold it into a tiny packet, and follow Prince Husain to his father's palace. This he did, and when the prince called him to present the gift, he opened it out, and as it grew and grew, he skipped among the evil counsellors, not forgetting the old woman, beating and driving them out with his iron bar.

Then he turned to the king. "O foolish monarch," he said, "I spare you because you are weak, not wicked, but you are no longer worthy to reign. My master Prince Husain and my mistress of the Jinn are now the king and queen." The old king hurried off and joined his hermit son, Prince Ali, in his far retreat. But Prince Hasan and Princess Nur al-Nihar, who had taken no part in the plot, were given the finest province of the new king's empire. Many were the offspring of both brothers; long and joyful and prosperous were their married lives. Wonderful are the ways of Allah!

THE TALE OF THE TWO LIVES OF SULTAN MAHMUD

THE STRANGEST OF TALES IS told of the Sultan Mahmud, who ruled the land of the Nile in days long gone. All the gifts that fortune can grant to mortal man seemed to be his; youth, beauty, power and glory, wisdom in ruling, loyal friends, damsels of melting loveliness, exquisite landscapes wherever he looked, pleasures of his choice. Yet a nameless dejection and melancholy weighed him down. He would sit alone, desiring only death.

One day, when in this mood of dire depression, he was seated in a room which had four windows, each facing a different direction. The view from each was of wondrous beauty, but such was his despair that he could think only of the uselessness of being.

He did not even look up when his Grand Wazir came to him, saying, "O lord of time, an ancient holy man from the most distant west has come to our gates and desires to speak with you. It may be that he will have the power to disperse your royal grief."

The Sultan faintly nodded, and the wazir led in a being that seemed more of a wraith or shadow than a living man. If he *were* a living man, thought the Sultan, he was one that had known the earth not for a mere hundred years but for centuries. His skin was parchment over a cage of bones; his beard grew to the ground, but his dark eyes burned with a living fire which could see through all hypocrisy and deceit. They pierced the young man's soul.

This ancient sage neither bowed nor wasted words, but said straightaway, "Peace be with you, Sultan Mahmud. I am sent by my brothers, the saints of the distant west, to bring light into your darkness, to open your eyes, awaken your mind, and to make you aware of the gifts you hold from Allah – and can lose." Then he gripped the hand of the young king and took him to one of the four windows. "Open it!" he said. "Now look."

The young man did as he was told – and saw with horror a vast army riding down from his own mountain citadel, waving naked swords. Already the leaders were climbing the walls and calling for Mahmud's death. The air shook with noise and violence, and the Sultan, watching aghast, realised the horrible truth, that his trusted men had come to take over his kingdom.

"Allah knows all!" he cried. "This is the hour of my doom!"

At once the old man shut the window, then opened it again. The young man looked, amazed. No angry army was to be seen, only the mountain citadel, quiet and peaceful, its minarets clear against the noonday sky. Before he had time to speak he was led to the second window, overlooking the city.

"Open," ordered the sage, "and see what you will see." Again Mahmud obeyed – and leapt back in terror. The whole of his fair city, the mosques, the domes, the terraces, all the great parks and noble buildings were being devoured by roaring flames. And as he gazed, the sheet of fire raced towards the palace. The Sultan buried his head in his arms.

"Allah alone is great!" he said. "Tomorrow the fairest city on earth will be blackened waste; desert will join desert again – and all who lived here, all their works and thoughts, will have vanished utterly, with no memorial."

Then the old man put out his hand, closed the window, and reopened it. The fire might never have been. There, before the Sultan's eyes, was the lovely city of Cairo, its graceful buildings and flowering trees.

Now he was led to the third window and made to open it. This one looked over the Nile, a scene which always refreshed the Sultan's mind. Yet what was this? The river had broken its banks and great tides advanced on the city. The swollen waters had almost reached the palace; they were lapping against the walls; the lower storeys were beginning to melt and crumble; the whole place was about to topple over – he could feel the grinding lurch. Then the old man closed the window. He opened it again – and the flood might never have been. Down below the river flowed on, in peaceful shining strength.

And now the king was made to open and gaze through the fourth of the windows. This one looked over the great green plain beyond the city gates, a paradise of running streams, flowering bushes, singing birds, orange and lemon trees, roses and jasmine and sweet herbs. But now to his shocked eyes it had become a scorched and desert waste, crawling with snakes, the starving hyenas and jackals vainly seeking shade from the aching rocks. Then the old man closed the window and opened it – and there was the plain stretching to the horizon in all its flowering freshness and loveliness.

The Sultan did not know if he was in a nightmare dream, or if his mind was crazed, or if some spell was upon him. But before he could voice his questions, the old man led him to a little fountain in the room.

"Bend down and look!" ordered the sage. The young man did so, and his mentor forced his head into the water.

He found himself at the foot of a mountain which overlooked the sea. He still wore his crown and royal robes, but they were wet from shipwreck. A group of rough labouring men stood laughing and pointing at him. A mounting rage against the old saint filled Mahmud.

"Vile enchanter!" he cried. "When Allah returns me to my kingdom, you will be fitly punished." He walked towards the grinning peasants and said, "I am the Sultan Mahmud!" But they laughed all the more. At length, one who seemed the leader or chief among them, came up to him, took off his crown and royal robes and tossed them into the sea.

"Poor fellow," he said kindly. "You must have been hot and uncomfortable in all that. Come, I'll give you some proper clothes." And Mahmud was obliged to put on a coarse blue cotton robe, and a head covering of drab felt. "Now, come and work for us, stranger," the man went on, "for whoever does not work must starve."

"I do not know how to work," said Mahmud.

"Then you must do the work of an ass," said the man, "for that needs no knowledge. You can start by taking burdens."

The day had come to an end, and the peasants loaded on their "ass" their spades and rakes and pickaxes – an enormous load. Hooting children kicked at Mahmud as he staggered along, and tormented him with sharp sticks. He was shut for the night in a dusty old stable, smelling of mould and dirt; and in the morning he found that he was indeed an ass, with long ears, hoofs and tail. First, they tried him for ploughing. But when he was rebellious, they beat him and gave him to the miller who blindfolded him and made him turn the mill, without rest, day after day. This made him almost blind, perpetually giddy, and tortured by a migraine in his head. All he had to eat was mouldy beans.

For five years he suffered this slavery and abuse, the hunger, the curses and the whip. But one day the chain broke, and he found himself once more in human shape. He looked around; he was in the market place of an unknown city, and he was weary to the bone, as if he had walked a long distance. An elderly merchant invited him to rest in his shop.

"You are a stranger, I see," said the man. "Are you staying long in our city?"

"Wherever there is other food than mouldy beans," said Mahmud, "I will happily stay."

The merchant laughed. "Oh, good food is plentiful here, as you will find. But first the law obliges young male newcomers like yourself to do what I shall now explain to you. You must stand outside the hammam at that corner yonder, and as each woman comes out you must ask if she is married or single. If she is single, you will become her husband instantly: such is the law of the land. But it is also the law that you must not omit one woman from your questioning. The penalties are grave."

In his life as a Sultan, Mahmud had encountered only the most exquisite of damsels, and he cheerfully took his place at the hammam door. Straightaway a lovely girl of no more than thirteen years came down the steps.

"Ah, this will mend all my woes!" said Mahmud to himself. So he bowed, and said, "Dear young mistress, are you married or single?"

"I was married last year," she replied, and went her way.

Next came a hideous old woman whom he could scarcely bear to look upon. Should he risk the question? It was an even chance so, trying not to see her as he spoke, he asked, "Are you married or single?"

"I am married, handsome one," said the crone, looking as though she could devour the young man.

"I congratulate you, worthy aunt," he said and silently offered a prayer to Allah on behalf of her unlucky spouse.

Then a third woman came through the door, a monument of old age and ugliness, who seemed to him a hundred times more foul and disgusting. Only the hope of luck and the fear of he knew not what dire penalty made him speak at last.

Faintly he put the question: "Are you married or single?"

"Single, O beloved," she replied, and advanced with a frightful leer. The dreadful creature was about to cover his face with kisses when, with an enormous effort, he jerked up his head.

And there he was, in his own palace, with the Grand Wazir on his right hand, and the ancient saint on the left. A lovely girl, one of his favourites, was handing him a cup of sherbet on a golden salver. He was a Sultan! – not a homeless shipwrecked pauper, not a poor tormented ass, not the wretched husband of a monster. All his long experience had lasted only a few moments while his face was in the water. How pleasant to be himself, a Sultan, young and free, with endless power of choice.

Then the old man spoke. "Sultan Mahmud," he said, "as I told you before, I was sent to you by my brothers, the saints of the distant west, to make you aware of the gifts which Allah has showered upon you. Has my journey been in vain?" And he vanished – whether by door or window none can tell. Mahmud fell on his knees, thanking the saint again and again. Those visions! They might have been real! He was aghast. But now all self-pity and gloom had flown away; happiness filled his heart and the wish to give joy to others.

Such were the two lives of Sultan Mahmud, the one which was, and the one which seemed to be, but – thanks to Allah – was not.

THE TALE OF ALI BABA
AND THE FORTY THIEVES

ONCE, LONG AGO, IN PERSIA, there lived two brothers, Kasim and Ali Baba. Their father was a poor man, and had nothing to leave them when he died. But the boys had different characters. Kasim, the older and sharper-witted, having no taste for toil and poverty, married a wife who liked his looks and brought enough money to set him up as a merchant with a fine shop in the market place. Ali Baba, the younger, however, was content to live very modestly and work hard at a humble job; he was a woodcutter. But he was so careful and industrious that, after a time, he was able to buy an ass, then two, then three, to carry the faggots back to the town. He also acquired a wife, though she brought no dowry, and they lived together happily enough and had both sons and daughters.

One day, while he was cutting wood in the forest, a strange turn came to Ali Baba's fortunes. He heard the sound of galloping horses coming towards him – tirump! tirump! – and being of a cautious nature, he climbed into a high tree where he could watch unseen. A wise move, this! For, a few minutes later, a villainous band of riders reached the clearing. They were frightful to look at, with swarthy faces, rolling eyes, forked black beards and long moustaches – brigands and outlaws every one of them. At a signal from the chief, they all dismounted, fastened their horses to trees, took off the heavy saddle bags, slung them over their shoulders, and filed towards a nearby rocky mound.

Then the chief cried out the strange words, "Open Sesame!" At once the sheer rock gaped before them, and, one by one, they passed into the hill. Ali Baba counted them as they went; there were forty in all. When the last was inside, the captain followed, uttered from within the words, "Shut, Sesame!" and the rock closed, leaving no crack or seam.

Presently the rock face opened; the brigands emerged in single file, but now with empty saddle bags on their shoulders. When all were through, the chief again pronounced, "Shut Sesame," the rock closed, and off they rode. Ali Baba watched with staring eyes; but even when they had gone it was an hour or

more before he dared to climb down from his tree. And yet, once he was on the
ground, curiosity – and the call of Destiny – gave him a courage that he did not
know he possessed. He tiptoed to the rock, turning his head from left to right,
right to left, then, with a timorous boldness, uttered the words used by the
robber chief: "Open Sesame!" The secret door yawned open! And facing him
was no cellar of darkness but an airy gallery leading to a splendid hall,
cunningly lit from hidden slits in the roof.

And the light fell on treasure, heaped and piled everywhere in that splendid
hall. No man, no monarch even, can have beheld such treasure: the gleaming
gold, the glittering jewels, the delicate work of royal craftsmen, the lustrous
silks and sumptuous tapestries – much of it still unsorted – brought in by
generations of robbers over who knows how many centuries. Ali Baba stood
transfixed.

At last he cried, "Allah, who knows all, has chosen a humble woodcutter to
pluck this fruit that he may feed his family; thus may crime be turned to
innocent uses!" Then, with no further doubt or scruple, he set about filling
with gold coins as many bags as he felt that his animals could carry. He used
the magical formula to open and close the door, disguised the sacks with a
covering of brushwood, and took them home, calling to his wife to help with
the unloading. But it soon became clear to the poor woman that she was
moving not faggots of wood but coins. Had her husband joined a robber band?

"Woe upon us!" she cried out. "We are all undone!"

"Foolish woman!" said Ali Baba. "All that I have here comes by the will of
Allah. Listen and you shall hear." And he told of the strange happenings.

"Now," he said, "we must quickly bury our find; the neighbours must not know. For if the brigands come to learn of this our lives will all be lost."

So the wife's lamenting turned to cries of joy, and she was seized with a wish to know exactly how much gold they had acquired. "O husband," she said, "first let me borrow a measure. And while you are digging a hole to bury the coins, I shall be counting them, so that we shall know our sons' inheritance and our daughters' dowries."

Ali Baba knew that to argue with a woman was a waste of time. "Go quickly then," he said, "but mind – not a word of this to anyone."

"You may be sure of that," said she, and hurried off to the wife of Kasim, her husband's wealthy brother, and asked to borrow a measure. Kasim's wife, a mean and vulgar woman, who had always ignored her humble relatives, would have refused the loan if she had not been puzzled and curious. What could the wretched creature want it for? She lent the thing, but first she rubbed some suet on the underside, a ruse which was to have fearful consequences, as you will see.

When Ali Baba's wife reached home she promptly started to count the coins, making a mark on the wall for each full measure. After some hours, this was done, and, as she did not wish to offend her haughty sister-in-law, she went to return the loan without delay. The wife of Kasim eagerly took the measure, and as soon as she was alone she turned it over. There she saw, not grains of wheat or barley, but a dinar of bright gold. Her face turned yellow and purple; her eyes became pins; her lips were pressed as thin as the blades of knives. Then she opened them to scream with rage. How, she thought, does a beggarly woodcutter come to have so much gold that it has to be shovelled out like corn? Unable to wait, she sent her servant to fetch Kasim from work. Scarcely had he arrived when she pushed the dinar under his nose and screeched out a garbled tale of his brother's hidden wealth.

When Kasim grasped what the woman was saying, he turned quite saffron yellow from jealousy and set off for his brother's home. Not even pausing for greetings (though years had passed since they had met) he poured forth anger and abuse, saying, "O louse on a beggar's rags, how dare you pretend to be poor and humble when you have to measure your gold by the bushel? Why have you kept the truth from your own kinsfolk?" And he held out the measure with the dinar still stuck beneath.

Ali Baba was troubled by Kasim's displeasure. "Brother," he said mildly, "I think you forget how many years you have turned away from myself and my family, as if you had no time for a humble woodcutter. However, we come from the same parent and I gladly offer you half of what I possess." Then he related the story of the robbers' cave and what he had found within. But the greedy Kasim was not content with the offer. Far better, he thought, to collect the goods in person. So he insisted on knowing all the details.

"If you give me false directions," he added, "I will report you to the law as an accomplice of thieves." So Ali Baba gave his brother all the facts he possessed. Without a word of thanks, Kasim rushed off to prepare for the expedition.

At the first gleam of dawn he set out for the hill with ten mules, each carrying great wooden boxes and sacks. Reaching the rock he tied the mules to trees with trembling hands. Then, shaking with greed, he cried out, "Open Sesame!" and a hole yawned in the rock. He stepped within and, using the magic words, he closed the gap behind him so that no one else could see and share the loot. If only he had known the doom contained in that one act! For when the greedy fellow had crammed sack after sack full of treasure, with every intention of coming back for more, and had staggered to the entrance place, he was so bemused that the words had left his mind.

"Open Barley!" he called hoarsely. The door stayed shut. What was wrong? It was a grain of sorts, he knew. He tried once more.

"Open Wheat! Open Oats! Open Rye!" Nothing happened. The name that mattered never returned to his mind. Now he no longer cared about the gold, only about escape; he screamed, he wailed, he rushed to and fro like a madman.

The wretched Kasim was still there, running up and down, beating his head against the wall, when the forty thieves returned. Seeing the waiting mules their minds were already inflamed with suspicion; they leapt from their horses and rushed with naked swords towards the rock. The captain uttered the two essential words and in they went. They saw the leather sacks all filled with gold; they saw Kasim. And so he met his end.

The men wiped their swords and sat for a while to determine what to do. Never again must a stranger learn the secret of their den. But since they were men of action rather than thought, they did not waste much time. They decided to cut the body into six parts, laying three on one side of the door, three on the other; that should scare any further predators! Then they rode off in search of yet more plunder.

Now when night fell and Kasim had not returned, his wife became filled with dread. She rushed to the house of Ali Baba and asked him for his help.

"If only he had let me be his guide," said the kindly brother, and at the first light of dawn he started out for the rock. A terrible stench assailed his nose; there were ominous trickles of blood in the dusty earth. Fearfully, he uttered the words, "Open Sesame!" and the door yawned open to reveal – O horrid sight! – his brother's body, chopped into several parts.

One thought now filled his mind, to give the corpse an honourable burial. So he carefully gathered the portions into sacks, loaded them on his asses, and very discreetly took them into the courtyard of his home. First he went to his sister-in-law, and told her of his frightful discovery.

"But if the nature of his death is known," he added, "the robbers will track us all down and our doom is sealed. However, if you keep a shut mouth and do just as I tell you, all will be well."

Now in Ali Baba's house was a slave girl, Morgiana. She had lived there since her infancy, and the couple had brought her up as if she were their own daughter. Their goodness had its reward. For not only was she helpful in every way, never tired, never out of humour, she was also quick in wit, full of invention, a solver of difficulties, yet discreet beyond the nature of womankind – and a pleasure to behold. Ali Baba called this damsel to him, with his finger on his lip, and told her all that had passed. Then he asked her to apply her mind to the problem: how to announce the death and burial of Kasim without revealing the manner of his end. At once the intelligent girl devised a plan. She went to the apothecary's shop, sighing and lamenting, and asked for a special potion known to help serious ailments.

When the man asked who was ill, she said, "Alas, alas, my master's brother lies mortally sick; his face is yellow; his eyes are dull; his skin is cold as a toad; a rattling sounds in his throat. Your potion is our last hope."

The chemist gave her the medicine, but next day she was back again, weeping noisily, and asking for another potion, one to be used only when life had well-nigh gone. As she returned through the streets, she spread the news of the illness to all the women around; as she intended, the gossip took root and grew. So no one was surprised to hear soon after that Kasim was no more; the fever had carried him off. But a problem still remained. If the body was seen to be hacked into several parts, belief in a natural death might be quite hard to sustain. And the news would certainly reach the robber band. So the thoughtful girl went to a cobbler's shop in a run-down part of the city where she and the family were unknown.

First, she put a gold dinar into the old man's hand. Then she said, "We have great need of your skills, good sir. The task may perhaps seem strange, but have no fear. When you have done what is to be done, another gold dinar will be yours. Only – you must agree to be blindfolded while I take you to and from the place. All that you are to do is a little matter of stitching. Your conscience can be clear."

It was long since the old man had seen so handsome a coin, and he allowed

from Ali Baba and the Forty Thieves

himself to be led through the streets, a scarf over his eyes, to the cellar of Ali Baba's house. There, he was put to the task of sewing together the several portions of the body, and this he did. Morgiana led him back to his shop, giving him a second and a third dinar, and the old man, though wondering much, was well content. Home again, the invaluable girl washed the body according to the rites and wrapped it round in shrouds. The funeral ceremony was well attended, the Imam himself appearing, for Kasim was known to be a man of substance. As for the widow, Ali Baba kindly took her in as his second wife, and this was approved by all.

But what of the forty thieves? Not only did they find the body gone, but they realised, for the first time, that gold had been taken from their coffers.

The captain called the men together, saying, "Someone in this city knows our secret, so carefully kept for centuries by our ancestors. This villain must be tracked down and destroyed. How to find him? First, we will listen for news of one recently buried, whose body was in six pieces. For this purpose, a member of our band will go about discreetly, disguised as a dervish or travelling merchant, and give his ear to gossip. But beware! Whoever undertakes this mission must have both wit and courage, for if he fails, his life will be the forfeit. In a crisis such as this, there are no second chances. Who is the first to offer?"

In spite of the warning, a sturdy thief at once volunteered. He set out at dawn, and on the outskirts of the city passed the shop of the cobbler, who began work earlier than most.

"Honest friend," said the seeming dervish, "you have nimble fingers for one of your years."

The cobbler, delighted with this praise from the holy man, replied, "O dervish, thanks be to Allah, I can still thread a needle; what is more, I can even sew together the six parts of a dead body, without the aid of light."

The robber almost swooned with joy. "O master of your honoured craft," said he, "what can you mean by that? Where would such a body be found?"

"I know what I know," said the cobbler, "but there are times to speak and times to be silent. I say no more. Besides, my memory is always bad at this time of the morning."

The robber thought, "I must be subtle and wily." He clasped the man's hand, and in doing so placed a golden dinar in the palm. Then he said, "A secret is a secret, and I would be the last to cause you to break your word. But, just as a point of interest, do you happen to know the position of the house where you performed this remarkable feat?"

"It is strange that you should ask this," said the cobbler, "for I was led to it blindfold, and brought back in the same manner. Yet, if my eyes were covered, as before, I might more easily find my way than by sight – though of course my lips must be sealed."

"O most excellent sheikh of the needle!" said the robber. "That would be a wonder beyond belief; I cannot think it possible."

"So you doubt me?" said the old man, now quite vexed. "Come, and I will show you. Place this scarf over my eyes, and I shall trace the path, step by step." They started off, the old man saying, now and then, "Ah yes, this is the post I tripped against. Here is the noise of a coppersmith's hammer. Here is – yes – the smell of an ass's stable. Here is the house itself; the third step down to the cellar has a broken edge."

The robber was overjoyed. He gave the man another dinar, made a chalk mark on the door, and hastened back to the forest, where he told his news to the eagerly waiting band. The captain gave him a special nod of approval, then addressed his men.

"Now, my bold fellows," he said, "you must go to the town in groups of twos and threes, mingling with the crowds, then gradually assemble at the house. There will be no chance then for the villain to escape."

But that same morning, the girl Morgiana had gone out to buy provisions, and had seen the chalk mark on the door.

"This did not write itself," she thought. "It may be nothing; it may be something – but Allah helps the prudent." So she fetched a piece of chalk and made a similar mark on every door in the street. Then she went about her work.

Early next day the robbers came to the town as their leader had commanded – but which was the house? For all in the street had the same white mark. The chief, enraged, ordered his men back to the cave, and there, by common consent, the unfortunate volunteer was condemned to death and beheaded. In spite of this, another reckless fellow, certain that he could do better, offered his services. He too found the cobbler and was taken to the house of Ali Baba, where he made a discreet red mark. But this did not escape the vigilant eye of Morgiana, who marked all the neighbouring houses in the same way. This luckless robber also lost his head.

The captain had no wish for his band to dwindle further, and knowing well that wit can do what force alone can not, he set out for the town himself. The cobbler, whose store of dinars increased with every journey, traced the path to the dwelling once again. But the captain made no mark on the door. Instead, he gazed at it carefully, until every detail was fixed in his mind; then he returned and called his men together.

"Listen," he said. "You are to go in twos and threes to different villages, and bring back thirty-eight wide-necked jars, each large enough to contain a man. One jar must be filled with olive oil to allay suspicion; the others will hold yourselves – a man with a sword to be concealed in each."

When this was done, the jars were carried by mules to Ali Baba's house. There was no need to knock, for the kindly woodcutter was sitting outside in the pleasant evening air.

The robber chief halted the procession and, in the most courteous manner, said to Ali Baba, "O honoured master, I have travelled far with a load of oil to sell at the market, but I do not know the city and have found no place to lodge. If you would permit the use of your courtyard for my wares and horses, Allah will count it among your merits in Paradise."

Ali Baba at once replied, "O worthy merchant, you are welcome; my house this night is yours." And while the stranger went to the yard to arrange the unloading, Ali Baba went within to order a delicate feast to be prepared.

But what the man was really doing was giving his men the plans for the night's attack, and the signal which they must await – the throwing of some pebbles from the window. Then the false merchant returned to the house, ate well, and lay down to enjoy a few hours' sleep.

Now it chanced that the slave girl Morgiana, working in the kitchen, found herself short of oil. Then she remembered the many great jars in the yard.

"Surely," she thought, "our guest will not miss a cupful." She went to the nearest jar, removed the top, and lowered the measuring vessel. O horror! It touched – not a smooth liquid but a solid, moving thing, which said in a human voice, "Is it time, master?" Then, in a lower voice, "Pebble? It's more like a rock!"

Any other damsel would have shrieked; not so Morgiana. Keeping her voice as gruff as she could, she whispered, "Not·yet; keep as still as you may before the order comes." Then she moved from jar to jar, discovering that, in all but

one, an armed man was hiding. There were thirty-seven in all. Straightaway she devised a plan. From the single jar of oil she filled a cauldron and set it on to boil. When it was ready, she took it, bucket by bucket, to the yard, opened each jar, and poured the boiling oil on the robber's head. No cries were heard, for each was stifled at once. No man can escape from his destiny!

At midnight, the robber chief woke, fresh and ready for action. He went to the window and threw out some stones, but no sign came from the jars, only, as he now perceived, a nauseous smell of burning oil and meat. A dread arose in him. He crept down to the yard and peered first into one vessel, then another, then another. His enemy had outreached him! Filled with rage and terror he leapt the courtyard wall, fled along the dark streets, through shadowy alleys and byways, until he reached his cave, where he sat in smouldering silence, brooding on his next move.

In the morning Morgiana went calmly about her work until her master woke at his usual time. Then she told him all that had come to pass: the chalk marks, the false merchant, the oil jars and the rest.

Amazed, he cried out, "O daughter of benedictions, you have repaid a thousandfold the bread that you have eaten. Henceforward you are no slave but our eldest child." Then they buried the bodies in a great pit, and returned to their peaceful lives.

But the robber chief was not defeated. He put together rich fabrics and other such treasure from the cave and opened a shop near that of Ali Baba's oldest son, doing the youth many favours.

One day the young man said to his father, "I do not know how to repay my neighbour Husain for all the help he has given me in the market. Sometimes, too, he has asked me to share his midday meal. Should we not offer him an evening's hospitality in return?"

"You are right, my son," said Ali Baba. "I wish only that you had spoken earlier. Invite this good man to dine here tomorrow evening."

The boy ran eagerly back with the invitation, but the so-called merchant replied, "I would gladly come, my son – only I have taken a vow never to eat salt in any form."

"That is an easy matter," said the youth. "The meal will contain no salt." The order was passed on to the women of the kitchen.

Morgiana thought it a strange request, and when she brought in the food she gazed closely at the curious visitor. He had, she thought, a familiar look – and then she remembered, and understood why he would eat no salt, for this bonds a host and guest. She made her plan. When the meal was over she entered again, but now in the guise of a dancer, hung about with golden bells and glittering sequins, a jewelled dagger hanging at her belt. Behind her was the household slave boy, young Abdullah, playing a tambourine. The girl began to show her skill, first in cunning slow motion, then in rapidly whirling measures, always with matchless litheness and grace. She danced in the manner of the Greeks, the Persians, of the Ethiopians; then came the dance of veils, then the wild and riveting dagger dance itself. And the men watched as if spellbound.

At last she stopped, smiled, took the tambourine from the boy and held it out to her master in the manner of professionals. Ali Baba was puzzled, but put in a dinar; his son did likewise. But as Husain felt in his purse for a coin the damsel raised her dagger and stabbed him to the heart.

"Mad woman, what have you done?" cried Ali Baba in horror.

But Morgiana, calmly wiping the dagger on a silken scarf, said, "O my masters, this is a time for rejoicing, and for giving thanks to Allah. Your guest was no merchant but the robber chief himself, who came to destroy you, but by Allah's goodness was destroyed himself."

Then Ali Baba kissed the girl between the eyes, saying, "Once again you are my saviour. Will you consent to marry my son, and so be doubly my daughter? He is a handsome lad, you will agree."

"Be it so, honoured master," said the lively girl, and it was so. The wedding took place without delay, and the villain's body was added to those in the pit.

For a full year Ali Baba kept away from the secret cave, in case any further brigand lurked in wait. Then he decided to see what he might see, and set forth with his son and his indispensable daughter-in-law. She pointed out that the path to the cave was overgrown with shrubs and plants and bushes, unbruised by human foot.

"We may enter safely!" she declared. The magic words were spoken; the door gaped open, and centuries of treasure were revealed, a noble inheritance for the young people. Thus did Allah make a humble woodcutter the wealthiest and most honoured man in his town. Great are the ways of Allah who knows all!

THE TALE OF THE MAGIC BOOK

A TALE IS TOLD IN ancient annals that a night of sleepless melancholy came to the Khalifah Harun al-Rashid. Neither damsels, nor music, nor the fragrance of his garden could divert his mind, and he called for his wazir, Jafar.

Jafar reflected, and then said, "When all else is of no avail, one thing yet remains – a book. A library of books is the most delightful garden in the world; it holds for each who walks within uncounted joys and wonders and every kind of solace to the heart."

"Ah, Jafar, you are right," said Harun; "I had not thought of that." And they made their way to the hall of books. While servants held torches, Harun picked up one volume, then another, from the coffers and shelves of scented wood. At last he opened a very old tome indeed, almost crumbling. But as he turned the pages he began to laugh quite violently, then weep, then laugh, turn and turn again.

Unthinkingly, Jafar remarked, "O Prince of the Faithful, what has made you laugh and weep at the same time?" Harun was vexed at the question.

"O dog of dogs, what business is this of yours?" he cried. "Now, unless you can find a man who can tell me why I laughed and wept, and the whole contents of the book as well, your head will leave your shoulders. Go!"

Jafar had little doubt that his master's wrath would melt in time, and be washed away by need of his wazir. But he thought it prudent to vanish for a while. He left his wife and harem in his father's care, and started out for Damascus, a city which he was curious to see. Unattended, on a mule, like any humble traveller, he reached his goal on the tenth day and wandered through the lovely streets, fragrant with myrtle, rose, laurel and jasmine, admiring the fine buildings, until he reached a great house whose magnificence made him stop. It was set in a matchless garden, where, seated on a couch in a silken tent, was a young man of exquisite beauty, dressed in a rose-coloured tunic. Guests around him moved and feasted; a damsel at the young man's side sang love songs to the lute.

As Jafar watched, as if spellbound, the young man noticed him and said to one of his slaves, "Go to that stranger, speak to him courteously, and ask if he will join our company." And when Jafar approached, the graceful youth stood up, holding out both hands in welcome; he made him sit at his side, and the finest of food was brought to him. At last, when the guests had gone, the young man sent for horses, giving his guest a mare that a king's ransom could not buy, and they rode to a fair villa, lit with coloured lanterns. Here they feasted again, listened to songs whose sweetness turned the blood to ice and fire, and talked until the dawn.

Then the youth (whose name was Attaf the Generous) said, "O my friend, while you are in this city, my home is your home; you are my brother of brothers."

And so began a time of unmarred joy, when the two were almost never apart. In the day they would ride out and visit the tombs of great departed men, and other places of interest; then they would sing, make verses, talk and talk, hold feastings, and at night sleep side by side. Whatever Jafar lacked in gold or finest clothes or any other need, Attaf would instantly supply. So passed four months. But a moment came when Jafar felt unease. Had Allah dispersed the anger of his master? Was this dream-life the whole of his destiny? He asked his friend if he might walk alone for a few hours, to calm his troubled thoughts.

"Whatever you desire, dear brother," said Attaf. "But let me give you a purse of dinars for almsgiving as you go."

So Jafar roamed by market, mosque and street, turning his thoughts within him, until, quite weary, he saw a marble bench with a fine rug over it, and so sat down to rest. It stood before a splendid house with windows framed in gold and silver, and curtained in finest silk. As he gazed, he saw a curtain drawn aside by a small white hand, which held a little golden watering pot: from this the basil, jasmine, gillyflowers and other sweet-smelling plants were sprinkled and refreshed. But the soul of Jafar was touched by something more, for suddenly he saw the damsel's face. It was one to destroy all reason.

"Stranger," said the girl at last, "you devour this house with your eyes, yet it is not yours to devour. Why do you linger?"

Jafar replied, "I am putting together some verses in honour of the owner of the hand that holds the sprinkling jar."

"You waste your time," said the girl with a teasing smile, and closed the window, drawing the curtains together. Jafar, however, was left in a turmoil of spirit, and it was many hours before some sense returned, and he could make his way back to the house of his friend.

All night long he tossed with fever, a vessel on the stormy seas of love.

In the morning Attaf spoke to him, saying, "You had no sleep, my friend. I beg you to tell me your trouble. If you do not, you show neither trust nor affection." And so persuasive was he that at last Jafar opened his heart, and told of the girl watering flowers at the window, and how, since seeing her, his peace of soul was utterly destroyed.

For an hour or more Attaf sat silent. This girl was none other than his own beloved wife, who lived with her servants in a separate house. Then he said to himself: "Allah's will be done. A friend and guest must have whatever is his desire. If I fail to give him this, I am mere rubbish, sand and dust."

Then he turned a calm and pleasant face to Jafar, saying, "O my brother, torment yourself no longer. I know the family of this girl, and I also know that she was divorced from her husband a few days ago. Leave the matter to me; I will make the arrangements on your behalf." So saying, he left, and made his way to his wife's dwelling, and asked a servant to bring his father-in-law. When the old man came, he said, "Dear uncle, Allah has shown me the way of light. A desire has come upon me to journey to Mecca, to the tomb of the Prophet. In order to leave no distracting worldly ties, I must declare my divorce from your daughter."

The old man was aghast. "What need is there for such extremes? However long your absence on this holy journey, your wife remains your wife."

But Attaf said, "I have made an oath, and that cannot be broken." The father wept; the young wife too, being forced to taste the bitter waters of desolation. For Attaf was not only her husband but her cousin; they had loved each other since childhood, and he was the light of her soul.

Attaf hid his grief and returned to Jafar, saying, "Brother of my heart, I have visited the family and have spoken in your cause. Rejoice! For soon you will be wed." Then Jafar rose and feasted with good appetite. After this, Attaf said, "It must not be thought that I am trying to marry this girl to a stranger, a man of no standing or possessions. Therefore I intend to settle you in a sumptuous caravan just outside the city, with many fine horses and slaves, and will spread report that you are a mighty personage in Baghdad, maybe the wazir Jafar himself – why not? – on an official visit from the Khalifah. The leading citizens will go to meet you and you will receive them as befits a man of rank. Then you must say that you have heard of the beauty of a certain amir's daughter, and would like to wed with her." Attaf had no notion that his friend was in truth the Grand Wazir Jafar, nor that he might ever be repaid. He did what he did from the goodness of his heart.

Jafar lost no time in arranging the marriage contract, the dowry and the feastings, and with this good fortune achieved, he felt that Allah was smiling upon him, and that the Khalifah might have forgotten his wrath. So, all negotiations being done, and farewells said, his caravan set out for Baghdad, the girl enclosed in a jewelled palanquin. They had not travelled many hours when Jafar, hearing the sound of hooves, looked back to see a rider racing towards them. It was none other than Attaf; unable to endure the parting from his friend, he had come to say yet another farewell. Jafar rejoiced, halted the caravan, and caused a feast to be made. Meanwhile, the young bride, wondering at the delay, put her head out of the window and saw Attaf and Jafar feasting together. At once the truth became clear. Jafar was the man who had gazed upon her when she was watering her plants. Her beloved cousin and husband was so noble of soul that he had put his friendship with this man before all else, and for love of the stranger had yielded him her very self. She determined to tell the facts to her new unwanted spouse.

And so, when the caravan next made a stop and Jafar came to the palanquin to see that all was well with the lady, she said to him, "It is not your place to speak to me. I am the cousin and wife of Attaf; our hearts have been entwined since childhood, and only the laws of friendship have made him do this deed. If you are also a friend, you will hand him back a gift as painful to him as to me."

Jafar looked into his mind and saw the course of these happenings, and how much he had been at fault.

He wept and cried aloud, "Strange are the ways of Allah! O woman, from this moment you are a sacred trust, forbidden to me, to be returned to your own husband." He put her in the care of special servants to be guarded night and day and the caravan went on towards Baghdad.

Now it happened that the Khalifah had soon regretted his anger and had longed to see his friend and wazir again. Search parties had been sent forth to find the outcast, but without success. So when Jafar appeared, in wealth and splendour, Harun rejoiced, and was afire with impatience to hear his story. Then Jafar related it, from first to last, and the Khalifah was amazed.

"This man Attaf is a jewel of men, a model to all. I greatly wish to meet so rare a being. We will send for him straightaway. In the meantime you must divorce the woman and return her to her husband when he comes. If you do not, your friend may become your foe; if you do, you have a friend for life." So, on the advice of his master, Jafar installed the girl in a fine house with handsome furnishings, slaves, all that she might need.

But Destiny held other paths for Attaf. When he returned to Damascus, jealous tongues were already wagging against him.

One and another went to the naib saying, "Be on your guard against that man. You must know that he is so close a friend of the wazir Jafar that he accompanied him well beyond the city walls, in order that he could arrange for the wazir to procure him an edict of the Khalifah to depose you from your place. You will be wise to act against the traitor before his plan can bear its evil fruit."

"This shall be done!" said the naib. Guards were sent to drag Attaf from his house, to beat him with rods and sticks, and to bring him to the naib. His home was ransacked; all his possessions, goods and slaves were taken from him, and when he asked why this had come about his enemies jeered, saying, "Are you so ignorant of Allah's justice that you can plan to depose a naib of Damascus and go unpunished?"

Then the youth was led to the executioner's block. But just as the blade was about to fall, one of the amirs stepped forward, raised his hand and said, "O naib, do not too suddenly cut off this young man's head. Heedless haste is a trick of Satan. Have we a proof that those who speak against him are not liars, or have heard false report? Moreover, Jafar has the ear of the Khalifah. When he hears of this, how safe will your own head be?"

The naib saw the wisdom of this advice; he halted the execution, but to avoid dispute, ordered Attaf to be cast into prison. There in a dark dungeon, chained by the neck, he was left and forgotten. One night, the dungeon master who brought in his bread and water, omitted to lock the door. The light from the crack gave the poor victim an impulse of hope; with a sudden effort he broke the chain, crept out, crawled through passages, and found the door to the outer world, with a large key hanging on a hook nearby. In a moment he was free, and the moonless night was his friend. In the morning he mingled with the crowds and took the road for Aleppo, unable to rest until Damascus was well behind him. In Aleppo he fell in with some wayfarers who were journeying to Baghdad. Keeping close to these, he reached the fabled city.

Not knowing where to go, Attaf sat down in the nearest mosque, an abject figure, ragged and starved, with dirty turban and unkempt hair and beard. As he sat there thinking of his ill luck, a beggar squatted down nearby, and from a sack drew forth a roasted chicken, a loaf, olives, dates, a cucumber, sweetmeats – a feast indeed. The ruffian started to eat, while Attaf watched in anguish and at last began to weep.

The beggar said with scorn, "O dirty bearded sniveller, you may fill an ocean with your tears for all I care; you will not get a crumb from me. But I *will* give you some advice. If you want to eat the best of food, tender lamb, luscious pastries, you have only to go to the house of Jafar the Grand Wazir. When in Damascus he received hospitality from a man named Attaf, and it is for his sake that he feeds all who come. They say that Jafar never rises or lies down without invoking the same Attaf's name."

"Wonderful are the ways of Allah!" said Attaf. Then he went to the shop of a paper merchant and begged the gift of a piece of paper, and the loan of a reed pen. The good man provided these things, and Attaf wrote:

> *Let no man be proud, for in one day he may be cast from untold wealth to beggary. O Jafar my brother, you would not know me now, so greatly am I diminished in all my being by hunger, thirst, poverty, misery, torment, beatings, false imprisonment and long and sore foot travelling. Now I come to your door in the name of Allah, and of our friendship and love. Your brother Attaf speaks.*

Then he asked the way to Jafar's house and stood a while outside it, too fearful of the guards, and too full of shame at his appearance to go further. Then a eunuch, large and richly dressed, came from the door. Attaf kissed the man's hand and asked his help. "What do you want?" said the eunuch.

"I ask you of your goodness to take this letter to the master of the house, and to tell him that his brother Attaf is at the door."

Enraged at the seeming beggar's impertinence, the eunuch cried out, "Shameless liar! Imposter!" Taking his stick he beat the poor suppliant till he fell to the earth, covered with blood.

But a second eunuch, of a different nature, came forward, saying, "For shame! The man says that he is Jafar's brother. Are not all men brothers? Only goodness of heart distinguishes one from another." He bent over Attaf, raised him up, wiped the blood from his face and asked, "How can I help you?"

"I desire only that this paper be carried to Jafar," Attaf said faintly.

The good-hearted eunuch took the letter in his hand and carried it to the hall where Jafar sat with his friends and counsellors, drinking sweet wine, reciting verses and listening to the music of the lute.

At that moment the wazir rose to his feet, lifted his glass and said, "Never can I forget my friend of friends, my brother of brothers, the noble Attaf, the greatest of all men I have ever known. He gave me, a newcomer to his city, horses, slaves, damsels, coffers of gold, and all that was dear to him. He did all this with no idea that the man he helped might be of power and substance. Would he were here now." The eunuch listened joyfully to these words, then, bowing low, he handed the letter to Jafar. The wazir opened and read it – but the shock of joy was so great that he fell forward. The crystal cup in his hand shattered to pieces, one fragment entered his forehead and blood gushed forth.

Jafar's companions lifted the unconscious man and bound his wound, then one picked up the fallen letter.

"Where is the writer of this evil document?" he cried. "By Allah, he shall be given five hundred lashes, then thrown in prison for the remainder of his life."

The slaves ran out, calling, "Who is the writer of this paper?"

Attaf, still waiting at the gate, said, "I am the man, my masters." At once they seized him, gave him five hundred strokes with rods, and cast him into prison, causing the words, "For life" to be written on his chains.

Two months later, it happened that a son was born to the Khalifah, and in celebration, alms were given to the poor and the prisons emptied. Almost dead, filthy and starving, Attaf tottered forth from the dark cell.

Quite dazzled by the daylight, he cried out, "Allah be praised! My suffering must come from some fault in myself, when I was unworthy of the many blessings that the Lord had given me. May I be pardoned! But what am I now to do? If I leave for my own city, I will surely die of weakness on the road. If by chance I reach the gates, I will be beheaded by the naib. If I stay here, I must beg, but because I am a stranger, the beggars will not let me into their guild. All that is left for me is to await my destiny." So he sat for a while outside a mosque, but left it when night fell, remembering the words of the Prophet: "The house of Allah is built for prayer, not for slumber." Wandering through the empty streets he found a ruined house, and crawled inside for shelter. But all at once he tripped over – he knew not what; then he saw, by a glimmer of moonlight, that it was the body of a man, with a bloody knife lying beside.

As Attaf stood in horror, several of the police guard passed with torches, Attaf called to them, showing them the body.

"Villain! Why did you kill him?" they cried. But he was too shocked to answer. Then they bound his arms, and threw him into a dungeon. A report was sent to the wazir Jafar, saying that the prisoner had been found in a ruined building by the body of the murdered man; that his silence when questioned must be taken as a confession of the crime. Jafar signed for the execution without much thought, and next morning Attaf was led to the block.

The headsman swung his sword; it was about to descend, when a voice said, "Stay your hand, executioner. Is it true that this man comes from Damascus?" The speaker was none other than Jafar.

"He does indeed," said the executioner.

"Tell me," Jafar asked the prisoner, "did you ever by chance know of a man called Attaf, famed for his good and generous heart?"

"I did indeed," said Attaf. "He was scourged by Destiny, and drank from a bitter cup." Then he related all the happenings that had brought him so near to death, not once but many times. And then he cried out, "O my lord Jafar, my one-time brother, do you not know me? I am that same Attaf."

Jafar uttered a cry and clasped the poor prisoner in his arms. So many questions were to be asked and answered – they hardly knew where to begin. As they stood there, dazed with joy, an elderly man rushed up, with henna-dyed beard and a blue cloth on his head.

He was shouting out, "That man is innocent. I did the deed!"

"What is your story?" said Jafar.

"I brought up the murdered man from boyhood," said the stranger. "He took my money and gifts, but he was faithless and disloyal, consorting with the lowest of the low, and boasting of his depravity. At last when his taunts and boasts and treachery were not to be endured, I slew him. Now I come to save this innocent man."

"You have done well," said Jafar. "There is a doubt about the case, and where there is doubt it is best to leave well alone. Go with Allah, and seek from Him any pardon you desire."

Jafar took Attaf to the hamman, and, when he was clean and rested, provided him with handsome robes, then brought him to Harun al-Rashid saying, "My lord, here is Attaf the generous, whom you wished to meet. He was my host and benefactor in Damascus, and through my coming suffered untold ills." And the Khalifah listened with wonder, weeping much as he heard the tale, though he could not refrain from laughing at the episode of the henna-bearded man.

"Now, Jafar," said he, "what do you consider you owe your friend?"

"I owe my blood and my life," said Jafar, "so I am his slave always. I owe him also countless millions in gold. So I rejoice to say that until I can pay this sum, he must stay here in Baghdad. There is the matter too of a cousin, who is also his wife, who eagerly waits his coming." The wazir then led Attaf to the house of the young girl, and husband and wife were reunited in perfect love and joy. The Khalifah sent orders to Damascus that the naib was to be cast in chains in a dungeon, while he considered his fate.

Attaf spent many months in Baghdad, and every day the Khalifah found more and more to value in his company. But so many friends in Damascus begged for Attaf's return that Harun at last was obliged to let him go, with many magnificent gifts and a great train of mules and camels for the journey. When the young man reached his native city, night was approaching, yet it seemed to be day, so brightly was it illuminated in his honour. From the richest to the poorest all were out to welcome him, so greatly was he loved. Though the Khalifah had ordered the naib's death, Attaf had this commuted to

lifelong banishment. No other cloud ever darkened the sky of this good man.

The magic book? The whole affair had slipped from Harun's mind, and Jafar, wisely, never referred to it. So why should we do so?

from The Uninvited Guest

THE TALE OF THE UNINVITED GUEST

THERE WAS ONCE A NOTED glutton named Tufail, who was also known for his habit of attending feasts to which he had not been asked.

This tale is but one of a thousand told of his saucy tricks: a leading citizen invited a few chosen friends to a dinner whose main course was an exquisite mingling of many kinds of fishes. As the guests were about to start, they heard the all-too-familiar voice of Tufail at the door.

"Allah preserve us!" said one. "And may He also preserve our good dinner!"

"Let us at least keep the largest fish from his maw," said the host. "Quick! Hide it in that dark corner and just leave the little sprats and such. When he has devoured these, happily he will go, and we can feast in peace."

The big fish had scarcely been hidden when Tufail entered, assured and beaming. He surveyed the great dish and took from it one small sprat. The waiting guests gave one another enquiring looks. What was he up to *this* time?

"So, friend Tufail," said the host at last, "you appear not to like our fish."

"Ah," sighed Tufail, "well may you say that! I have had a considerable bone to pick with them ever since my unfortunate father was drowned at sea and his body was consumed by the gluttonous creatures."

"Then you have now a fine chance of avenging that behaviour," said a guest.

"You may be right," returned the wily Tufail, whose experienced nose and eye had already perceived the hidden fish in the corner. "But wait – this little sprat seems to have something to tell me." He lifted it to his ear. "Yes? . . . Yes? . . ." he murmured. Then at last he turned to the company. "Do you know what the little fellow said? I'll tell you." In a small high voice he went on: "O master, I am much too young to have eaten your worthy father, now in the care of Allah. If you wish for revenge, take it upon the great fish in that corner, for there lies the real offender, who gobbled your worthy parent."

The host and guests collapsed with laughter, knowing that they were no match for the irrepressible glutton. They set the great fish before him, saying, "What must be must be. Eat! and may it give you indigestion!"

from The Sea Rose of the Girl of China

The Tale of the Sea Rose of the Girl of China

THERE WAS ONCE, IN OLDEN days, in the land of Sharkastan, a king called Zain al-Muluk, known as far as the world's horizons for his noble heart, his valour in battle. Though still young himself he had two sons already halfway to manhood. Then a third was born, who outshone them in grace and beauty as the moon outshines the stars. He was given the name Nurgihan.

The king delighted especially in this child and called upon the royal astrologers to cast his horoscope. They gravely brought their findings to the court.

"The prince's lot is a brilliant one, lit with good fortune and joy. But it is also written in the Book of Destiny that if you, his royal father, look upon him during his boyhood, you will at once be blind."

The king felt as if struck by a thunderbolt. He had the child and mother taken to a far distant palace, where the boy's path might never cross with his. But who can outwit the will of Allah? One day the young prince was hunting in the forest, and rode far out of his way pursuing a deer. On that same day, the king was also hunting and he too was led by his quarry into untried paths. In a green clearing the two came face to face, and the father was at once struck blind, imprisoned without reprieve in the land of night. All the great doctors of the east were called to the palace, but the malady was not one to be mended by physicians. Then the most gifted soothsayers were consulted. Slowly and with downcast looks they brought their answer.

"Only one thing can restore the king's sight, and the chance of finding it is so small that he had best put it from his thoughts. We speak of the sea rose that belongs to the girl of China."

"Tell me more of this wondrous flower," said the king.

"All that we can learn," the chief sage answered, "is that in the very heart of China lives the Princess Brow of Lilies, daughter of the Emperor Firuz-Shah; in her private garden is the only tree in the world of the magic sea rose, whose flower can bring sight even to those born to blindness. But according to the signs, not only is the place well-nigh impossible to reach, but the tree has Efreet guardians of such might that even Jinn of highest power would dread to risk an encounter."

For all that warning, hope rose in the king's heart, and he sent forth criers, far and wide, saying that whoever found and brought to him the fabulous sea rose should have a half of his empire. Many set out, but most returned in failure; the others were never heard of again. Among those who started on the eastern road were the three princes, but the oldest two returned after many months, sullen and angry: their paths, they said, had been blocked at every turn, leading them back to where they had begun.

But the young Prince Nurgihan was determined to let no obstacle stand in his way, nor ever to return without the prize. Was he not the unwitting cause of the malady? He mounted his swiftest horse, and with the sun for guide, rode on towards the east. At last he came to a thick dark forest. Strange trees loomed over him, some with grinning heads instead of fruits; others with grey clay nuts, which cracked and brought forth fearsome birds, with golden beaks and eyes.

Suddenly he found himself facing a huge and hideous creature, an aged Jinnee, seated on the ground against an enormous carob tree. The young prince gave a deep bow, and, in the most elegant words that he could bring to his lips, made courteous greeting. The giant, unused to such civilities, was quite enchanted by the stranger's beauty, patted the earth beside him and asked the boy to sit down. But what finally moved the being's heart to its very core was a cake made of sugar and butter, which the prince had handed him from his pack as a token of friendship.

When at last no crumb remained, the Jinnee declared in an ecstasy, "This piece of human food comes straight from Paradise! What can I offer you in return? If you do not accept some favour as a poor return for that matchless gift, you leave me the most worthless of the Jinn, a toadstool on the earth, mere mud, a thing of dust."

The prince replied, "O crown of all the Jinn, most eloquent of spirits, your golden words ring like bells. And since you so graciously offer me a wish, I would ask to be transported to the garden of the Princess Brow of Lilies, in the heart of China, where I may find and pluck the fabulous sea rose." But as soon as he heard these words the giant uttered a terrible groan, turned cold as ice and fell over in a swoon. The prince tried every means to revive him but without success, until he thought to place a second sugar cake in the half-open mouth. At once the great Jinnee opened his eyes, sat up and having fully savoured the delicious item, he remembered the request.

"O friend and benefactor," he began, "I must tell you that the sea rose of the royal Chinese damsel is guarded day and night by certain aerial spirits, winged Efreets of unmatched power, shielding it from bruising rain, burning sun, the beaks of birds, and – if any ever came so near – from thieving human hands. So even if you were to reach the garden (which none has ever done) you would still be faced with the terrible vigilance of these guards. I am greatly perplexed about the matter, but if another of those quite exceptional cakes were made available it might rouse inspiration."

The prince handed another cake to the giant who consumed it with sounds of ecstasy, then leaned his mighty head upon his fist in order to think. Suddenly he sat up.

"Your cakes have unfailing powers," he said. "With their help, I have solved the problem. Seat yourself here – " he curved his arm – "and we will fly to China. I have devised a brilliant way of distracting those guardians of the rose; we will throw them one of those amazing sugar cakes."

"What will be will be," said the undaunted prince, and in a few moments he was borne aloft in the uppermost air, speeding over half the eastern world. Only minutes later they were hovering over the heart of China, and the amiable Jinnee prepared to set down the prince at the entrance of the royal maiden's garden.

"Have no fear," said the giant. "I now propose to divert the guardian spirits with the cake which you will give me. I thank you –" he took the cake – "though I have to say that I am sorely grieved at the thought of handing it over. When you have finished your business, you will find me waiting at the gate."

The prince entered the garden (though with some caution) and felt that he was in Paradise itself, so ravishing were the scents, the sounds, the colours of the flowers. In the midst was a rippling lake of rosewater, and in the centre of this lake, on a single stem, was a flower, red as fire. It was the sea rose.

The prince cast aside his clothes, dived into the fragrant water and pulled up the flower with its roots. Then he swam back, quickly dressed and hid the prize in his robes. He was about to return to the gate to meet his giant friend when his eye was caught by a delightful pavilion built beside the water. He peered within and saw a jewelled couch shaded by delicate curtains in lustrous changing colours. They were not quite closed, and he just perceived behind their shelter a young girl of matchless beauty lying on heaped cushions, fast asleep. Her cloud of hair was the violet black of midnight; her white hand, with its back against her brow, was lily and narcissus on the pale magnolia of her face. This priceless jewel of maidens was none other than Brow of Lilies, Princess of China; the sea rose was her flower. Almost swooning in rapture, the young prince gazed and gazed. But sense returned to him; every moment of delay held peril; he must escape before the guardian Jinn returned.

Yet how could he bear to leave without a sign? He took a ring from his finger and exchanged it for her own, then reached the gate of the garden just in time. The giant was waiting anxiously and they soared into the air.

"Most generous of spirits," said the prince, "might I ask if you would take me not to the forest but to the palace of my father, who is waiting in his darkness for the flower?"

"This too can be arranged," replied the giant, "for the fee of one more cake." By luck, one more remained; the giant joyfully swallowed it, set his course westward and westward, and in a matter of minutes set down his passenger at his father's gate.

Nurgihan at once sought an audience with his father, and when before him drew the marvellous flower from his robes and placed it in the blind king's hand. The monarch raised the fragrant sea rose to his face and sight returned to him; his eyes were bright as stars, and saw more clearly than ever they had done before. The royal father hardly knew how to express his joy. He clasped his son to his heart, and ordered heralds to proclaim that henceforth his empire was equally shared with his son, Prince Nurgihan. Rejoicings and celebrations were ordered through the land for an entire year.

The prince did not forget the flower of his good fortune. He hollowed out a fountain basin in the garden with a lining of pure gold, and filled it with water of a rare fragrance. The sea rose was set in the centre, and there it throve, an enchantment to all the senses.

But now our minds must fly far to the east, where Princess Brow of Lilies was left sleeping in her pavilion by the lake. Morning came. She opened her eyes, rose from her bed, combed out her long hair and stepped into the garden to taste the first delicious freshness of the day. Her one thought was of her flower. But she saw no flower – it was gone entirely, leaf, stem, root and all. She clasped her hands in anguished disbelief – then saw that the ring she wore was a strange one, not her own. The truth shot into her mind: the thief of the rose had also stolen a glance at her as she slept – a triple thief, for had he not also taken her ring and left his own?

"By Allah!" she said. "I may be young and a girl, but I will not accept this affront. If I have to go to the ends of the earth I shall find and recover my sea rose, and punish the thief and intruder."

So she and her girl slaves disguised themselves as young warriors and set out westward, everywhere seeking for clues. At last, by many chances, they reached the kingdom of King Zain al-Muluk, father of Prince Nurgihan. The streets were full of music and feasting and bright decorations, and the princess asked a passer-by if this was the daily custom.

"We are rejoicing for a special matter," she was told. "Our king was cured of blindness by a magic flower, brought to him from the heart of China by our young Prince Nurgihan. Now it grows in the palace gardens, and the prince visits it all day long, sighing and dreaming."

Brow of Lilies knew at once that the end of her quest was near. Still dressed as a youth she asked the way to the royal garden and there she saw her sea rose rising from the scented water of the golden pool, a marvel to all the senses.

"Now," she decided, "I will hide in these flowering bushes to see the impudent fellow for myself."

Before long the prince returned to the garden to gaze upon the rose. But so dazzling was his beauty that the maiden almost lost her wits.

"Woe is me!" ran her thought. "The taker of my rose and ring has stolen my heart as well. How can I, alone in a strange land, seek justice for my wrongs?" She went back to her attendants, asked for paper and ink and wrote a letter which contained the phrase: "O cruel taker of all I own, I accuse you most of the stealing of my heart." Then she wrapped this round the stranger's ring, and told her favourite little slave to take it to the prince.

The young man was sitting by the pool of the sea rose, thinking, as always, of the sleeping girl in China. When the messenger brought the letter and the ring, his heart beat violently. The damsel must be near! Swiftly he wrote an answer in words which would hold true meaning only for that one receiver. He told her that his heart was no longer his, that he was wasting away with longing. Then he gave the note to the little waiting slave.

The girl hurried back, and handed the prince's letter to Brow of Lilies, saying, "O mistress of the moonlight and the dawn, I bring you excellent news. The prince is as lost with love for you as you are for himself."

When Brow of Lilies had read the letter and heard her attendant's word, she told her slaves to remove her boy's disguise, and to prepare her in the most beguiling of women's clothes for her meeting with the prince. But her beauty had no need of the adornment. Now she made her way once more to the pool of the sea rose, and the prince came forward to meet her. All the words ever used in the poetry of love would not be enough to convey the wonder of that moment and that hour. And long years after their marriage, the beauty of the pair did not diminish nor the ecstasy that each felt for the other on that day. Was this the power of the sea rose? Only Allah can tell.

THE TENDER TALE OF PRINCE JASMINE AND PRINCESS ALMOND

THERE WAS ONCE IN AN eastern land a mighty king, held by all to be wise as time, glorious as the rising sun; his name was Nujum-Shah. He had seven sons, unmatched in princely skills and qualities. But the youngest was the flower of them all, a youth of ravishing beauty and goodness of heart; Prince Jasmine was his name. No foot was fleeter in the kingdom, no hand more sure with the sword. And none made sweeter music on the flute.

This prince had been chosen from his brothers to guard the vast buffalo herds of his father, and he did this well, knowing each beast by name. One day, as he watched his charges, playing tunes that might make the lame foot leap and the heart turn over, a venerable dervish approached him on a donkey, and asked if he might draw a little milk from a buffalo cow.

"O holy man," said the prince, "most willingly would I meet your wish, but to my grief the buffaloes were milked less than an hour ago and all are dry."

"Nevertheless," said the dervish, "to Allah all things are possible. Call on the Holy Name, and try that animal yonder." The boy did as he was told, and the buffalo cow gave a further pail of foaming milk.

When the dervish had quenched his thirst, he smiled, and said, "O pattern of princes, your gift will be returned a hundredfold, in ways unguessed at. I come as a messenger of love: to find a youth, seen in the dreams of a fairy girl, a magical princess whom I met one early morning in her garden. Her name is the Princess Almond, daughter of King Akbar. But I must tell you now, O handsome herd boy, that this rare jewel of damsels has no rest day or night because of the dream I spoke of. In that dream she saw a royal youth of peerless beauty, and that youth was a likeness of yourself. Enough! I say no more. May Allah lead you by pleasant paths to your destiny."

The dervish rose and was gone, but he left the prince in a torment of passion for the lovely Princess Almond. Too restless to stay in the work which had filled his days, he took his flute and wandered away, through green plain and thorny waste, over surging waters and towering cliffs, nearing all the time –

though he did not know it – the kingdom of King Akbar, the home of the Princess Almond, the place of his desire. Meanwhile, the princess pined and dwindled in her malady of love, and neither her parents nor the royal physicians could find a way to cure her or distract her mind. But when her maidens took her into the garden and sang and danced, she grew more calm, and her favourite little slave was able to give her a piece of news.

"Dear mistress," said the girl, "a young flute player has come to our land from the kingdom over the mountains. He stands like a young cypress, proud as a tulip, yet pliant as a blade of wheat. His name is Jasmine. What has brought him here, over perilous crags and cliffs, across wide and treacherous waters, that the very swans and wild ducks dare not enter? Only the cause of love."

As she listened to these beguiling words, the sickness of the princess fell away. Her eyes grew bright. The dream had taken living form, and had journeyed to her door, a youth of matchless beauty, an enchanting maker of music. She called her favourite attendant, asked for pen and paper, and wrote a letter of love and longing to the young prince of her dream, now so close at hand. Then she gave it to the little slave girl to take to the charming stranger.

She found him in a wood, playing his flute and composing verses of love. First she placed the letter in his hand; then, as he stood amazed, his heart on fire at the delectable words, she added certain instructions, which the princess had not committed to paper. Following these, he glided out in the evening shadows, made his unseen way to the Princess Almond's garden, lightly climbed the wall and hid in the branches of a certain tree. As night came to the garden, so too did the princess, her dress of violet-blue merging with the violet shades of night. As she stood there, trembling, a fruit of entire perfection dropped from the branch above; it was the lovely boy, already seen in dream.

Words have not been devised to describe the ecstasy of these two young people as they gazed on one another, and sweetly kissed, hand in hand. At last, when the whispering sounds of night brought prudence into their minds, they devised a plan which would keep them near to one another, and even allow them to meet in open light. To bring this plan about – for delay was not to be endured – the princess at once went back to the palace and asked to be admitted to the king. The father loved his daughter, and greeted her with joyful tenderness, asking, however, why she had come at so late an hour.

"O light of the earth, dear father," she replied, "I wish to ask a favour. After taking an evening walk with my maidens, my sickness began to leave me; I looked around at our fields with their cattle and sheep and saw much that needed attention. Yet I found no shepherd or herdsman. While these thoughts

from The Sea Rose of the Girl of China

were in my mind, my maidens spoke to me of a shepherd who has journeyed into our kingdom, seeking work, one who is young, diligent and careful for his flock. If you agree to employ this man, my mind will be at rest."

The king laughed. "Little daughter," he said, "I can refuse you nothing. Shepherds are not usually engaged in the middle of the night, but one time is as good as another if the bargain is sound. To show my delight in your recovery, I shall see this herdsman, and if he is all that you tell me, I shall take him into my service."

"Dear father," said Almond, "the young man is even now at the palace gate, for he has as yet no shelter but the open sky."

So the king had the young man brought before him. What he saw was a youth of rarest grace and beauty – not, however, in the least like a herd boy.

The princess saw her father's thoughts, and quickly said, in musing tones, "Dear father, the outside is not always a key to what is within. I am told that this young man has worked only for kings and princes, and that every kind of animal thrives under his care."

"Allah's ways are strange," said the monarch, still somewhat perplexed, "but there is a purpose in all things, and I keep my word. Now, my daughter, you may go to your bed with a clear untroubled mind."

And so Prince Jasmine became the royal shepherd, taking his sheep and cattle to pasture, tending their needs, calling them together at dusk by the playing of his flute. Then he would lead them back to the stables of the king. But thereafter, every evening, he would secretly meet the Princess Almond in her garden. Who would wish for a life of greater sweetness? Yet with the day comes night, with the fairest rose, a thorn. In her love for the lovely herd boy, Almond would send her slaves to the pastures with gifts of food and drink. One day, unable to wait for nightfall, so great was her longing to feast her eyes upon the boy, she carried the dish herself: a silver dish from the king's own table, laden with delicate fruits and nuts and sweetmeats. She handed it to Jasmine, then hurried away, fearful of curious eyes in the open daylight. She had hardly gone a minute when the prince saw an old man approaching, somewhat out of breath. This was the princess's uncle, a jealous and surly old man who hated music and dancing and young people at their play. Seeing the silver dish full of delicacies his face grew purple.

"What is this, shepherd?" he demanded.

Jasmine, thinking no evil, replied, "Good sir, if you are hungry, take the dish and eat." The old man seized the dish and rushed with it to the king.

And that was how the love between the Princess Almond and the herd boy came to be known. The king, in high rage, sent for his daughter.

220

"Shame of our house!" he cried. "With your sugared words and melting eyes, you have snared your father's mind. Who can be safe from women? Wives and daughters are a pitfall and a gin; they come from a twisted rib. They have neither reason nor honour. When they are wayward it is our duty to beat them. What am I to do with a daughter who dallies and wantons with a mere shepherd? Go from my presence, until I have decided on your punishment."

Then the king devised a plan to rid himself of the shepherd boy. He sent for his sons and told them to decoy the miscreant into a certain wood. The shepherd boy would not know that this wood was shunned by the boldest of citizens. For there lurked unknown terrors, monsters, frightful beasts born of unnatural couplings. Most feared of all were two horned pig-deer, the bane of every living thing that crossed their path.

But the young man knew nothing of this. So when the royal brothers brought the order to Jasmine that the king desired the herds to try the lush green pasturing in this wood, he cheerfully drove his charges through the trees, then sat down in a clearing and began to play his flute. The two pig-deer, lured at first by the human smell, but charmed still more by the music, settled down before him, and gazed up into his face in enraptured trance. When it was time to leave the forest they still went with him, one upon his right, one on his left. He took them to the king's palace where, in a special cage, he presented the pair to the king.

"It may be that Allah intends the youth to live," thought the monarch. And in token of the miracle and the gift, he revoked the sentence of death.

This did not please the brothers. To break any further bond between the herd boy and their sister, they arranged to marry her to a detestable cousin, none other than the son of that disastrous uncle – the cause of all her trouble. Wedding celebrations were announced throughout the kingdom. What could the princess do? The fateful day came all too soon. Clothed in splendid bridal robes, with golden ornaments, she sat like a dead thing, pale as a lily, cold as a stone, silent in a torrent of festive noise, weighed down by grief and loss.

But among the palace servants watching the wedding procession was the shepherd boy, Jasmine himself. His eyes met hers; the glance said many things and left her with the seed of hope.

Now it was night, and the Princess Almond was led to the marriage chamber. In the short moment before the bridegroom entered the room, she glided swiftly out by another door where Jasmine awaited her. Hand in hand, lighter than birds, they vanished into the friendly dark, fragrant with flowers, lit with guiding stars. Nothing more was ever heard of them in the palace. But fortunate is the dreamer who meets in dreams such happiness as theirs!

ᕼOW THE TALES CAME TO AN END, AND WHAT BEFELL THEREAFTER

WHEN SHAHRAZAD CAME TO THE end of this story the king exclaimed, "That was a noble tale! It lodges in my heart. O Shahrazad of the golden voice, how much has a king been able to learn from your tellings! For a thousand nights and one you have made past times live again, the wisdom, follies and wonders. You have made me reflect on the strange chances of Destiny, on the behaviour of men, whether princes, merchants or beggars. You have dispelled all thoughts of my own misfortunes, as a mist disappears in the sun; joy has returned to me, and a desire for life."

Then Shahrazad whispered some words to her little sister, who glided from the room, light as a leaf, then reappeared, followed by a slave woman carrying twin infants, while a third crawled in on all fours.

Shahrazad took the children from the nurse and set the three down on the royal couch, saying, "O king of the centuries, behold your three sons whom Allah has granted to us during these thousand days. Your oldest boy is two years old; these twins are almost one."

The king was quite amazed, and could find no word to say.

Then little Dunyazad, who had been making much of the infants, turned to him and boldly asked, "Are you about to cut off my sister's head, and leave these three little kings without a mother?"

"Have no fear, young girl," said the king, with tears running down his cheeks. "O Shahrazad, marvel of women, I swear to you that even before I knew of these children, you had won my heart. I found you pure and holy, subtle, ingenious, wise, discreet, a banisher of woe and darkness, a bringer of light and cheer. May Allah bless you and all your line before you and all who are yet to come."

Then Shahrazad said, "O virtuous king, I beg you to send for the wazir my father, to know that I have been so generously saved from execution, and to share in our rejoicing." The king at once sent for the old man, who entered carrying a shroud for the dead over his arm, thinking that his daughter's end had come at last.

from Prince Jasmine and Princess Almond

But the king embraced him, saying, "O father of Shahrazad, Allah has caused your daughter to be the salvation of a people, and the joy of a king's days." After this, the monarch ordered a fleet of messengers to go to his brother, King Shahzaman of Samarkand, bidding him to join in the celebrations. The city was made bright with flags by day and with torches all the night; the finest incense filled the streets, of nard and musk and ambergris; the air was made melodious by flute and drum, cymbal, fife and dulcimer. Even the poorest had a share in the feasting.

When the king had welcomed his brother, and they had eaten together and were ready for talking, he began to tell him of the thousand nights and one that he had passed with Shahrazad, and he recounted a selection of the episodes, anecdotes, proverbs, poems, marvels, jests, wise sayings. Shahzaman was struck with wonder.

"Brother," he said, "you have made me determined to marry; I will have the little sister – I do not know her name – of your Shahrazad. For the past three years, since my return from here, I have followed your example, taking a virgin girl to my bed each night and in the morning having her slain, in this way appeasing the wrong that was done to me. Now, with my new wife, I shall need no more of that."

This news was told to Shahrazad, who said at once, "If your brother is to marry our little Dunyazad, there is one condition. He must agree to stay with us here, for I could not bear to be parted from my sister, whom I brought up and educated, nor could she bear to part from me." And Shahmazan straightaway agreed.

"I, too, long to stay here," he said, "to be with my brother; Allah will find a successor for my throne of Samarkand."

"Who but the father of our wives?" replied Shahryar. And the wazir was made the King of Samarkand.

Then said King Shahryar, "I too have a condition. If you are to stay here, dearest brother, you must share my reign and kingdom, day by day about." And this too was agreed.

So began long years of pleasure and delight for the royal four. But one thing more must be told, how King Shahryar called together all the most skilled recorders and scribes of the eastern world, ordering them to set down the tales of Shahrazad, from first to last, in letters of gold. This manuscript was kept in a golden coffer, under especial care, but copies were sent through the kingdom as an instruction to the people and their descendants, century after century. Such is the wondrous history of the stories you have heard!